Pro PHP

Patterns, Frameworks, Testing and More

Kevin McArthur

D1473586

Apress®

Pro PHP: Patterns, Frameworks, Testing and More

Copyright © 2008 by Kevin McArthur

ISBN-13 (pbk): 978-1-59059-819-1

ISBN-10 (pbk): 1-59059-819-9

ISBN-13 (electronic): 978-1-4302-0279-0

ISBN-10 (electronic): 1-4302-0279-3

Printed and bound in the United States of America 9 8 7 6 5 4 3 2 1

Lead Editors: Jason Gilmore, Tom Welsh
Technical Reviewer: Jeffrey Sambells
Editorial Board: Clay Andres, Steve Anglin, Ewan Buckingham, Tony Campbell, Gary Cornell,
    Jonathan Gennick, Kevin Goff, Matthew Moodie, Joseph Ottinger, Jeffrey Pepper, Frank Pohlmann,
    Ben Renow-Clarke, Dominic Shakeshaft, Matt Wade, Tom Welsh
Project Manager: Beth Christmas
Copy Editor: Marilyn Smith
Associate Production Director: Kari Brooks-Copony
Production Editor: Katie Stence
Compositor: Susan Glinert
Proofreader: Lisa Hamilton
Indexer: Broccoli Information Management
Artist: April Milne
Cover Designer: Kurt Krames
Manufacturing Director: Tom Debolski

Distributed to the book trade worldwide by Springer-Verlag New York, Inc., 233 Spring Street, 6th Floor, New York, NY 10013. Phone 1-800-SPRINGER, fax 201-348-4505, e-mail orders-ny@springer-sbm.com, or visit http://www.springeronline.com.

For information on translations, please contact Apress directly at 2855 Telegraph Avenue, Suite 600, Berkeley, CA 94705. Phone 510-549-5930, fax 510-549-5939, e-mail info@apress.com, or visit http://www.apress.com.

Apress and friends of ED books may be purchased in bulk for academic, corporate, or promotional use. eBook versions and licenses are also available for most titles. For more information, reference our Special Bulk Sales—eBook Licensing web page at http://www.apress.com/info/bulksales.

The source code for this book is available to readers at http://www.apress.com.

Jill—my wife, my muse, and my raison d'être—I write for you.

Contents at a Glance

About the Author xvii

About the Technical Reviewer xix

Acknowledgments xxi

Introduction xxiii

PART 1 ■■■ OOP and Patterns

■CHAPTER 1   Abstract Classes, Interfaces, and Programming by Contract 3

■CHAPTER 2   Static Variables, Members, and Methods 11

■CHAPTER 3   Singleton and Factory Patterns 21

■CHAPTER 4   Exceptions 31

■CHAPTER 5   What's New in PHP 6 41

PART 2 ■■■ Testing and Documentation

■CHAPTER 6   Documentation and Coding Conventions 55

■CHAPTER 7   Reflection API 73

■CHAPTER 8   Testing, Deployment, and Continuous Integration 105

PART 3 ■■■ The Standard PHP Library (SPL)

■CHAPTER 9   Introduction to SPL 127

■CHAPTER 10   SPL Iterators 143

■CHAPTER 11   SPL File and Directory Handling 163

■CHAPTER 12   SPL Array Overloading 179

■CHAPTER 13   SPL Exceptions 189

PART 4 ■■■ The Model-View-Controller (MVC) Pattern

■CHAPTER 14   MVC Architecture 201

■CHAPTER 15   Introduction to the Zend Framework 215

■CHAPTER 16   Advanced Zend Framework 235

■CHAPTER 17   The Zend Framework Applied 259

PART 5 ■■■ Web 2.0

■CHAPTER 18   Ajax and JSON 273

■CHAPTER 19   Introduction to Web Services with SOAP 285

■CHAPTER 20   Advanced Web Services 299

■CHAPTER 21   Certificate Authentication 313

■INDEX 329

Contents

About the Author xvii

About the Technical Reviewer xix

Acknowledgments xxi

Introduction xxiii

PART 1 ■■■ OOP and Patterns

■CHAPTER 1   Abstract Classes, Interfaces, and Programming
                     by Contract 3

                     Abstract Classes 3
                     Interfaces 6
                     The instanceof Operator 8
                     Programming by Contract 9
                     Just the Facts 10

■CHAPTER 2   Static Variables, Members, and Methods 11

                     Static Variables 11
                     Static Usage in Classes 12
                              Static Members. 12
                              Paamayim Nekudotayim 13
                              Static Methods 16
                     The Static Debate 18
                     Just the Facts 18

■CHAPTER 3   Singleton and Factory Patterns 21

                     Responsibility and the Singleton Pattern 21
                     The Factory Pattern 23
                              The Image Factory 24
                              The Portable Database. 27
                     Just the Facts 29

▪CHAPTER 4   **Exceptions** 31

Implementing Exceptions 31
    Exception Elements 31
    Extending Exceptions 34
Logging Exceptions 35
    Logging Custom Exceptions 35
    Defining an Uncaught Exception Handler 36
Exception Overhead 37
Error Coding 37
Type Hinting and Exceptions 38
Rethrowing Exceptions 39
Just the Facts 40

▪CHAPTER 5   **What's New in PHP 6** 41

PHP Installation 41
Unicode in PHP 6 44
    Unicode Semantics 44
    Unicode Collations 46
Namespaces 47
Late Static Binding 48
Dynamic Static Methods 50
Ternary Assignment Shorthand (ifsetor) 50
XMLWriter Class 50
Just the Facts 52

PART 2 ▪▪▪ **Testing and Documentation**

▪CHAPTER 6   **Documentation and Coding Conventions** 55

Coding Conventions 55
PHP Comments and Lexing 57
    Types of Comments 57
    More About Doccomments 57
    Lexing 58
    Metadata 58
PHPDoc 59

DocBook 62

    Creating an XML File for DocBook 62

    Parsing a DocBook File 63

    Using DocBook Elements. 67

Just the Facts 71

CHAPTER 7   **Reflection API** 73

Introducing the Reflection API 73

    Retrieving User-Declared Classes. 74

    Understanding the Reflection Plug-in Architecture. 76

Parsing Reflection-Based Documentation Data 81

    Installing the Docblock Tokenizer. 81

    Accessing Doccomment Data 82

    Tokenizing Doccomment Data 83

    Parsing the Tokens. 84

Extending the Reflection API 86

    Integrating the Parser with the Reflection API. 86

    Extending Reflection Classes 88

    Updating the Parser to Handle In-Line Tags 96

    Adding Attributes 99

Just the Facts 102

CHAPTER 8   **Testing, Deployment, and Continuous Integration** 105

Subversion for Version Control 105

    Installing Subversion 106

    Setting Up Subversion 106

    Committing Changes and Resolving Conflicts. 108

    Enabling Subversion Access 110

PHPUnit for Unit Testing 110

    Installing PHPUnit 110

    Creating Your First Unit Test 111

    Understanding PHPUnit 112

Phing for Deployment 115

    Installing Phing 115

    Writing a Phing Deployment Script. 116

Xinc, the Continuous Integration Server 118

    Installing Xinc 118

    Creating the Xinc Configuration File 119

    Starting Xinc 120

Xdebug for Debugging 120

Installing Xdebug 120

Tracing with Xdebug 121

Profiling with Xdebug 123

Checking Code Coverage with Xdebug 123

Remote Debugging with Xdebug 124

Just the Facts 124

PART 3 ■■■ **The Standard PHP Library (SPL)**

■**CHAPTER 9**   **Introduction to SPL** 127

SPL Fundamentals 127

Iterators 128

Iterator Interface 128

Iterator Helper Functions 129

Array Overloading 130

ArrayAccess Interface 130

Counting and ArrayAccess 131

The Observer Pattern 131

Serialization 135

SPL Autoloading 137

Object Identification 140

Just the Facts 141

■**CHAPTER 10**   **SPL Iterators** 143

Iterator Interfaces and Iterators 143

Iterator Interfaces 143

Iterators 146

Real-World Iterator Implementations 158

Parsing XML with SimpleXML 158

Accessing Flat-File Databases with DBA 159

Just the Facts 161

■**CHAPTER 11**   **SPL File and Directory Handling** 163

File and Directory Information 163

Iteration of Directories 166

Listing Files and Directories 166

Finding Files 168

Creating Custom File Filter Iterators 169

SPL File Object Operations 171
    File Iteration... 172
    CSV Operation.. 172
    Searching Files 176
Just the Facts 177

■CHAPTER 12 **SPL Array Overloading** 179

Introducing ArrayAccess 179
Introducing ArrayObject 180
Building an SPL Shopping Cart 182
Using Objects As Keys 184
Just the Facts 188

■CHAPTER 13 **SPL Exceptions** 189

Logic Exceptions 189
Runtime Exceptions 191
Bad Function and Method Call Exceptions 192
Domain Exceptions 192
Range Exceptions 193
Invalid Argument Exceptions 194
Length Exceptions 194
Overflow Exceptions 195
Underflow Exceptions 196
Just the Facts 198

PART 4 ■■■ The Model-View-Controller (MVC) Pattern

■CHAPTER 14 **MVC Architecture** 201

Why Use MVC? 201
MVC Application Layout 203
    From the Web Server.................................... 203
    Actions and Controllers 203
    Models.. 203
    Views... 203

Criteria for Choosing an MVC Framework 204

Architecture of the MVC Framework. 204

MVC Framework Documentation 204

MVC Framework Community. 205

MVC Framework Support. 205

MVC Framework Flexibility 205

Roll Your Own MVC Framework 205

Setting Up a Virtual Host 206

Creating an MVC Framework. 207

Just the Facts 213

■CHAPTER 15   **Introduction to the Zend Framework** 215

Setting Up the Zend Framework 215

Installing the Zend Framework 215

Creating a Virtual Host 216

Bootstrapping 217

Creating Controllers, Views, and Models 219

Adding an Index Controller. 219

Adding a View 220

Defining Models 221

Adding Functionality 224

Using the Request and Response Objects 224

Using Built-in Action Helpers. 226

Using Built-in View Helpers 227

Validating Input 229

Just the Facts 233

■CHAPTER 16   **Advanced Zend Framework** 235

Managing Configuration Files 235

The Array Approach 235

The INI Approach 236

The XML Approach 237

Setting Site-Wide View Variables 237

Sharing Objects 238

Error Handling 238

Application Logging 239

About the Technical Reviewer

JEFFREY SAMBELLS is a graphic designer and self-taught web application developer, best known for his unique ability to merge the visual world of graphics with the mental realm of code. After obtaining his Bachelor of Technology degree in graphic communications management with a minor in multimedia, Jeffrey enjoyed the paper-and-ink printing industry, but he soon realized the world of pixels and code was where his ideas would prosper.

Jeffrey has previously published articles related to print design and has contributed to award-winning graphical and Internet software designs. His latest book, *AdvancED DOM Scripting* (friends of ED, 2007; 1-59059-856-6, http://advanceddomscripting.com), was an instant success. In late 2005, Jeffrey became a PHP 4 Zend Certified Engineer. He updated the certification to PHP 5 in September 2006 to become one of the first PHP 5 Zend Certified Engineers! Jeffrey also maintains a blog at http://jeffreysambells.com, where he discusses his thoughts and ideas about everything from web development to photography.

Jeffrey currently lives and plays in Ontario, Canada, with his wife Stephanie, his daughter Addison, and their little dog Milo.

Acknowledgments

This book is based upon a decade of innovation by a community of thousands of developers. I would like to thank each of them, and offer this book as a modest contribution to our great work.

I would like to thank David Fugate for giving me the opportunity and guidance needed to write this book.

Thank you to Michael Geist, whose actions and advice have allowed me to achieve real change in the face of tremendous adversity.

I also have to thank my friends and family for their support. Without you, I could never have achieved so much.

Finally, to everyone at Apress who made this book possible, and who have helped many other writers to publish high-quality publications: you have my sincerest thanks. Without all of you, this book would never have been written.

Introduction

Over the past decade, PHP has transformed itself from a set of simple tools for web site development to a full-fledged object-oriented programming (OOP) language. PHP now rivals mainstream languages like Java and C# for web application development, with more and more enterprises turning to it to power their web sites. The reasons for this are clear: PHP has found the right combination of an easy-to-learn language and powerful features.

In this book, you will learn how to make the most of your PHP programming, from a detailed understanding of OOP theory to frameworks and advanced system interoperability.

Who Should Read This Book

This is an advanced book. I have needed to choose carefully which information to include and what readers should be expected to know already. Readers should have a solid understanding of HTTP and PHP—that is, you should understand how to make web pages and build forms, and you should understand key concepts like the HTTP request cycle.

If this doesn't sound like you, I recommend reading *Beginning PHP and PostgreSQL 8* by Jason Gilmore and Robert Treat (Apress, 2006; 1-59059-547-3). It is an excellent introduction to PHP programming and a definite must-read for any would-be developer.

If you are comfortable at the intermediate to advanced level, then this book is for you.

How This Book Is Organized

Each chapter builds on lessons learned in previous chapters, but recognizes that readers will have a wide variety of skill levels. If you think you already know the content covered in a chapter, I encourage you to skip ahead, but before you do, be sure to read the "Just the Facts" section at the end of each chapter. This section provides a terse summary of what was covered in the chapter. But note that even the most seasoned programmers are likely to find something worth learning in each chapter.

The book is organized into five parts:

Part 1, OOP and Patterns: This part provides a foundation for advanced OOP concepts. It dives right in and tells you all you need to know about abstract classes, interfaces, static methods, and patterns like the singleton and factory, as well as exceptions. The part concludes with an introduction to the new features in PHP 6.

Part 2, Testing and Documentation: This part covers all those interesting "peripheral" concepts, like test-driven development and automated deployment. It teaches you about writing great documentation and includes introductions to several documentation standards, including PHPDoc and DocBook. You will find information about the reflection API and learn how to extract metadata from your programs. Finally, you'll learn about continuous integration and how to use tools like Phing and Xinc to improve your development workflow.

Part 3, The Standard PHP Library (SPL): The SPL contains some of the most advanced PHP code ever written. It offers language support for advanced OOP concepts like indexers and iterators, and also provides structures for exceptions and patterns like observer/reporter. The information in this part will allow you to create much more elegant and well-formed classes than would normally be possible.

Part 4, The Model-View-Controller (MVC) Pattern: MVC is probably the most useful development pattern for PHP developers. It allows you to structure your applications and work in teams using the best resources to get the job done. A strong understanding of this pattern is probably the single most important job qualification for any PHP developer, so this book makes a special effort to fully explain it. This part of the book also introduces you to the Zend Framework, an MVC-based framework embraced by thousands of PHP companies. It starts with a complete walk-through of how to get a framework application up and running, and then presents the core concepts and advanced features of the Zend Framework.

Part 5, Web 2.0: This part covers all the things you need to know about Web 2.0. You will find information about Ajax and JSON, SOAP web services, and SSL client authentication. This part includes a lot of really useful tutorials, based on personal experience.

Contacting the Author

Please feel free to contact the author at `Kevin.McArthur@StormTide.ca`. You can find the latest information about this book at `http://www.stormtide.ca/pro-php-book` or on the Apress web site, `http://www.apress.com/book/view/9781590598191`. Last but not least, you can chat with the author via IRC by visiting #PHP EFnet.

PART 1

OOP and Patterns

CHAPTER 1

■■■

Abstract Classes, Interfaces, and Programming by Contract

In this chapter, you will learn about abstract classes, interfaces, and a technique known as programming by contract. These are object-oriented programming (OOP) mechanisms that allow you to write code that does more than just perform calculations or present output. These constructs give you the ability to define conceptual rules about how classes interact, and they provide a foundation for extension and customization in your applications.

Abstract Classes

*Abstract class*es involve the use of a common *base class* when you want to leave certain details up to its inheritors—specifically, when you need to create a foundational object whose methods are not fully defined. You will find that by using abstraction, you can create very extensible architecture within your development projects.

For example, file-format parsing lends itself particularly well to the abstract approach. In this case, you know that the object will need a set of methods, like getData() or getCreatedDate(), in order for it to interoperate with other classes; however, you want to leave the parsing methods up to inheriting classes that are designed for a specific file format. By using abstract classes, you can define that a parse() method must exist, without needing to specify how it should work. You can place this abstract requirement and the fully defined methods in a single class for easier implementation.

You might think of abstract classes as partial classes because they do not define the implementation for all the methods they declare. Instead of implementing all methods, an abstract class has the added ability to define abstract methods, which are method prototypes lacking a body. These methods will be implemented when the class is derived. However, an abstract class doesn't need to consist solely of abstract methods; you're free to declare fully defined methods as well.

■**Note** A method's *prototype* is the signature by which it is defined, exclusive of the body. This includes the access level, the function keyword, the name of the function, and the parameters. It does not contain the brace ({ }) characters or any code inside. An example is `public function prototypeName($protoParam);`.

Because an abstract class does not define the implementation for every method it declares, it cannot be instantiated directly with the new operator. Instead, a separate class must be created that extends the abstract class and overrides any previously declared abstract prototypes. In extending the class, you will be able to create specialized objects that still maintain a common set of functionality.

To get the most out of abstract classes, you should remember the following rules:

- Any class that contains even one abstract method must also be declared abstract.

- Any method that is declared abstract, when implemented, must contain the same or weaker access level. For example, if a method is protected in the abstract class, it must be protected or public in the inheriting class; it may not be private.

- You cannot create an instance of an abstract class using the new keyword.

- Any method declared as abstract must not contain a function body.

- You may extend an abstract class without implementing all of the abstract methods if you also declare your extended class abstract. This can be useful for creating hierarchical objects.

To declare a class as abstract you use the abstract modifier in the class declaration. The code presented in Listing 1-1 defines one abstract class with both a fully declared method and an abstract method that will be implemented later.

Listing 1-1. *Defining a Basic Abstract Class*

```
abstract class Car {

  //Any base class methods

  abstract function getMaximumSpeed();

}
```

This class by itself is not particularly useful because it is abstract and cannot be instantiated. To make this class useful and obtain an instance, you must first extend it. For example, you can create a class named FastCar that inherits from Car and defines a getMaximumSpeed() method, as shown in Listing 1-2.

Listing 1-2. *Inheriting an Abstract Class*

```
class FastCar extends Car {

  function getMaximumSpeed() {
    return 150;
  }

}
```

Now you have a class, FastCar, which can be instantiated. Next, you can create another class, named Street, which will use this common functionality, as shown in Listing 1-3.

Listing 1-3. *Using Abstract Common Functionality*

```
class Street {
  protected $speedLimit;
  protected $cars;

  public function __construct($speedLimit = 200) {
    $this->cars = array(); //Initialize the variable
    $this->speedLimit = $speedLimit;
  }

  protected function isStreetLegal($car) {
    if($car->getMaximumSpeed() < $this->speedLimit) {
      return true;
    } else {
      return false;
    }
  }

  public function addCar($car) {
    if($this->isStreetLegal($car)) {
      echo 'The Car was allowed on the road.';
      $this->cars[] = $car;
    } else {
      echo 'The Car is too fast and was not allowed on the road.';
    }
  }

}
```

The Street class includes an addCar() method, which is designed to take an instance of a derived Car. Now you can use the Street class and pass an instance of the FastCar class to the addCar() method, as shown in Listing 1-4. The addCar() method makes a call to the isStreetLegal() method, which will then call the getMaximumSpeed() method defined in the FastCar class.

Listing 1-4. *Using an Abstract Class*

```
$street = new Street();
$street->addCar(new FastCar());
```

Using an abstract class makes it possible to know that all Car-derived objects will implement the getMaximumSpeed() method and share common functionality. If a class inherits from Car and does not define the method, it will result in a syntax error, and the program will not run. This restriction allows you to guarantee compatibility at the instantiation layer, rather than needing to later debug the code to find out why an object does not contain the method.

Abstract classes are not without their limitations, however. PHP supports extending from only a single base class, so you cannot derive from two or more abstract classes. The ability to extend from two or more base classes is commonly called *multiple inheritance* and is illegal by design in PHP. The reasoning is that descending from multiple classes can cause unwanted complexity when two or more classes define fully defined methods with the same prototype. When you find that you want to descend from two or more abstract classes, an alternative is to split out the base class methods and use interfaces to achieve the same goals, as described in the next section.

Interfaces

An *interface* is a class-like structure that allows you to declare which methods an implementing class must declare. For example, interfaces are often used to declare an API without defining how it will be implemented.

While similar to an abstract class, an interface may contain only method prototypes and must not contain any fully defined methods. This prevents the method conflicts that can arise with abstract classes and allows you to use more than one interface for a given implementing class. However, since you cannot define fully defined methods, if you wish to provide default functionality for inheritors, you must also provide a non-abstract base class separately.

To declare an interface, you use the `interface` keyword:

```
interface IExampleInterface {}
```

■**Note** Many developers choose to prefix interface names with a capital `I` to clearly distinguish them from classes, both in code and in generated documentation.

Instead of extending from the interface as you would an abstract class, use the `implements` keyword:

```
class ExampleClass implements IExampleInterface {}
```

If you mark a class as implementing an interface and fail to implement all the interface's methods, you will see an error similar to this:

```
Fatal error: Class ExampleClass contains 1 abstract method and must therefore
be declared abstract or implement the remaining methods
(IExampleInterface::exampleMethod)
```

This error means that if any method in an interface is not declared, it is assumed that the method is abstract. And since any class containing an abstract method must also be abstract, the class must be marked as abstract to be parsed successfully. To resolve this error, implement any methods that are declared abstract in the base class but that are not implemented in the inheriting class. You should implement the methods instead of marking the class `abstract`, because marking it abstract would prevent the class's instantiation and just push the error further downstream.

You must implement all methods in an interface such that a complete class can be formed and such that other classes may be allowed to depend on the existence of all the methods defined in the interface. Failing to implement even one interface method defeats the purpose of defining a common interface and thus is not permitted.

As noted, one benefit of interfaces over abstract classes is that you may use more than one interface per class. When you wish to implement two or more interfaces in a class, you separate them with commas. For example if you had an array style object that you wanted to be both iterable and countable, you might define a class like this:

```
class MyArrayLikeObject implements Iterator, Countable {}
```

It is entirely possible to achieve the same operation as abstract classes using interfaces. Usually, you will use an abstract class where there is a logical hierarchy between the child and parent classes. You will generally use an interface where there is a specific interaction you wish to support between two or more objects that are dissimilar enough that an abstract class would not make sense.

For example, suppose you want to convert the code in Listings 1-1 through 1-3 from their abstract form. First, create an interface called ISpeedInfo:

```
interface ISpeedInfo {
  function getMaximumSpeed();
}
```

This interface defines the getMaximumSpeed() method, replacing the abstract method in Car.

Next, remove the abstract method from the Car class. Then change the declaration of FastCar to include implements ISpeedInfo, as follows:

```
class Car {
  //Any base class methods
}

class FastCar extends Car implements ISpeedInfo {
  function getMaximumSpeed() {
    return 150;
  }
}
```

This code will result in nearly identical operation as the prior abstract approach. The only important difference is that in the abstract approach, you can be assured that an implementing class has the getMaximumSpeed() method. In the interface approach, the class Car as defined does not necessarily know that its inheritor implements ISpeedInfo. Consider the code in Listing 1-5.

Listing 1-5. *Using a Class Without Implementing a Required Method*

```php
interface ISpeedInfo {
  function getMaximumSpeed();
}

class Car {
  //Any base class methods
}

class FastCar extends Car implements ISpeedInfo {
  function getMaximumSpeed() {
    return 150;
  }
}

class BadCar extends Car{}

$a = new BadCar();
echo $a->getMaximumSpeed();
```

The code in Listing 1-5 will generate the following error:

```
Fatal error: Call to undefined method BadCar::getMaximumSpeed()
```

This is because BadCar does not implement ISpeedInfo, and Car does not check for the interface before calling getMaximumSpeed(). This error condition can be detected by using the instanceof operator, as described in the next section.

The instanceof Operator

The instanceof operator is a PHP comparison operator. It takes parameters on the left and right, and returns a Boolean value. This operator is used to determine if an instance of an object is of a specific type, inherits from a type, or implements a specific interface.

■**Note** The word *type* refers to the runtime definition of a specific class. A type is created any time a class or interface definition is parsed by PHP.

For example, to avoid the error shown in the previous section, generated by Listing 1-5, you can use instanceof to determine if the inheritor of Car implements ISpeedInfo, as shown in Listing 1-6.

Listing 1-6. *Using the instanceof Operator*

```
class Street {
  protected $speedLimit;
  protected $cars;

  public function __construct($speedLimit = 200) {
    $this->cars = array(); //Initialize the variable
    $this->speedLimit = $speedLimit;
  }

  function isStreetLegal($car) {
    if($car instanceof ISpeedInfo) {
      if($car->getMaximumSpeed() < $this->speedLimit) {
        return true;
      } else {
        return false;
      }
    } else {
      //The extended class must implement ISpeedInfo to be street legal
      return false;
    }
  }

  public function addCar($car) {
    if($this->isStreetLegal($car)) {
      echo 'The Car was allowed on the road.';
      $this->cars[] = $car;
    } else {
      echo 'The Car is too fast and was not allowed on the road.';
    }
  }

}
```

As shown here, you use the `instanceof` operator on the `Car` instance. If it returns `true`, you then know that it is safe to call any method that is defined in the interface.

Now that you've learned about abstract classes and interfaces, let's talk about programming by contract.

Programming by Contract

In simple terms, *programming by contract* is the practice of declaring an interface before writing a class. This can be particularly useful for guaranteeing the encapsulation of your classes.

Using the programming by contract technique, you will be able to identify the capabilities you are trying to implement before building your application, much in the same way an architect creates plans for a building before it is constructed.

Development teams frequently program by contract because of the many workflow improvements this technique brings. By defining the interaction of classes before any implementation begins, the team members know exactly what their objects must do; it is then fairly trivial to implement the required methods. When the interface is fully implemented, testing of the class will be conducted using only the rules defined in the interface.

In the car example you've seen in previous sections, the ISpeedInfo interface could be considered a contract, as it is the only point of API interaction of which either class, Car or Street, needs to be aware. The Street class will test for this contract before accepting the object for interaction. One developer could then be assigned to create a Car class and another to create a Street class, and the two would not need to collaborate on the implementation beyond the IStreetInfo interface.

In Chapter 7, we will revisit this concept of programming by contract in the context of application plug-ins.

Just the Facts

Abstract classes are classes that are declared with the abstract keyword. They allow you to defer declaring a method's implementation by marking it as abstract. To declare a method as abstract, you simply omit the body, including all braces, and terminate the line with a semicolon.

Abstract classes cannot be directly instantiated—they must be derived. If a class inherits from an abstract class, it must also be declared abstract when it does not implement all the abstract methods in the base class.

Interfaces are like abstract classes in that you can declare method prototypes without method bodies. They differ from abstract classes in that they must not declare any methods with method bodies. They also have different usage syntax. Instead of extending from an interface, you use the implements keyword to put in force an interface's rules on a class.

In some cases, you will want to determine if a class is of a certain type or if it implements a specific interface. The instanceof operator is particularly useful for this task. The instanceof operator checks three things: if an instance is of a specific type, if an instance derives from a specific type, and if an instance or any of its ancestors implement a specific interface.

Some languages have the ability to derive from multiple base classes, which is called multiple inheritance. PHP does not support multiple inheritance. Instead, it gives you the ability to declare multiple interfaces per class.

The ability of interfaces to declare rules that classes must follow is extremely useful. The programming by contract technique uses this capability to enhance encapsulation and optimize workflow.

CHAPTER 2

■ ■ ■

Static Variables, Members, and Methods

This chapter discusses the static keyword as it is applied to variables, classes, and methods. You will learn about the scope resolution operator (::) and its implication in object-oriented design. Finally, I will touch on the often heated debate about the usage of static classes in application design.

To get the most from this chapter, you should already be familiar with variable scope; that is, you should understand global, function, and class scope, and the use of the $this variable within classes.

Static Variables

A *static variable* is a variable that exists only in function scope, but that does not lose its value when the function is finished executing; that is, it remembers its value the next time the function is called.

To declare a variable as static, you simply prefix the variable with the static keyword, as shown in Listing 2-1.

Listing 2-1. *Declaring a Basic Static Variable*

```
function testing() {
  static $a = 1;
  $a *= 2;
  echo $a . "\n";
}

testing();
testing();
testing();
```

Executing Listing 2-1 produces the following output:

```
2
4
8
```

In this example, the testing() function stores the value of $a internally after each execution. The next time the testing() function is called, the old value of $a is restored, multiplied by 2, and echoed anew.

Notice that variable's default value is initialized to 1. This assignment will occur only the first time the variable is initialized. It will not be called with each execution of the function.

■Note It is illegal to default a static variable to the product of an expression. An *expression* is anything that is not a value itself. For example, (1+1), $variable, and anyfunc() are examples of expressions.

You are probably thinking that this doesn't seem particularly useful, as you could just as easily use a global variable to achieve the same result. However, global variables are accessible by all functions, and as such, can cause conflicts if two or more functions use a similarly named variable that is designed to be independent. Also, using a static variable doesn't require any more syntax space than importing a global variable, so when only one function needs to access the variable, using a static variable instead of a global variable is preferred.

Static Usage in Classes

The static keyword is used in classes in two key ways: for static members and static methods. Within classes, you can use the scope resolution operator to access different scope levels.

Static Members

A *static member* is a class variable that is best thought of as belonging to the class and not any specific instance of a class. Unlike a normal instance variable, a static member retains only one value for all instances; that is, all instances share the one member. Listing 2-2 demonstrates the declaration and access of a static member.

Listing 2-2. *Declaring a Static Member*

```
class MyObject {

 public static $myStaticVar=0;

 function myMethod() {
  self::$myStaticVar += 2;
  echo self::$myStaticVar . "\n";
 }
```

```
}
$instance1 = new MyObject();
$instance1->myMethod();
$instance2 = new MyObject();
$instance2->myMethod();
```

Executing Listing 2-2 produces the following output:

```
2
4
```

This is the result because the static member variable is shared among all instances of the class.

Notice the use of the :: scope resolution operator and the self scope instead of $this. This is because $this refers only to the current instance of the class, whereas self:: refers to the class itself. Let's take a closer look at this scope resolution operator.

■**Note** Unlike with $this, when using static variables, you must include the $ symbol after the scope resolution operator.

Paamayim Nekudotayim

Say what? OK, I know, *paamayim nekudotayim* is even hard to read. It literally means "double colon" in Hebrew. The good news is that you can forget the name right now.

The paamayim nekudotayim symbol, also known as the scope resolution operator, is specified by a double colon (::) and is used to access different scope levels within classes. This operator takes a scope on the left and a member on the right.

You can use two magic scopes with the scope resolution operator: self and parent. Additionally, PHP 6 introduces static scope.

The code shown earlier in Listing 2-2 illustrates access to the self scope. This scope refers to the current class, but unlike $this, it does not refer to a specific instance of a class. It cannot be used outside a class and is not knowledgeable of its position in an inheritance tree. That said, self, when declared in an extended class, can call methods declared in a base class but will always call the overridden method. This is demonstrated in Listing 2-3.

Listing 2-3. *Accessing Functions in a Parent Class with self Scope*

```
class MyObject {

 function myBaseMethod() {
  echo "I am declared in MyObject\n";
 }

}
```

```
class MyOtherObject extends MyObject{

 function myExtendedMethod() {
  echo "myExtendedMethod is declared in MyOtherObject\n";
  self::myBaseMethod();
 }

}

MyOtherObject::myExtendedMethod();
```

Executing Listing 2-3 produces the following output:

```
myExtendedMethod is declared in MyOtherObject
I am declared in MyObject
```

In an extended class, you may want to call a method that is defined in the base class but that is then overridden. For example, you might do this when you want to extend a class to add extra functionality to an existing method. To achieve this, you use the parent scope, as demonstrated in Listing 2-4.

Listing 2-4. *Using parent Scope*

```
class MyObject {

  function myMethod() {
    //Standard functionality
    echo "Standard Functionality\n";
  }

}

class MyOtherObject extends MyObject{
  function myMethod() {
    //Add some new functionality
    echo "New Functionality\n";

    //Then call the original myMethod that is defined in MyObject
    parent::myMethod();
  }
}

$obj = new MyOtherObject();
$obj->myMethod();
```

Executing Listing 2-4 from the command line produces the following output:

New Functionality
Standard Functionality

Static members can also belong to parent classes specifically. If you were to declare a member both in MyObject and MyOtherObject, you could also use parent:: to access the parent variable from the child class. In this case, both the parent and child classes maintain separate values for the static member. Listing 2-5 demonstrates how to override a static variable in a parent class and what effect it will have on program execution.

Listing 2-5. *Overriding Static Variables*

```
class MyObject {

 public static $myStaticVar=0;

 function myMethod() {
  self::$myStaticVar += 2;
  echo self::$myStaticVar . "\n";
 }

}

class MyOtherObject extends MyObject {

 public static $myStaticVar=0; //Override myStaticVar

 function myOtherMethod() {
  echo parent::$myStaticVar . "\n";
  echo self::$myStaticVar . "\n";
 }

}

$instance1 = new MyObject();
$instance1->myMethod();
$instance2 = new MyObject();
$instance2->myMethod();
$instance3 = new MyOtherObject();
$instance3->myOtherMethod();
```

Executing Listing 2-5 produces the following results:

```
2
4
4
0
```

All of the prior examples use instances of classes to access methods. You may also pass a class name to the left of the :: operator to access a member statically and avoid needing to create an instance. This will save you writing instantiation code, and it can be more efficient, as each instance of a class takes up a small amount of system resources. Calling a class method statically is demonstrated in Listing 2-6.

Listing 2-6. *Calling a Class Method Statically*

```
class MyObject {

 public static $myVariable = 10;

}

echo MyObject::$myVariable;
```

Running Listing 2-6 has the following result:

```
10
```

Note again the use of the $ symbol when accessing myVariable via the :: operator. This is because PHP currently does not support the use of dynamic static variables—that is, variable variables that are static. When using $this->$variable, the member that is accessed is the value contained in $variable. Accessing a variable without the $ symbol will actually be looking for a class constant, and constants cannot be accessed via $this.

The introduction of the static:: scope in PHP 6 allows you to stop using self:: and parent::. When you mean to refer to the final functional class, use static::, which will perform a computation immediately prior to code execution to determine the most descendant member. This process is called *late binding*, and it allows you to override a static variable in a child class and access the final member from a function declared in the parent, as you'll see in the next section.

Static Methods

Static methods follow the same rules as static variables. You mark them with the static keyword, and you use the scope resolution operator (::) to access them via the class's name.

Static methods have one key difference from non-static methods: you no longer need to have an instance of the class to call your method. Listing 2-7 shows an example of using a static method.

Listing 2-7. *Invoking a Static Method*

```
class MyObject {

 static function myMethod() {
  //Do something useful
 }

}

MyObject::myMethod();
```

PHP 6 introduces a few new changes to the operation of static methods. First, you may no longer use the :: operator to access methods that are not marked static. Correctly marking your methods as static or non-static is now much more important than it was in previous versions of PHP. Additionally, the static:: scope can also be applied to static methods. This allows you to statically call a method of an inheriting class from within a parent class, as shown in Listing 2-8.

Listing 2-8. *The static Scope in PHP 6*

```
class MyObject {

 static function myMethod() {
  static::myOtherMethod();
 }

 static function myOtherMethod() {
  echo 'Called from MyObject';
 }

}

class MyExtendedObject extends MyObject {

 static function myOtherMethod() {
  echo 'Called from MyExtendedObject';
 }

}

MyExtendedObject::myMethod();
```

Listing 2-8 generates the following output:

```
Called from MyExtendedObject
```

The code in Listing 2-8 will properly call `myOtherMethod` inside `MyExtendedObject`. Prior to PHP 6, it was not possible to call the method in the extended class from the parent, and `self::` would always result in a calling from `MyObject`.

Sometimes it is difficult to know when to use a static method versus a non-static one. One rule of thumb is that you should use a static method any time the method does not include the `$this` variable. If you don't need an instance, you should probably use a static class instead of unnecessarily instantiating classes. Further, you cannot use `$this` from within a static method, as the method belongs to no-specific instance.

The Static Debate

The usage of static classes is a controversial subject. Some developers make it a rule to never use the scope resolution operator on a class name. I personally feel this is extreme, and you will find static classes used throughout all major OOP frameworks. The static debate centers around a design principle called Inversion of Control (IoC).

IoC is a design principle that tries to get rid of all interdependence in OOP. This principle is important in complex systems, and allows for objects to be more polymorphic and encapsulated. The less interdependence, the easier it is to test a component in isolation.

The problem with static classes and IoC is that static accessors, by their very nature, define bindings between two classes, as the name of the class is hard-coded. This means that a class cannot be easily simulated when trying to test another class in isolation.

■Note In PHP, it is not possible to use a variable as a class name for the scope resolution operator. `$classnameinvar::somemethod()` is invalid and will result in a parse error.

Just the Facts

Static variables are modified function variables that do not lose their value when a function's execution is complete. You create a static variable with the `static` keyword and may provide a default initialization value; however, that initialization value may not be an expression. Static variables can be useful for eliminating variable-naming conflicts that may occur when using global variables to simulate static variables.

The `static` keyword can also be used in classes to modify properties and methods. When used on a property, it changes the property from holding a value per instance to holding a single value that is intrinsic to the class itself. This value can also be considered shared between all instances of a class.

To access static methods, you use the paamayim nekudotayim operator (::), which is also called the scope resolution operator. The left side of this operator takes a class name or one of the magic scopes: self, parent, or in PHP 6, static. The right side takes a static method, variable, or constant. The self magic scope, when used from within a class, refers to the class itself. The parent magic scope refers specifically to the parent class and can be especially useful for accessing methods in the base class that may have been overridden.

Static classes can have consequences to certain types of testing. The IoC design principle is limited when static classes are used in PHP. This is because static usage can lead to binding classes together by name, and that makes isolated testing of components more difficult. In the end, however, most PHP applications do not utilize IoC principles, and static usage is typically preferred.

CHAPTER 3

Singleton and Factory Patterns

Patterns are like recipes for OOP developers, with each pattern providing the required ingredients. You will customize the elements of the pattern to solve your particular programming challenges.

Patterns are useful to OOP developers because they can help you create a stable API but still maintain a desired level of flexibility. A pattern can help you define which object is responsible for a specific task, or even allow you to change a class completely without changing any of the code that interacts with your class. The former is called *responsibility*, and the latter *polymorphism*. You're probably already aware of these concepts in theory, but this chapter will help you understand the PHP syntax required to implement them in your applications.

This chapter introduces you to the two most commonly used patterns: the *singleton* and *factory* patterns. The singleton pattern is known as a *responsibility pattern*, and it is used to create a single point of functionality within an application. The factory pattern is important in polymorphic design. When properly applied, the factory pattern can make your applications more portable, loosen object interdependencies, and allow for future flexibility. For example, by implementing polymorphism through the factory pattern, you will be able to substitute a new experimental class for an established one and test new features in a safe and stable manner.

Responsibility and the Singleton Pattern

In OOP, it is often advantageous to have one object be the only responsible entity for a specific task. For instance, you might want to make a single object responsible for communicating with your database. The singleton pattern is considered a responsibility pattern because it delegates control for creation to a single point. At any given time, there will always be one, and only one, instance of the class existing anywhere within the application. This can help you prevent creating multiple connections to a database or unnecessarily using extra system resources. In more complex systems, use of the singleton pattern is especially useful in keeping your application's state synchronized.

All singleton classes have at least three common elements:

- They must have a constructor, and it must be marked private.

- They contain a static member variable that will hold an instance of the class.

- They contain a public static method to access the instance.

Unlike a normal class, a singleton class cannot be directly instantiated within other classes. Instead, a singleton class may instantiate only itself. To achieve this restriction, the __construct() method must be marked private. If you try to construct a class with a private constructor, you will get an accessibility level error.

To be useful, a singleton class must provide other classes with an instance on which they can call methods. Instead of creating a copy of the instance, a singleton class will return a reference to the instance the singleton has stored internally. The result is that the singleton class prevents duplication of memory and resources that would be better used in another area of your application. As part of the pattern, you must also prevent an object from being copied or cloned by creating a blank, private __clone() method.

The method that returns the instance reference is commonly named getInstance(). This method must be static and must instantiate the class if it has not already been instantiated. The getInstance method detects if the class has been initialized by utilizing the instanceof operator and the self keyword. If the static member that holds the instance is null or is not an instance of the class itself, then an instance will be created and stored to the instance holding variable.

Listing 3-1 shows an example of a singleton class designed to encapsulate a database connection object.

Listing 3-1. *Centralizing Database Connection Responsibility*

```
class Database {

  private $_db;
  static $_instance;

  private function __construct() {
    $this->_db = pg_connect('dbname=example_db');
  }

  private __clone() {};

  public static function getInstance() {
    if( ! (self::$_instance instanceof self) ) {
      self::$_instance = new self();
    }
    return self::$_instance;
  }

  public function query($sql) {
    //Run a query using $this->_db
    return pg_query($this->_db,$sql);
  }

}
```

This example begins with the declaration of two variables: an instance variable $_db, that will be populated when the object is constructed, and a static variable $_instance, which will hold the only instance of the class.

Next are the private __construct() and __clone() magic methods. The private constructor prevents the object from being created from an external context using the new operator. Similarly, the private __clone() method closes a small loophole in the PHP language that could make a copy of the object and defeat singleton responsibility.

Next, the getInstance() static method is declared. This is the real meat of the singleton pattern. This function checks if the static instance variable already holds an instance of the class. If it does not contain an instance of itself, the class is instantiated and stored in $_instance. The next time the code is called, $_instance will hold an instance of the class, and the class will not be instantiated again. Finally, the reference to the instance is returned.

So, now you've seen how to declare the singleton class. But how do you use it? Listing 3-2 demonstrates the use of a singleton class from another context.

Listing 3-2. *Using a Singleton Class*

```
$db = Database::getInstance();
$db->query('SELECT * FROM example_table');
```

By calling getInstance(), $db now holds a reference to the internally stored instance. With the instance, you can call any non-static method defined in the singleton class.

If your class does not need a __construct() method, the singleton pattern is not appropriate. In that case, you should use a purely static class. Simply provide a private constructor with no body and omit the getInstance() and $_instance members. This will prevent instantiation, so you are assured a single point of responsibility by eliminating the obtaining of an instance when the code is used. Listing 3-3 shows an example of a purely static class.

Listing 3-3. *Using a Purely Static Class That Cannot Be Instantiated*

```
class SomeClass {

  //Prevent the class from being used as an instance
  private function __construct() {}

  public static function SomeMethod() {
    //Do something
  }

}
```

The Factory Pattern

Factories are any class that contains a method whose primary purpose is to create another object. Factories are critically important to the practice of polymorphic programming. They allow you to substitute classes, change configuration on the fly, and generally make your application more nimble. The successful mastery of the factory pattern is important for any advanced PHP developer.

The factory pattern is typically used to return different classes that conform to a similar interface. A common use for factories is to create a polymorphic provider, allowing you to decide which class should be instantiated, based on application logic or a configuration setting. For example, you could use such a provider to extend a class without needing to refactor any other part of the application to use the new extended name.

Typically, a factory pattern has one key ingredient: a static method, which is by convention named `factory`. However, this is merely a convention, and a factory method may be given any name. The static method may take any number of arguments and must return an object.

Listing 3-4 demonstrates the most basic possible factory class.

Listing 3-4. *Creating a Basic Factory*

```
class MyObject {
    //Your object that will be returned from the factory
}

class MyFactory {
  public static function factory() {
    //Return a new instance of your object
    return new MyObject();
  }

}
```

The factory would then be invoked like this:

```
$instance = MyFactory::factory();
```

Well, that's nice, but unfortunately, totally useless. It's time to examine a couple of real-world scenarios where you might employ a factory.

The Image Factory

Picture, if you will, a drawing program. You want to be able to draw an image contained in a file to the screen. Each image file is in a totally different file format and it is not appropriate to place image-parsing code for every conceivable image type in a single class. In this case, you will need to create a class for each image type: `Image_PNG`, `Image_JPEG`, and so on. Each class should be contained in a separate file. All of these image classes should contain a few common methods to get the image height, width, and raw image data. However, how they each parse their files to get this information will differ greatly. You can use an interface to define the common functionality and create a factory pattern to make your API easier to use, as shown in Listing 3-5.

Listing 3-5. *Image File Parsing with Factories*

```
interface IImage {

  function getHeight();
  function getWidth();
  function getData();

}
```

```php
class Image_PNG implements IImage {

  private $_width, $_height, $_data;

  public function __construct($file) {
    $this->_file = $file;
    $this->_parse();
  }

  private function _parse() {
    //Complete PNG specific parsing
    //and populate $_width, $_height and $_data
  }

  public function getWidth() {
    return $this->_width;
  }

  public function getHeight() {
    return $this->_height;
  }

  public function getData() {
    return $this->_data;
  }

}

class Image_JPEG implements IImage {

  private $_width, $_height, $_data;

  public function __construct($file) {
    $this->_file = $file;
    $this->_parse();
  }

  private function _parse() {
    //Complete JPEG specific parsing
    //and populate $_width, $_height and $_data
  }

  public function getWidth() {
    return $this->_width;
  }
```

```php
  public function getHeight() {
    return $this->_height;
  }

  public function getData() {
    return $this->_data;
  }

}

class ImageFactory {

  public static function factory($file) {
    $pathParts = pathinfo($file);
    switch(strtolower($pathParts['extension'])) {
      case 'jpg':
        $ret = new Image_JPEG($file);
        break;
      case 'png';
        $ret = new Image_PNG($file);
        break;
      default:
        //Problem
    }
    if($ret instanceof IImage) {
      return $ret;
    } else {
      //Problem
    }
  }

}
```

Now, when you use the factory method with your image file name, you will get a different object depending on what type of file you pass in. Since all the Image_* classes implement IImage, you can use a consistent set of method calls on the returned instance.

```php
$image = ImageFactory::factory('/path/to/my.jpg');
//$image is now an instance of Image_JPEG
echo $image->getWidth();
```

In the example, ImageFactory is a factory class because it returns a class instance. The type of class is determined by file extension using the pathinfo() function.

Because it is a factory, the resulting application does not need to know the details of how these images were parsed. All it needs to know is that each object returned by the factory supports the IImage interface.

Using this technique makes it significantly easier to consume your API, because it has only one class and one method. Without the factory pattern, the consumer of your API would need to determine which class should be called, and then call a specific class, replicating the factory's behavior.

This factory also makes it easy to make changes in the future. Adding another supported image type requires only modification of the single factory method. Without the factory pattern, you would need to update every block of code that consumed your API. In the next example, we will examine this concept, often called *future-proofing*, in more depth.

The Portable Database

In PHP applications, you will typically use a relational database to store the data your application creates and references. One of the biggest problems with databases is the inability to interact with them in a portable and interchangeable manner. If you've ever ported an application from one database to another, you've probably needed to refactor an extremely large amount of code, because the possible need for such a change was not considered when the application was developed.

With applications that use a database, the factory pattern can help you in two ways:

- It will make it easy for your software to support many different database platforms, a feature which will help to expand your customer base.

- If your software is in-house, it will guarantee that if you need to change databases, porting the application to another platform will be a trivial job.

Listing 3-6 demonstrates the concept of using a database factory. You may wish to create a database table called user to test it. This table should define a single varchar column named email.

Listing 3-6. *Using a Factory for Database Portability*

```
interface IDatabaseBindings {

  public function userExists($email);

}

class PGSQL implements IDatabaseBindings {

  protected $_connection;

  public function __construct() {
   $this->_connection = pg_connect('dbname=example_db');
  }

  public function userExists($email) {
    $emailEscaped = pg_escape_string($email);
    $query = "select 1 from users where email = '". $emailEscaped ."'";
    if($result = pg_query($query, $this->_connecion)) {
      return (pg_num_rows($result) > 0)?true:false;
```

```php
    } else {
      return false;
    }
  }

}

class MYSQL implements IDatabaseBindings {

  protected $_connection;

  public function __construct() {
    $this->_connection = mysql_connect('localhost');
    mysql_select_db('example_db', $this->_connection);
  }

  public function userExists($email) {
    $emailEscaped = mysql_real_escape_string($email);
    $query = "select 1 from users where email = '". $emailEscaped ."'";
    if($result = mysql_query($query, $this->_connecion)) {
      return (mysql_num_rows($result) > 0)?true:false;
    } else {
      return false;
    }
  }

}

class DatabaseFactory {

  public static function factory() {
    $type = loadtypefromconfigfile();
    switch($type) {
      case 'PGSQL':
        return new PGSQL();
        break;
      case 'MYSQL';
        return new MYSQL();
        break;
    }
  }

}

//--- Usage ---

$db = DatabaseFactory::factory();
$db->userExists('person@example.com');
```

The code creates a DatabaseFactory class that will instantiate and return IDatabaseBindings-compatible objects. The application will be written to the specification in IDatabaseBindings, and the implementing classes will be responsible for actually executing the queries that operate with the specific database. This example creates two classes: a PGSQL class for the PostgreSQL layer and a MySQL class for the MySQL layer.

The rest of the application will be kept completely oblivious to which database it is interacting with and will interact directly only with the instance returned by the factory, based on the rules defined in the IDatabaseBindings interface.

Just the Facts

In this chapter, you learned that patterns are like recipes for developers. Patterns require the inclusion of key elements to behave as expected. We focused on two key patterns: the singleton and factory.

The singleton pattern allows you to define a central point of responsibility. The singleton class holds an instance of itself in a static variable and vends it by a getInstance() static method. This method returns a reference to that variable, as well as performing the initial instantiation if it has not previously been done. This delayed instantiation is called *lazy loading*. A singleton class should also mark its constructor with a private modifier to prevent direct instantiation. To close a loophole that could create a copy of the singleton, the __clone() magic method must also be defined and marked private.

The factory pattern allows you to create a class that is designed to instantiate and return instances of other classes depending on differences in input or application configuration. The factory pattern contains one method, factory(), which, by definition, must return an object. You saw a couple examples of where the factory pattern can be useful—specifically, in file-format abstraction and database portability.

■ ■ ■

CHAPTER 4

Exceptions

Introduced in PHP 5, exceptions are a critical part of any OOP application. The term *exception* refers to the entire machinery of try, catch, and throw statements, and the Exception class. This machinery is designed to help you define when a problem occurs and what the code should do when a problem is encountered.

Exceptions give you control over how your program generates and handles errors. Exceptions also make your programming life easier by providing details about the context of the exception. By using exceptions, you will be able to create more robust applications that are fault-tolerant and that can inform an administrator when problems arise.

In this chapter, I will show you how to use built-in exceptions, as well as how to extend exceptions in your own applications.

Implementing Exceptions

An exception should be used for any type of error that is not supposed to occur in normal code execution. For example, you might implement an exception in a section of code that connects to an external database, to handle the possibility of a database connection failure.

Exception Elements

Exceptions are implemented by the addition of three keywords: try, catch, and throw, as well as the creation of the built-in Exception base class. These language constructs allow you to run error-prone sections of code and recover from failure.

try

The try keyword is used to define a block of code in which to watch for exceptions. You use the try block with braces, just as you would use any other block statement, such as if, while, or for. A try block has the following form:

```
try {
  //Code
}
```

The code within this block will be run until it completes or an exception is thrown. If an exception is thrown, the rest of the code is skipped, and execution resumes at the catch block.

catch

The catch block defines what to do in the case of an exception. It allows you to define the type of exception to catch, as well as access the details of the exception that was caught. Here is an example:

```
catch (Exception $e) {
  echo $e;
}
```

In this example, $e is now an instance of the Exception class. As discussed shortly, Exception is the highest ancestor of any type of exception, so catching Exception will catch any type of exception.

You may define multiple catch blocks when working with different types of exceptions. Always define the most specific type first, as catch blocks are evaluated in sequential order, with the first block executed first.

throw

throw is used to cause an exception to occur and abort processing at that point. You must pass an instance of Exception to throw. You can throw an exception stored in a variable or create the instance inline.

Both of the following forms are equivalent:

```
$a = new Exception("Error message");
throw $a;
```

or

```
throw new Exception("Error message");
```

You will typically use the first form when using custom exceptions (discussed in the next section). In these cases, you will sometimes need to set various properties of the exception before throwing it. You can use throw with any Exception-derived class.

Exception

Exception is the base class for all exceptions. You can extend from Exception to define custom exceptions. (Chapter 13 discusses some of the extended, built-in exceptions that are available.)

Exception's constructor optionally takes an error message and an error code. The error message is self-explanatory, but error codes deserve some explanation.

By providing an error code, you can later decide pragmatically what to do in the event of an exception. By inspecting the code returned, you can numerically map exceptions without needing to make your programming dependent on the error strings, which may be changed from time to time. This technique is demonstrated in the "Error Coding" section later in this chapter.

Once constructed, an exception knows several key things: where it was constructed, what code was executing at the time of construction, and the error message and the error code. Table 4-1 lists the methods that provide this data.

Table 4-1. *Exception Methods*

Method	Description
getMessage()	Returns the exception message, which is a string describing the error state
getCode()	Returns the error code
getFile()	Returns the source file in which the error occurred; useful for locating where an exception was thrown
getLine()	Gets the line in the source file where the exception was thrown; should be used with getFile()
getTrace()	Returns an array containing the context backtrace, which is a list of all the methods that are currently executing and their order
getTraceAsString()	Same as getTrace(), but returned as a string instead of an array
__toString()	Returns the entire exception represented as a string

The getTrace() method is very useful because each key in the array also contains the file, line, function name, and most important, all the arguments with which the function was called. Using the backtrace information, you can see all the upstream data that caused the problem, simplifying debugging. The getTrace() method is similar to the built-in function debug_backtrace().

Listing 4-1 demonstrates exception logic in the context of a database connection.

Listing 4-1. *Throwing an Exception While Connecting to a Database*

```
function connectToDatabase() {

  if(!$conn = pg_connect(…)) {
    throw new Exception("Could not connect to the database");
  }

}

try {

  connectToDatabase();

} catch(Exception $e) {

  echo $e->getMessage();

}
```

When thrown, this exception generates the following message:

```
Could not connect to the database
```

First, the code in Listing 4-1 creates a function that has a potential for failure. If the database is inaccessible, the connection function will return `false`, and an exception is thrown. The `throw` keyword is used with an `Exception` class object and tells the application when an error has occurred. Once an exception is thrown, instead of completing the function, the execution jumps to the `catch` block, where the application is told to echo the error message.

Extending Exceptions

Nonspecialized exceptions are great, but exceptions can be so much better. In Listing 4-1, it would be much more useful if you could examine why the database connection failed. To be able to get this information, you need to integrate `Exception` with the appropriate function. For example, `pg_last_error()` provides the reason for a PostgreSQL error.

Listing 4-2 demonstrates how to create a custom exception to use when connecting to a PostgreSQL database.

Listing 4-2. *Creating a Custom Exception Class*

```
class DatabaseException extends Exception {

  protected $databaseErrorMessage;

  public function __construct($message=null, $code = 0) {
    $this->databaseErrorMessage = pg_last_error();
    parent::__construct($message, $code);
  }

  protected function getDatabaseErrorMessage() {
    return $this->databaseErrorMessage;
  }

}
```

This code defines a `DatabaseException` class that extends from `Exception` and that declares a new method. This method will record the `pg_last_error()` in context and expose it for later access.

When creating this class, you must be careful to call the base class's constructor, as failing to do this can result in unreliable and often unstable behavior within PHP.

Listing 4-3 shows how to use this new exception.

Listing 4-3. *Throwing a Custom Exception*

```
function connectToDatabase() {

  if(!$conn = pg_connect(…)) {
    throw new DatabaseException("Friendly Message");
  }

}

try {

  connectToDatabase();

} catch(DatabaseException $e) {
  echo $e->getMessage() . "\n";
  echo $e->getDatabaseErrorMessage();

}
```

When thrown, this exception generates the following message:

```
Friendly Message
Unable to connect to PostgreSQL server: Access Denied for user. . .
```

This example exposes not only a friendly message, but also the technical details of why the connection failed. In most circumstances, you will wish to hide the technical details in a production environment, and expose the technical error message only when debugging.

Logging Exceptions

It is often advantageous to log exceptions to a file for later review. You can accomplish this in either of two ways:

- Create a custom exception base class for your application.

- Define an uncaught exception handler.

Let's look at both techniques.

Logging Custom Exceptions

To define a logging base class, you need to subclass Exception and add a log() method. Place a call to this logging method in your overridden constructor. Listing 4-4 demonstrates how to create this logging method.

Listing 4-4. *Creating a Logging Exception Base Class*

```
class LoggedException extends Exception {

  public function __construct (
              $message=null,
              $code=0,
              $file='/var/log/phpException.log')
  {
    $this->log($file);
    parent::__construct($message, $code)
  }

  protected function log($file) {
    file_put_contents($file, $this->__toString(), FILE_APPEND);
  }

}
```

■**Note** For details on the file functions used in Listing 4-4, see the PHP manual at http://www.php.net/manual/en/ref.filesystem.php.

You can then use LoggedException in place of Exception in all your invocations or custom exceptions. This will log all exceptions, even those that are caught. This is not always desirable, as you may wish to log only exceptions that were not caught or that were rethrown by a catch block. In these cases, you will want to use the PHP function set_exception_handler(), as described in the next section.

Defining an Uncaught Exception Handler

The set_exception_handler() function defines what to do when an exception makes it all the way up your call stack to the main function entry without being caught. Usually, you will see a message like this:

```
Fatal error: Uncaught exception 'Exception' in file.php:2
Stack trace:
#0 {main}
  thrown in file.php on line 2
```

This is the built-in exception handler. It can be useful, but it can also expose sensitive information, such as database login credentials. It is advantageous to disable this handler in production environments, by using php.ini, .htaccess, or ini_set(). Alternatively, if you wish to know about the exceptions that occur but still not display those exceptions, you can use the set_exception_handler() function to substitute your own logging function that does not display information.

To use the set_exception_handler() function, you must declare a single function that takes a single parameter. This function's name is then passed to set_exception_handler() as a string. You must, however, declare the function before calling set_exception_handler(), or you will encounter an error.

Listing 4-5 demonstrates how to use the set_exception_handler() function.

Listing 4-5. *Creating a Logging Exception Handler*

```
function exceptionLogger($exception) {
  $file = 'var/log/exceptionLog.log';
  file_put_contents($file, $exception->__toString(), FILE_APPEND);
}

set_exception_handler('exceptionLogger');
```

Now, since you have overridden the default exception handler, your uncaught exceptions are logged and not displayed to the screen.

Exception Overhead

While incredibly powerful, exceptions come at a price. When an exception is thrown in PHP, many mechanisms must be initialized, including the exception class instances and code back-traces. If your exceptions log to a file, even more weight is added. The power of exceptions can make it tempting to overuse them.

You should not use exceptions to control routine application flow, because that would adversely affect the performance of your application. An example of when not to use an exception is when searching a database for a login credential and not finding the user. In this case, you should just return null or false to indicate failure. This is the standard approach of returning mixed results from a PHP function: valid results to indicate data and false or null to indicate failure. In other words, when a PHP function fails to locate what it is looking for, it is common to return null or false instead of that value.

Error Coding

As mentioned earlier, you may want to use error codes to control pragmatic decisions. However, as your applications get larger, you will want to centralize the strings in the error messages so that they can be easily updated or even internationalized.

There are literally dozens of ways you can achieve this, but they all share a common quality: mapping of the error code to a string. You can also create an exception-derived class that will make operating with coded exceptions easier. Listing 4-6 shows one of the simplest possible implementations of error coding.

Listing 4-6. *Creating an Error Coding Custom Exception*

```
class DatabaseException extends Exception {

  const ConnectionFailed = 1;
  const LoginFailed = 2;
  const PermissionDenied = 3;

  public function __construct($code=0) {

    switch ($code) {
      case DatabaseException::ConnectionFailed:
        $message = 'Database connection failed';
        break;
      case DatabaseException::LoginFailed:
        $message = 'Login to the database was rejected';
        break;
      case DatabaseException::PermissionDenied:
        $message = 'Permission denied';
        break;
      default:
        $message = 'Unknown Error';
    }

    parent::__construct($message, $code);

  }

}

try {
  if( ! $conn = pg_connect(…)) {
    throw new DatabaseException(DatabaseException::ConnectionFailed);
  }
} catch (Exception $e) {
  //Output the standardized error message on failure
  echo $e->getMessage();
}
```

With this custom exception, all of your error message strings are centralized in one place. This will allow you to update the database connection error messages without needing to dig through a large volume of code.

Type Hinting and Exceptions

In Chapter 1, you learned about types and the instanceof operator. *Type hinting* is effectively instanceof meets method signature; function(type $param) would be a type-hinted function.

Type hinting is especially important when working with customized exceptions. By using type hinting and multiple catch blocks, you will be able to catch certain types of errors before others.

As explained earlier, catch blocks allow you to specify the type of exception to be caught, and you can have multiple catch blocks. Think of this as if the instanceof operator were applied to each catch block; if it returned true, then that block would be the one that was executed.

Listing 4-7 shows how to implement multiple catch blocks with different exception types.

Listing 4-7. *Type Hinting Exceptions*

```
class firstException extends Exception {}
class secondException extends Exception {}

try {
  //Code that throws exceptions
} catch (firstException $e) {
  //What to do when firstException is thrown
} catch (secondException $e) {
  //What to do when secondException is thrown
} catch (Exception $e) {
  //What to do for all other exceptions
}
```

Rethrowing Exceptions

Sometimes you will want to catch an exception, look at some of its properties, and then throw it again. This is often useful to check an error code and decide whether it should be fatal.

Listing 4-8 demonstrates how to catch an exception, check its error code, and rethrow the exception.

Listing 4-8. *Rethrowing an Exception*

```
function demonstration() {
  try {
    //Some code that throws exceptions
  } catch (Exception $e) {
    if($e->getCode() == 123) {
      //Do something special for error code 123
    } else {
      throw $e;
    }
  }
}
```

This code will allow any exception that does not have the code 123 to bubble up to the uncaught exception handler. The code 123 can then be handled in a special way, without making a special subclassed exception.

Just the Facts

In this chapter, you were introduced to exceptions. You learned that the keywords try, catch and throw, and the built-in Exception base class allow you to run error-prone sections of code and recover from failure.

The try keyword defines a block of code to run, watching for thrown exceptions. You can define multiple catch blocks for different types of exceptions.

You can throw the built-in Exception class using both variable and inline invocations. Properties that are available for inspection when an exception occurs include the message, code, and trace information.

You can create custom exceptions for your applications by extending the built-in Exception class. A key example is making your custom exceptions log to a file.

You can override the built-in exception handler by defining a set_exception_handler() callback function and also get that to log all uncaught exceptions to a file.

Exceptions, however, come with a certain amount of overhead. You should avoid excessive use of exceptions to control program flow.

You can centralize your error messages through the use of an error-coding class. This allows you to create more manageable applications as your systems grow.

Type hinting applies to exceptions, and you can implement multiple catch blocks with different exception types.

Finally, you can catch, inspect, and rethrow exceptions to the uncaught exception handler.

■■■

CHAPTER 5

What's New in PHP 6

P HP 6 is a major upgrade to the PHP language. The core focus for PHP 6 is native Unicode support, which will allow you to seamlessly use multiple languages within your applications. Programmers in non-English-speaking countries will even be able to name their functions and classes in their own native language. Unicode support is quickly becoming extremely important, as more and more of your applications will be targeting users worldwide.

Beyond multilanguage support, PHP 6 also adds some advanced OOP concepts, such as namespaces and late static binding. If properly used, these features will allow you to better organize your classes and methods.

PHP 6 also serves as a chance to break some backward-compatibility and clean up existing functions. You will find support for `register_globals`, `magic_quotes_gpc`, and `safe_mode` removed, along with the PHP 4 ze1 compatibility mode. The parameter ordering of a few functions has also been updated to make the API more consistent.

Finally, PHP 6 includes several new classes like `XMLWriter`, which add new functionality to the PHP language.

■Note In tracking any open source project, it is often hard to predict how the language will evolve. This chapter is based largely on rumored information and proposed changes that may change before the final release of PHP 6. In order to keep current with these changes, I will try to maintain an up-to-date erratum on this chapter, which you can access in the Book Extras section on the web page for this book on the Apress site (`http://www.apress.com/book/view/1590598199`).

PHP Installation

Eventually, PHP 6 will be included in the package management systems for your operating system, but until then, some manual installation is required. Here, I'll focus on the manual installation of modules that are not under package management (at the time of this writing) on Debian/Ubuntu Linux-based operating systems. I will also assume that you are using the Apache 2.2 web server.

To get started, you will need some basic packages from package management. Install the following packages using `apt-get install`:

```
> apt-get install apache2.2-common apache2-mpm-prefork \
> apache2-prefork-dev apache2-src apache2-utils autoconf \
> bison flex g++ libtool libxml2-dev re2c
```

Once these packages are installed, you need to install the Unicode library ICU. At the time of this writing, the package-managed version of ICU is not compatible with PHP 6, so ICU 3.6 or higher must be manually installed. Fortunately, this installation is trivial:

```
> mkdir ~/icu3.6
> cd ~/icu3.6
> wget ftp://ftp.software.ibm.com/software/globalization/icu/3.6/icu4c-3_6-src.tgz
> tar xf icu4c-3_6-src.tgz
> cd icu/source
> mkdir /usr/local/icu
> ./configure --prefix=/usr/local/icu
> make && make install
```

After you've completed the installation of ICU, installing PHP 6 is simple. First, find a copy of PHP 6—sourced from http://snaps.php.net or (once the final version is released) from http://www.php.net. The snapshot file should be called php6.0-200XXXXXXX.tar.bz2. Use the following commands to install PHP 6:

```
> tar xf php6.0-200XXXXXXXX.tar.bz2
> cd php6.0-200XXXXXXXX
> ./configure \
> --prefix=/usr/local/php6 --with-apxs2=/usr/bin/apxs2 \
> --with-icu-dir=/usr/local/icu
```

■**Note** If you are a Debian/Ubuntu user, pay special attention to the cautions about your modified Apache installation. If you need additional functionality, like MySQL or PostgreSQL support, be sure to add it on the configure line. For a complete list of configuration options, pass the `--help` option.

Debian/Ubuntu users may need to execute the following command due to a quirk with the way these distributions package Apache 2.

```
> echo #AddModule placeholder placeholder >> /etc/apache2/httpd.conf
```

Finally, compile and install PHP 6:

```
> make
> make install
```

At this point, PHP 6 should be installed, but it is not fully set up. To confirm the installation is correct, use the following command:

```
> php --version
```

```
PHP 6.0.0-dev (cli) (built: Dec 13 2007 16:59:43)
Copyright (c) 1997-2007 The PHP Group
Zend Engine v3.0.0-dev, Copyright (c) 1998-2007 Zend Technologies
```

The final step in setting up PHP 6 is to integrate it with your web server. If you're using Debian/Ubuntu, you will want to follow its module format by creating the configuration files shown in Listings 5-1 and 5-2.

Listing 5-1. *Creating /etc/apache2/mods-available/php6.load*

```
LoadModule php6_module /usr/lib/apache2/modules/libphp6.so
```

Listing 5-2. *Creating /etc/apache2/mods-available/php6.conf*

```
<IfModule mod_php6.c>
  AddType application/x-httpd-php .php
  AddType application/x-httpd-php-source .phps
</IfModule>
```

After you have created these two configuration files, remove the automatically added content from /etc/apache2/httpd.conf. Then make this call:

```
> a2enmod php6
```

You now have PHP 6 installed and configured.

If you are not a Debian/Ubuntu user, the PHP installer should automatically update httpd.conf with the changes listed in Listings 5-1 and 5-2. You should confirm that these settings were added and are correct.

Next, to enable PHP 6, Apache must be reloaded. On Debian/Ubuntu systems, issue this command:

```
> /etc/init.d/apache2 force-reload
```

And here's the generic Apache 2 command to reload Apache:

```
> apache2ctl restart
```

To test your PHP installation, on the web server, create a .php file containing a call to the phpinfo() function, as shown in Listing 5-3.

Listing 5-3. *Getting PHP Information (/var/www/index.php)*

```
<?php
  phpinfo();
```

Then visit http://*example.com*/index.php, where *example.com* is the IP or domain name of your web server. You should see "PHP Version 6.0.0-dev" on the screen, as well as information about all the loaded modules.

Unicode in PHP 6

The single biggest change in PHP 6 is the introduction of Unicode text-encoding support. Unicode changes a lot of things in PHP because the conceptual length of a string is no longer connected to the number of bytes of storage it uses. Many characters in Unicode may be two or more bytes. This required reworking most string functions, such as `strlen()`, to support multibyte character strings.

Unicode Semantics

A string in PHP 5 normally allocates one byte (8 bits) per character, but in PHP 6, the strings can be Unicode 16-bit encoding. The 8-bit encodings, and any other encodings you may have used, are now considered binary format strings. New, normal strings are considered Unicode. Which one you use by default depends on a `php.ini` setting called `unicode.semantics`.

When `unicode.semantics` is set to on, normal string literals are Unicode. When it is set to off, string literals are 8-bit binary strings. I recommend enabling Unicode semantics at this time. To see whether Unicode semantics are on or off, execute this command:

```
> php -r "echo ini_get('unicode.semantics');"
```

```
1
```

If you see a 0 here instead, you will need to enable `unicode.semantics` in your `php.ini` file. You can use the command `php -i` to locate your `php.ini` file. If no `php.ini` file exists at the specified location, a sample file comes with the PHP distribution. Locate `php.ini-recommended` in the source package and rename/copy it to the location specified by `php -i`; for example, `/etc/php.ini` or `/usr/local/php6/lib/php.ini`.

Once Unicode semantics are enabled, you can use Unicode characters directly in your PHP scripts, and functions like `strlen()` will correctly count the length of your strings using Unicode, rather than the number of bytes in the string. Listing 5-4 demonstrates a Unicode example using Canadian Aboriginal Syllabics.

■**Tip** Linux and Mac users will already have a compatible font, but Windows users can find one on `http://www.tiro.com`. Without a proper font, the text in Listing 5-4 may appear as boxes or spaces.

Listing 5-4. *Unicode String Length*

```
<?php
$standard = "abcde";
echo standard . " " . strlen($standard) . "\n";

$unicode = "▽△△△▷";
echo $unicode . " " . strlen($unicode) . "\n";
```

```
With unicode.semantics=off
abcde 5
▽△△△▷ 15
With unicode.semantics=on
abcde 5
▽△△△▷ 5
```

You will notice that the Unicode characters actually form a string with a length equal to 5. When Unicode semantics are turned off, the Unicode string is reported as having a length of 15.

Even with `unicode.semantics` off, the `$unicode` string is still treated as Unicode in PHP 6, and your output will look correct.

It is possible to force binary handling of string data, even if the source file contents are Unicode and Unicode semantics are enabled. Listing 5-5 shows the same Unicode string as in Listing 5-4, but using the new binary string literal format.

Listing 5-5. *Binary String Literals*

```
<?php
$binary = b"▽△△△▷";
echo $binary . " " . strlen($binary);
```

```
á..á..á..á..á.. 15
```

Notice that the output is assuming that the input string is in binary, because of the b before the quotation marks. The output appears distorted on the screen because the encoding for binary strings uses the value of the `unicode.runtime_encoding` setting in the `php.ini` file—in this case, ISO-8859-1.

You can cast between binary and Unicode just as you cast between types, as demonstrated in Listing 5-6.

Listing 5-6. *Unicode Casting*

```php
<?php
$unicode = "été";
echo $unicode;

$binary = (binary)$unicode;
echo $binary;

$unicode2 = (unicode)$binary;
echo $unicode2;
```

```
été
  t
été
```

Note that not all characters can be converted to binary format. If you were to take the Canadian Aboriginal Syllabics from Listing 5-4 and try to convert them to binary mode, you would end up with all your text being replaced with question marks (3f bytes), because the question mark is the default error-substitution character.

Unicode Collations

In addition to generally supporting Unicode, PHP 6 will support Unicode collations. One feature of collations is that they allow you to sort a list based on the sorting rules of a specific language or region. Listing 5-7 demonstrates sorting in the traditional Spanish collation, which uses an extended 30-character alphabet, in which *ch*, *ll*, *ñ*, and *rr* are all considered separate characters. Because of these extra characters, *ll* is sorted after *l*, just as the letter *b* is normally sorted after *a*.

Listing 5-7. *Unicode Collation Sorting*

```php
<?php

$list = array('luna','llaves','limonada');

//Normal alphabetical sort, lla before lu
sort($list);
print_r($list);

//Collated sort, lla after lu
locale_set_default('es_VE@collation=traditional');
sort($list, SORT_LOCALE_STRING);
print_r($list);
```

```
Array
(
    [0] => limonada
    [1] => llaves
    [2] => luna
)
Array
(
    [0] => limonada
    [1] => luna
    [2] => llaves
)
```

Precisely which methods will be upgraded to support Unicode semantics is not yet clear. fopen() will likely be updated to extend the rt reading mode to read Unicode documents. Additionally, most of the string methods—strlen(), str_word_count(), and so on—will be updated, and you will be able to use various SPL iterators to iterate over strings by character or by word.

You can find more information about PHP 6 Unicode support at http://www.php.net/Unicode.

Namespaces

Namespaces are to PHP classes as directories are to files—they add structure and hierarchical organization to class libraries. Namespaces allow you to use the same class name for two distinct classes. For example, you might wish to have a class named Line, which draws a line on an image. However, the way your Line class would function would be very different for raster or vector images. The ideal solution is to use two classes, and with namespaces, you can give them both the same class name.

Namespaces make use of two key language constructs: namespace and use. To declare a namespace, specify the namespace name at the beginning of a file. All the classes and functions declared in this file will now belong to the namespace. The namespace line must be at the top of the file, before any other variable, class, or function declarations. Listing 5-8 demonstrates how to create a class within a namespace.

Listing 5-8. *Declaring a Namespace (Vector.php)*

```php
<?php
namespace Vector;

class Line {
  public function draw($x1, $y1, $x2, $y2) { . . . }
}
```

The scope resolution operator (::) has been overloaded for use with namespaces. For example, if you wanted to create a new instance of your Line class in the Vector namespace, you would use the scope resolution operator, as shown in Listing 5-9.

Listing 5-9. *Scope Resolution for Namespaces*

```php
<?php
require_once('Vector.php');

$line = new Vector::Line();
$line->draw(1,1,10,10);
```

You can use multiple levels of namespaces. For example, Graphics::Vector::Line is valid as a namespace name. The only restriction is that you may have only one namespace declaration per file.

As the namespace size grows, using namespaces can become a bit verbose. Fortunately, PHP also provides the use statement, which allows you to alias a specific namespace. Listing 5-10 shows how to use the use statement to shorten the instantiation of the Line class.

Listing 5-10. *Using the use Statement*

```php
<?php
require_once('Vector.php');

use Vector::Line as Line;

$line = new Line();
$line->draw(1,1,10,10);
```

You can also alias an entire namespace with the use statement.

Late Static Binding

It has been a long-standing issue with PHP's inheritance model that a parent class could not easily reference the final state of the class when extended. Consider the example shown in Listing 5-11.

Listing 5-11. *Unintended Inheritance*

```php
<?php
class ParentBase {
  static $property = 'Parent Value';
  public static function render() {
    return self::$property;
  }
}
class Descendant extends ParentBase {
  static $property = 'Descendant Value';
}
echo Descendant::render();
```

Parent Value

In this example, the render() method refers to self, which is ParentBase and not Descendant. There is no way from ParentBase::render() to refer to the final value of $property. To solve this problem, you would need to override the render() method in the descendant class as well.

With the introduction of late static binding, you can now use the scope keyword static to refer to the final value of a class property or method, as shown in Listing 5-12.

Listing 5-12. *Using Static Scope*

```php
<?php
class ParentBase {
  static $property = 'Parent Value';
  public static function render() {
    return static::$property;
  }
}
class Descendant extends ParentBase {
  static $property = 'Descendant Value';
}
echo Descendant::render();
```

Descendant Value

By using the static scope, you force PHP to look at the final class for all its property values. In addition to this late binding behavior, PHP also adds the get_called_class() function, which allows you to determine from which descendant class an inherited method was called. Listing 5-13 shows how you can get the current class calling context using get_called_class().

Listing 5-13. *Using get_called_class()*

```php
<?php
class ParentBase {
  public static function render() {
    return get_called_class();
  }
}
class Decendant extends ParentBase {}

echo Descendant::render();
```

Descendant

Dynamic Static Methods

The __call() functionality allows you to create a wildcard type method that will handle all undefined calls to methods to the class. The parameters of the method are the name of the called method and an array of the parameters passed to the method. You can now create dynamic static methods in the same manner as __call is used for non-static methods. With PHP 6, static functionality is handled by implementing the magic method __callStatic() as shown in Listing 5-14.

Listing 5-14. *Using __callStatic for Dynamic Static Methods*

```php
<?php

class MyClass {
  public static function __callStatic($name, $parameters) {
    echo $name .' method called. Parameters: '. PHP_EOL .
        var_export($parameters, true) . PHP_EOL;
  }
}

MyClass::bogus(1, false, 'a');
```

```
bogus method called. Parameters:
array (
  0 => 1,
  1 => false,
  2 => 'a',
)
```

Ternary Assignment Shorthand (ifsetor)

One of the more common operations when working with input data is the use of the ternary operator to provide a default value when an input is not present or fails to validate. You have likely seen code like this:

```php
$safe = $input ? $input : 'default';
```

This is wordier than needed, so the middle value has been made optional. You can now simply use the ifsetor syntax, ?:, like this:

```php
$safe = $input ?: 'default';
```

XMLWriter Class

Creating XML documents is a key part of modern web programming. You will often need to export data using XML formats. You have several existing options for creating XML documents, from SimpleXML to full-fledged Document Object Model (DOM) creation. However, these options have many limitations and, at times, frustrating and confusing APIs

The XMLWriter class is being introduced in PHP 6 to provide a simple, straightforward, and easy-to-use method for XML document creation. The API for this component has not yet been fully developed, and it is likely to change. You can find the latest reference information at http://www.php.net/xmlwriter.

Listing 5-15 is intended as a demonstration of how the API will eventually come together, but is not intended to be used as exact syntax. This listing builds a basic XHTML document for the output stream.

Listing 5-15. *A Sample XHTML Document*

```php
<?php

//Instantiate and set indentation options
$xml = new XMLWriter();
$xml->openURI('php://output');
$xml->setIndentString('  ');
$xml->setIndent(true);

//Start the document and set the DTD
$xml->startDocument('1.0', 'UTF-8');
$xml->startDtd('html','-//W3C//DTD XHTML 1.0 Strict//EN',
               'http://www.w3.org/TR/xhtml1/DTD/xhtml1-strict.dtd');
$xml->endDtd();

//Create the HTML document

$xml->startElement('html');
$xml->writeAttribute('xmlns', 'http://www.w3.org/1999/xhtml');
$xml->writeAttribute('xml:lang', 'en');
$xml->writeAttribute('lang', 'en');

$xml->startElement('head');
$xml->writeElement('title', 'An example XHTML document.');
$xml->endElement();

$xml->startElement('body');

$xml->writeElement('p', 'Hello, World!');
$xml->startElement('p');
$xml->text('This paragraph contains an inline ');
$xml->startElement('a');
$xml->writeAttribute('href','http://www.example.org');
$xml->text('link.');
$xml->endElement(); //a
$xml->endElement(); //p
```

```
$xml->endElement(); //body
$xml->endElement(); //html

$xml->endDocument();
$xml->flush();
```

```
<?xml version="1.0" encoding="UTF-8"?>
<!DOCTYPE html
PUBLIC "-//W3C//DTD XHTML 1.0 Strict//EN"
        "http://www.w3.org/TR/xhtml1/DTD/xhtml1-strict.dtd">
<html xmlns="http://www.w3.org/1999/xhtml" xml:lang="en" lang="en">
  <head>
    <title>An example XHTML document.</title>
  </head>
  <body>
    <p>Hello, World!</p>
    <p>This paragraph contains an inline
        <a href="http://www.example.org">link.</a>
    </p>
  </body>
</html>
```

Just the Facts

This chapter started with a guide for installing a preview release of PHP 6 from source, and then covered some of the upcoming features scheduled for PHP 6.

A major change in PHP 6 is Unicode support. This includes unicode.semantics, a new Unicode string type, and the ability to convert between traditional binary and Unicode strings. You can also sort Unicode-encoded arrays according to a localized collation.

PHP 6's namespaces can help you create a program hierarchy within your class libraries. Namespaces are created with the namespace statement. The use statement allows you to alias a specific namespace.

Late static binding expands PHP's inheritance capabilities. You can use the static scope to access a value overridden in a descendant class. The get_called_class() method enables you to create context-aware methods in base classes. Additionally, in PHP 6, a new magic method, __callStatic(), allows you to create dynamic static functions within your classes.

The ifsetor syntax for the ternary operator in PHP 6 enables a new shorthand format for ternary assignments.

The new XMLWriter class simplifies XML document creation.

Keep in mind that this chapter was written based on preview information about PHP 6, which is subject to change. You can access errata about this chapter in the Book Extras section on the web page for this book on the Apress web site (http://www.apress.com/book/view/1590598199). You can also find more details about PHP version information by referring to the PHP changelog.

PART 2

■■■

Testing and Documentation

CHAPTER 6

Documentation and Coding Conventions

Documentation is a crucial part of software development. It provides information regarding how to use the program, and can also help future maintainers and consumers of your program understand the decisions you made while developing the application. Documentation can also help *you* to remember design decisions you made when you later revisit your applications.

Documentation's importance is not limited to the communication of ideas. In PHP, documentation is also a key way to include *metadata* in your applications. Metadata, or data about data, is a key way to create advanced interactions between objects when you do not know the details of the objects beforehand. It's also a handy way of self-documenting applications that can be parsed into manuals automatically.

In this chapter, I will explain some of the common formats for PHP documentation, including PHPDoc and DocBook. These industry-standard formats, when correctly applied, will allow you to create easy-to-read code, generate manuals, and embed metadata in your applications. Note that you will need to understand the information presented in this chapter to take advantage of the powerful reflection features covered in the next chapter.

Coding Conventions

Coding conventions can be troublesome. Many developers have conducted lengthy arguments about why *their* way is the *best* way and any other methods are inferior. Although opinions on the subject may differ, one idea is universally accepted: consistency is king. Correctness is entirely in the eye of the beholder, but agreement is crucial. It's critically important that all members of a team follow the same conventions and apply them consistently. Most of the public projects, such as the Zend Framework and PEAR components, have clearly defined coding standards.

The sort of conventions I'm referring to are pretty basic. For the most part, they deal with where braces go and how functions and variables are named. They also include various documentation standards that will be discussed shortly.

For example, some developers like to put an opening brace on the same line as an element, like this:

```
function foo() {
}
```

Others prefer to place the brace on the next line:

```
function foo()
{
}
```

The Zend Framework and PEAR standards both call for the latter form, but they use the former form when working with control structures. For instance, you'll find code in the Zend Framework that looks like this:

```
if($x == 1) {
  $x += 50;
} else if ($x == 2) {
  $x += 55;
} else {
  $x = 60;
}
```

In PEAR packages, you'll find an almost identical coding style:

```
if($x == 1) {
  $x += 50;
} elseif ($x == 2) {
  $x += 55;
} else {
  $x = 60;
}
```

Pretty close, right? The only difference between the Zend and PEAR styles is that the `elseif` isn't spaced to `else if`. But neither follows the function-bracing standards just mentioned. Others may say that the correct format is to always use the brace-on-a-new-line approach, like this:

```
if($x == 1)
{
  $x += 50;
}
elseif ($x == 2)
{
  $x += 55;
}
else
{
  $x = 60;
}
```

Who's right? Technically, no one.

If you are trying to define the standards for a new application, the easiest way by far is to pick a project whose standards you like and follow them to the letter. For more information about the Zend and PEAR standards, see the complete references at http://framework.zend.com/ and http://pear.php.net/, respectively.

PHP Comments and Lexing

To get the most from your documentation efforts, it is important to understand the differences between different types of comments. Some types of comments just include information for programmers, and other types actually store their content with the program's data.

Types of Comments

PHP has several types of comments. *Single-line comments* are declared like this:

```
//This is an inline comment
```

Multiline comments have the following form:

```
/*
This is a multiline comment and
may span many lines
*/
```

A third form is known as a *doccomment*, which is declared like this:

```
/**
This is a doccomment, which is also often
called a docblock
*/
```

The two latter forms might look similar, but they have different parsing implications to PHP. The first form is just human-readable information that is not meaningful to PHP. The second form does something extra: it stores the data of the comment along with the program code, and this data may be used by other applications to get more information about how they should interact with your program. Let's take a closer look at how doccomments work.

More About Doccomments

Doccomments can be associated with certain programming elements, such as classes, functions, constants, variables, methods, and so on. To associate a doccomment with an element, you simply declare the doccomment block immediately prior to the element and ensure that there are no newlines between the closing asterisk (star) and slash and the element. Listing 6-1 demonstrates how to associate a doccomment with a function.

Listing 6-1. *Using Doccomments*

```
/**
This is a doccomment that is associated with a function
*/
function notimportant() {}

/*
This is not a doccomment because it does not start with a slash-star-star
*/
```

```
function notimportant{}

/**
This is a doccomment but it is not associated with the function
*/

function notimportant() {}
```

As you can see, doccomments are picky. If they are not placed immediately before the function, they will not be associated with that function.

Now you can write and associate doccomments, but what does that association actually do?

There is a key distinction between a normal comment and a doccomment. To understand that distinction, you need a little background on how the PHP parsing process works.

Lexing

While PHP is not a compiled language, it resembles compiled languages in that PHP code is converted into a binary format before actually being executed.

This transformation from programming language to executable code is called *lexing* because it transforms the lexical structure of PHP code into opcodes (numeric representations of PHP language elements). When the *lexer*—the part of PHP that performs lexing—encounters a normal comment, it understands that it is a comment and ignores it, discarding all the data within the comment. All discarded data is no longer present in the resulting binary format and cannot be accessed by other programs; therefore, regular comments aren't useful for embedding metadata.

On the other hand, a doccomment, like a function or class, is actually parsed and its data stored. It becomes part of the binary, and more important, when declared with a code element, becomes associated with that element. It is this association that is so critical for creating context for your data.

The context of comments is important because metadata is accessed by asking the program for the element's details and then checking the associated doccomment property. Without the association, you won't be able to use your doccomments in a programmatic way, and you might as well have just used a normal multiline comment.

The association of doccomments and programming elements provides the ability to embed extra metadata in your programs.

Metadata

Metadata is data that describes other data. In programming terms, that means metadata is information about your program. For example, all the method names within a class can be considered metadata.

By default, PHP includes metadata for most programming elements. However, you may need to embed more metadata than PHP normally does. For example, some systems use metadata attributes to include testing information, such as the expected output for a certain input.

While some other languages inherently support addition of extra metadata through programming elements called *attributes*, PHP doesn't include this ability. However, this ability can be simulated with the parsing of doccomments. For example, you can embed metadata that is not important to the execution of the application but is important to the creation of a manual about that code.

Using metadata in this way is especially useful in generating documentation automatically. One method of creating manuals from metadata is to use the PHPDoc standard. If you create doccomments that follow a specific format, a parser program can turn the comments into meaningful documentation automatically.

PHPDoc

PHPDoc (`http://www.phpdoc.org/`) is the most widely used solution for maintaining PHP documentation. If you've ever used a PEAR library or any kind of prepackaged PHP library, you will have undoubtedly run across PHPDoc.

PHPDoc defines a structure for doccomments that allows them to be parsed in a consistent manner. As HTML is to XML, PHPDoc is to doccomments. With it, you can create useful manuals from your in-line documentation.

PHPDoc consists of a set of rules regarding how to declare doccomments and is almost a language in itself. A PHPDoc block—a doccomment—can define dozens of different pieces of metadata. In this section, I'll cover only the basics and most commonly used parts of PHPDoc.

Like all doccomments, PHPDoc blocks must start with the slash-star-star comment declaration. Next, they may include normal descriptive information about the item you are documenting.

```
/**
I am a PHPDoc comment and I describe somefunction
*/
function somefunction() {}
```

This follows the format of all doccomments, so you are likely wondering what makes it special. The answer is tags!

Tags are specified by the @ symbol and a predefined identifier. They can occur at the beginning of a line or may be enclosed in curly braces ({}) and placed free-form anywhere within the comment. The allowable identifiers are predefined, and they form the rules for how a documentation parser will interpret your comments.

```
/**
I am a PHPDoc comment.
@param bool $foo Foo tells the function something
*/
function bar($foo) {}
```

Notice that a @param tag describes the function's $foo argument. This is metadata and can later be read by a parser to output documentation about $foo. The tag's format allows you to add some extra metadata, such as the type of the variable, the variable's name, and a description of what it does. All PHPDoc tags follow this same basic format.

The @param tag is just one tag of many. Table 6-1 lists the most commonly used PHPDoc tags applicable to PHP 5 and later. For the complete list, see `http://manual.phpdoc.org/`.

■**Note** Some of the PHPDoc tags in the official standard are not applicable when working with reflection-based parsers because these parsers can determine some attributes, like access, automatically.

Table 6-1. *Common PHPDoc Tags*

Tag	Description
@access public|private|protected	Describes the access level. This tag is not particularly useful for use with reflection, as the API can determine this ability automatically. In PHPDoc, it is used to allow you to omit generating documentation for private members.
@author Author Name [<author@email.com>]	Helps determine who is responsible for a particular element (I strongly recommend its use).
@copyright Copyright Information	Allows you to specify the copyright of the code.
@deprecated [version information]	Allows you to tell consumers of your code that an element is no longer to be used and has been replaced.
@example [path|url] description	Lets you reference an example of how to use the element. The second parameter can be a path or a full URL.
@filesource	Allows you to indicate that you want to make the source of the file available to the documentation. This tag can be included only in a page-level block and will be ignored elsewhere.
@global datatype description	Describes the global variable data type. This tag must immediately precede a global variable and is applicable only to phpDocumentor-parsed documentation. It is not useful for reflection-based parsing.
@ignore	Tells the parser to ignore an element and to not include it in documentation.
@internal	Allows you to hide certain information from public documentation. It can be used in-line as well as on a new line.
@license url [license]	Specifies the URL to the license this software is used under and optionally describes the license name.
@link url [description]	Includes a link in your documentation. This tag may be used in-line.
@param datatype $variablename[, . . .] description	Describes the parameters associated with functions and methods. This is probably the most important tag. The variable name argument can optionally include , . . . to indicate there may be an unlimited number of other parameters passed to the function. This tag may appear multiple times in a block. (See Listing 6-2 for examples.)
@return datatype description	Describes the type of data returned by a function or method. This is probably the second most important tag and is the only way in PHP to include metadata about the returned data. I recommend that you use this tag with all functions that return a value.

Table 6-1. *Common PHPDoc Tags*

Tag	Description
@see reference	Refers to the documentation of another element. You can use a variety of pointers, including a file, function name, class method, and many more. Multiple values can be separated by commas. This tag may also be used in-line.
@since version [information]	Allows you to tag the version in which this element first appeared.
@source startoffset [endoffset]	Allows you to include some of the source code for an associated element in-line with the documentation (the tag is in-line only). The start offset is the offset line number you want to include in your documentation, and the end offset is the number of lines you wish to include. If you omit the end offset, all the code starting at the start offset until the end of the element will be included.
@todo description	Includes information about work that remains to be done or a problem that needs to be resolved.
@var datatype	Documents the type of class variables that are also known as properties.
@version	Specifies the current version number of an element.

Listing 6-2 demonstrates a typical PHPDoc comment on a function.

Listing 6-2. *A PHPDoc Comment on a Function*

```
/**
 * This function adds two strings.
 *
 * It does this by taking the first string and
 * adding it to the second string, and
 * then returns the result.
 *
 * @param string $string1 The left string.
 * @param string $string2 The right string.
 * @return string A string containing concatenated inputs.
 * @todo Add a joining character parameter.
 */
function concatTwoStrings($string1,$string2) {
  return $string1 . $string2;
}
```

OK, so now that you have all these documentation blocks and tags, how do you use them to create a manual? One option is to use the phpDocumentor parser; another is to parse the information using reflection. Reflection will be covered in the next chapter. Here, let's see how to use phpDocumentor.

The easiest way to get the phpDocumentor parser tool is to install it from PEAR:

```
pear install PhpDocumentor
```

You will now have access to the phpdoc command. A good first try is this:

```
phpdoc -f somefile.php -t /path/to/output/directory
```

I suggest that you make the output path in your web root so that you can view the result from your web browser. The phpdoc command offers a lot of output options, such as the following:

- HTML:frames:default, for HTML frames output

- HTML:Smarty:default, for Smarty template output

- CHM:default:default, for Windows help file format

- PDF:default:default, for PDF output

You may specify these options with the -o option using the following format:

```
output:converter:templatedir
```

Using the -h option will show you all the options and arguments.

After you have run the phpdoc command, you will find an HTML file in the output directory. This file can be viewed with a web browser and will contain information about the code contained in your PHP file. I suggest you try some different combinations of the previously discussed tags and see how they affect the output.

Once you have your documentation working the way you want, you may wish to extend the PHPDoc tags. Although the phpDocumentor parser won't use them, you can define any otherwise unused tags and formats. When you build your own reflection parser, as described in the next chapter, you will be able to parse these custom tags to do whatever you wish. An example of a custom tag might be @lastmodified 01,23,2045. There really is no limit to what you might include in your application.

DocBook

You may need to create comprehensive documentation that would not be sensible to include in-line with your code. For example, some documentation may require examples or tutorials to fully understand. In these cases, PHPDoc is not as appropriate as DocBook.

DocBook is designed to create documentation that is readable and comprehensive. In practice, PHPDoc and DocBook are often used together harmoniously.

Creating an XML File for DocBook

DocBook is an XML application, just as XHTML is. It has elements and attributes, as you would expect, and it follows a specific Document Type Definition (DTD); that is, it has defined rules that translate the data at parsing time. DocBook uses Extensible Stylesheet Language (XSL) and stylesheets to transform the DocBook XML into a presentation format.

The file layout is pretty simple. First, you need to create an XML file that will contain the DocBook information. Like an HTML document, this file will contain elements and attributes. The basic structure of a DocBook XML file is shown in Listing 6-3.

Listing 6-3. *A Basic DocBook File*

```
<?xml version="1.0" encoding="UTF-8" ?>
<!DOCTYPE book PUBLIC "-//OASIS//DTD DocBook XML V4.4//EN"
  "/usr/share/xml/docbook/schema/dtd/4.4/docbookx.dtd">

<book>

<bookinfo>
  <title>Documentation</title>
  <subtitle>Cool Application</subtitle>
</bookinfo>

<chapter>
  <title>Chapter Title</title>
  <sect1>
    <title>Section Title</title>
    <para>Introduction to this section</para>
    <sect2>
      <para>Sections may have subsections</para>
    </sect2>
  </sect1>
</chapter>

</book>
```

Listing 6-3 demonstrates some of the more basic DocBook tags. As you'll notice, all DocBook files must contain a DOCTYPE declaration, which is the version of DocBook your documentation targets and the rules the file will follow. Next, you must define a root XML node, in this case, book. Next, all books contain information, so the bookinfo node describes these attributes.

All books contain chapters, and those chapters are logically enclosed in chapter tags. You may specify an unlimited number of chapters. Next, you can provide the chapter with a title.

Sections may be carved out of chapters, and even out of sections themselves. The sect1 element declares a first-level section. You can add subsections by nesting the sect1 through sect5 tags. Inside sections or chapters, you can declare paragraphs with the para tag.

The example in Listing 6-3 is straightforward and intentionally basic. You can do a lot more with DocBook, and we'll get to that, but first let's parse this file.

Parsing a DocBook File

To parse a DocBook file, you first need to install DocBook. You can do this in various ways depending on your operating system. I suggest that you use a package manager to install DocBook. For instance, on Debian, use the apt command:

```
apt-get install docbook docbook-xsl docbook-xml xsltproc
```

There are a lot of other DocBook-related subpackages, but these are the three packages you'll need to get started: DocBook XSL, DocBook XML, and the `xsltproc` tool.

Next, to parse your file, you will need to locate the `docbook.xsl` XSL stylesheet that you are going to use to transform your DocBook file. The file location depends on your distribution. The Debian default location is as follows:

```
/usr/share/xml/docbook/stylesheet/nwalsh/html/docbook.xsl
```

If the `docbook.xsl` file is not at this exact location, it will be close by. You will need to know the actual full path to this file to transform your document.

Next, execute the `xsltproc` program to transform your document according to the XSL stylesheet, like so:

```
xsltproc /path/to/docbook.xsl yourfile.xml
```

After running this command, you will also see some HTML output. This is the resultant form of DocBook processing, but it isn't very useful on the command line. To make it useful, you need to send it to a file, like so:

```
xsltproc -o yourfile.html /path/to/docbook.xsl yourfile.xml
```

You will now find `yourfile.html` in the directory, and you won't see the HTML on the command line; that HTML data is now in the file. You can open this file in a web browser, and voilà, instant manual! Figure 6-1 shows an example.

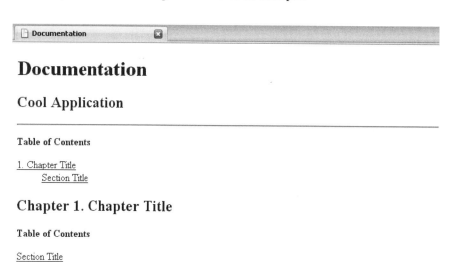

Figure 6-1. *Sample DocBook documentation in yourfile.html*

At this point, you have some HTML output, but it's all in one file, which may not be ideal. To break apart the file, say by chapter, you will need to create your own XSL file. This can be exceedingly complicated or fairly easy, depending on how fancy you want to get with the output. The stylesheet in Listing 6-4 demonstrates how to import the `chunk.xsl` stylesheet from the SourceForge DocBook project (`http://docbook.sourceforge.net`). Save this file as `yourfile.xsl`.

Listing 6-4. *A Chunking DocBook Custom XSL Stylesheet*

```
<?xml version="1.0" encoding="UTF-8"?>
<xsl:stylesheet xmlns:xsl="http://www.w3.org/1999/XSL/Transform"
  xmlns:fo="http://www.w3.org/1999/XSL/Format" version="1.0">

<xsl:import href="http://docbook.sourceforge.net/release/xsl/current/html/ ➥
chunk.xsl"/>
  <xsl:param name="use.id.as.filename">1</xsl:param>
</xsl:stylesheet>
```

Next, you will need to add `id` attributes to your DocBook file, as shown in Listing 6-5.

Listing 6-5. *DocBook File with id Attributes Applied*

```
<?xml version="1.0" encoding="UTF-8" ?>
<!DOCTYPE book PUBLIC "-//OASIS//DTD DocBook XML V4.4//EN"
  "/usr/share/xml/docbook/schema/dtd/4.4/docbookx.dtd">

<book id="mybook">

<bookinfo>
  <title>Documentation</title>
  <subtitle>Cool Application</subtitle>
</bookinfo>

<chapter id="mychapter">
  <title>Chapter Title</title>
  <sect1 id="firstsection">
    <title>Section Title</title>
    <para>Introduction to this section</para>
    <sect2 id="subsection">
      <para>Sections may have subsections</para>
    </sect2>
  </sect1>
</chapter>

</book>
```

Finally, use `yourfile.xsl` instead of the `docbook.xsl` with the `xsltproc` command, like so:

```
xsltproc yourfile.xsl yourfile.xml
```

If all went well, you should get this result:

```
Writing mychapter.html for chapter(mychapter)
Writing index.html for book(mybook)
```

You will notice that two files were created: an index document for the book and mychapter. html for the chapter. The index.html document will have links to the mychapter.html file automatically.

Now, you might be thinking that your DocBook file could get really large, and you would be right. Fortunately, DocBook supports linking XML files together by modifying the DOCTYPE with an ENTITY tag. Once the entity exists, you may use the &entity syntax to specify where to import the entity's data. Inclusion of external files is demonstrated in Listing 6-6.

Listing 6-6. *DocBook File with an Included Chapter*

```
<?xml version="1.0" encoding="UTF-8" ?>
<!DOCTYPE book PUBLIC "-//OASIS//DTD DocBook XML V4.4//EN"
  "/usr/share/xml/docbook/schema/dtd/4.4/docbookx.dtd"
[
  <!ENTITY chapter1 SYSTEM "chapter1.xml">
]>
<book id="mybook">

  <bookinfo>
    <title>Documentation</title>
    <subtitle>Cool Application</subtitle>
  </bookinfo>

  &chapter1;

</book>
```

Next, create a file named chapter1.xml, adding the content presented in Listing 6-7.

Listing 6-7. *A DocBook Chapter in an External File*

```
<chapter id="mychapter">
  <title>Chapter Title</title>
  <sect1 id="firstsection">
    <title>Section Title</title>
    <para>Introduction to this section</para>
    <sect2 id="subsection">
      <para>Sections may have subsections</para>
    </sect2>
  </sect1>
</chapter>
```

Reissuing the `xsltproc` command will work exactly as before, and the `chapter1.xml` file will be included.

Using DocBook Elements

The previous examples demonstrated using the elements for DocBook chapters, sections, and paragraphs. You can use many more elements to create comprehensive documentation. Here, we'll look at the more commonly used elements. For detailed information, see `http://www.docbook.org` and `http://docbook.sourceforge.net`.

The bookinfo Element

In Listing 6-6, you can see a `bookinfo` element that includes `title` and `subtitle` tags. The `bookinfo` element may include many more tags to give your documentation more detail. Listing 6-8 shows some of the more common `bookinfo` tags.

Listing 6-8. *DocBook bookinfo Tags*

```
<bookinfo>
  <title>A title</title>
  <subtitle>A subtitle</subtitle>
  <authorgroup>
    <author>
      <firstname>Kevin</firstname>
      <surname>McArthur</surname>
    </author>
    <corpauthor>Somecorporation Inc.</corpauthor>
  </authorgroup>
  <editor>
    <firstname>Joe</firstname>
    <surname>Somebody</surname>
  </editor>
  <date>
    Jan 1, 1970
  </date>
  <copyright>
    <year>2006</year>
    <holder>Somecorporation Inc.</holder>
  </copyright>
</bookinfo>
```

The chapter Element

The next thing in a book is a chapter. Listing 6-9 shows a basic `chapter` element.

Listing 6-9. *DocBook chapter Tags*

```
<chapter id="chapterid">
  <chapterinfo>
    . . .
  </chapterinfo>
  <title>Chapter title</title>
  <subtitle>Exploring chapter title</subtitle>
  <para>
    . . .
  </para>
  <sect1>
    <para>
      . . .
    </para>
  </sect1>
</chapter>
```

The chapterinfo tag behaves pretty much in the same way as the bookinfo tag, with a few exceptions. All chapters must have a title, and can optionally have a subtitle. The rest of the chapter is made up of sections and paragraphs.

The section Element

The section element may include sect1 through sect5 tags, which can be used to create logical sections for a chapter. The sect tags must be nested within one another, so a sect2 must have sect1 as a parent, sect3 must have sect2 as a parent, and so on. Each sect element may contain a title and any number of paragraphs or subsections up to sect5 depth. Listing 6-10 shows an example of a section element.

Listing 6-10. *DocBook section Tags*

```
<chapter>
  <sect1>
    <title>Section 1 Title</title>
    <para>Section one lead-in text</para>
    <sect2>
      <title>Subsection</title>
      <para>. . .</para>
    </sect2>
  </sect1>
</chapter>
```

The para Element

The para element is somewhat more complex than the previously discussed elements. Listing 6-11 shows some of the options for a para element.

Listing 6-11. *DocBook para Tags*

```
<para>
  This is a paragraph and can contain many elements.
  <itemizedlist>
    <listitem>
      <para>
        This is the first element in this list.
        <footnote>
          <para>This is a footnote to item 1</para>
        </footnote>
      </para>
    </listitem>
    <listitem>. . .</listitem>
  </itemizedlist>
  <example>
    <title>An example</title>
    <programlisting language="php">
      <![CDATA[<?php
        echo "hello, world";
      ?>]]>
    </programlisting>
  </example>
  The code <code language="php">echo "hello, world";</code> outputs
hello, world to the screen. For more information reference <ulink
url="http://www.somedomain.com/somefile.ext">Dave Smith's Tutorial</ulink>
  <citetitle>Dave's Reference</citetitle> describes this as:
  <blockquote>
    Material referenced from Dave's Reference.
  </blockquote>
  <table>
    <thead>
      <row>
        <entry>Header 1</entry>
        <entry>Header 2</entry>
      </row>
    </thead>
    <tbody>
      <row>
        <entry>Data 1</entry>
        <entry>Data 2</entry>
      </row>
    </tbody>
  </table>
  <note>Take note of some point</note>
  Data between literal tags is for specific data that should be taken literally
  and never translated. <literal>ObjectName</literal> is responsible for something.
  The information for x can be found in the Database
```

```
  <database>DatabaseName</database> in the table <database
  class="table">TableName</database> in the field <database
  class="field">FieldName</database>.
</para>
```

As you can see, you have a lot of options for the definition of a `para` element. This is, of course, an absurdly complex example, but it demonstrates the most common tags. Here are the items included in Listing 6-11:

Lists: `itemizedlist` is a grouping tag that contains items within the list. You can specify an unlimited number of `listitem` elements, each of which may have one or more `para` tags.

Footnotes: The `footnote` element adds a footnote. When parsed, footnotes substitute their text for a hyperlinked [*n*], where *n* is the current footnote index. At the end of the document, all your footnotes will be included with matching [*n*] text that is anchored to the original hyperlink.

Examples, code, and CDATA: The `example` tag lets you include PHP code within your documentation. The title of the example is contained in the `title` tag, and the actual code for the example is called a program listing and is enclosed by the `programlisting` tag. Notice, though, that the PHP data must be wrapped in CDATA. CDATA actually comes from XML and allows you to put brackets and other characters that would otherwise cause a problem inside an XML document. Without CDATA, most PHP code would cause validation issues with the XML document, and transformation would not be possible, so always remember to wrap your code inside CDATA delimiters. Similar to examples, you can also embed code in-line using the `code` tag. The `language` attribute defines what type of code the reference is.

Linking: The `ulink` elements add an underlined link from your documentation to another site. This is analogous to an `a` (anchor) tag in HTML; instead of `href`, the `url` attribute is used.

Citations: Sometimes, you will want to include material from another author or source. To do this, you can use the `cittitle` tag along with the `blockquote` tag to make it clear that the words cited are not your own.

Tables: The next item is the table model for DocBook. It's pretty much like HTML, but with slightly different element names. The table model in DocBook is not designed to be used for presentation, as in HTML. Instead, it is meant to be used when you have a set of data that is best expressed in a tabular format.

Notes and literals: You can use the `note` element to declare a note. Often, you will need to include the name of a function or class within your documentation. You should enclose any literal elements like these inside the `literal` tag. This tag can serve as notice to translators and editors that the information is to be taken literally and cannot be translated or edited.

Databases: When referencing databases, there is a great way to describe them in DocBook. First take a `database` element, and then customize it with a `class` attribute. The `class` attribute defines the information within the element to be one of the basic items in a database, like a field, primary key, data type, table, and so on. If you use this approach, the transformation will be able to create direct links to these items, or even present them in a graphical fashion.

There are literally hundreds of possible tags, and these are just the most common. Again, refer to the DocBook documentation for more details.

Just the Facts

In this chapter, you learned a lot about documentation. You learned that documentation is not only important for communicating ideas to other programmers, but can also be used for adding metadata to your applications.

You can use in-line, multiline, and doccomments comments in your code. Only doccomments are stored after lexing, and this is important for accessing the information programmatically.

PHPDoc is a way to embed metadata within your applications. The PHPDoc format is a standard in PHP documentation. Many PHPDoc tags are available, and you can also create your own tags. You will learn how to use PHPDoc information in the next chapter.

The DocBook standard is a comprehensive XML-based documentation type that defines the data markup for programming manuals. Its design is more focused on creating actual books, rather than commenting code within the program.

The next chapter covers the reflection API. In that chapter, you will build a reflection-based documentation parser using the doccomments that you learned about in this chapter.

■ ■ ■

CHAPTER 7

Reflection API

Reflection is one of the most powerful and perhaps one of the most underused features of the PHP language. If you're tasked with building complex, extensible applications, it's well worth your time to understand this powerful feature. Reflection can facilitate otherwise tedious and complicated tasks, such as autoloading plug-ins, automating documentation, and even extending the PHP language itself.

How can one feature offer such a wide array of capabilities? PHP's reflection API consists of a series of classes that allow you to access program metadata and interact with associated code comments. This gives you the ability to determine, for example, what methods a class implements. With this capability, you can create applications that load plug-ins without creating a rigid plug-in interface. This means that you can implement as few or as many methods of a supported API as you wish.

Reflection offers much more than the ability to review class metadata. It can also be used to create instances of classes, invoke functions, and pass arguments pragmatically. The reflection API even allows you to invoke static methods of classes dynamically. As mentioned in the previous chapter, reflection also can be used to create autodocumenting systems.

In this chapter, you will learn how, using reflection, you can create efficient plug-in-based systems. You will build a reflection-based documentation parser using the doccomments discussed in Chapter 6. Then you will learn how to add capabilities to the reflection API by extending the built-in classes. You will build a fully functional extended API that will parse your docblock comments into additional program metadata. Finally, you will learn how these techniques can be used to simulate attributes in the PHP language and allow for some very advanced OOP interaction.

Introducing the Reflection API

The reflection API is one of several built-in OOP extensions to PHP. It is a series of classes, exceptions, and interfaces that come together to allow you to analyze other classes, interfaces, methods, properties, functions, and extensions. This extension is appropriately named *reflection* and can be found in the PHP source under /ext/reflection, along with many useful examples and unit tests.

■**Note** You can find a complete reflection API reference at http://www.php.net/language.oop5. reflection. You may also wish to use the http://lxr.php.net/source/php-src/ext/ reflection/ source browser to see how the API works internally and view some of the more advanced usage scenarios included with the extension.

Rather than just telling you about the class declarations, I'll show you how to use reflection to expose the class declarations with PHP itself. To see a complete and up-to-date export of the entire reflection API, create the following script:

```php
<?php
  Reflection::export(new ReflectionExtension('reflection'));
?>
```

This will print out a very long listing, detailing every single class, method, and parameter for the entire reflection API. This export was achieved through the use of the Reflection class's export() method.

Nearly all parts of the reflection API implement the interface reflector, and ReflectionExtension is no exception. Reflection::export() prints a recursive output of the reflector passed into it, and since all reflectors must implement export() themselves as part of the interface, it is called all the way down the tree.

In this case, you start with with ReflectionExtension, which will, in turn, export all its classes and interfaces and then all their methods and parameters.

You can even use reflection to create an export of every single built-in PHP class. To do this, first you need to determine which classes are loaded. Fortunately, PHP provides the get_declared_classes() function for just this purpose:

```php
<?php
foreach(get_declared_classes() as $class) {
  Reflection::export(new ReflectionClass($class));
}
?>
```

The get_declared_classes() function returns all classes, even the built-in classes, but what if you want to get just your own user-declared classes?

Retrieving User-Declared Classes

All you need to do to retrieve just the classes you declared is to reflect on each class to determine if it is a user-defined class. Listing 7-1 demonstrates how to do this.

Listing 7-1. *Reflecting Only User-Defined Classes*

```php
class userClass {
  public function userMethod($userParameter='default') {}
}
```

```
foreach(get_declared_classes() as $class) {
  $reflectionClass = new ReflectionClass($class);
  if($reflectionClass->isUserDefined()) {
    Reflection::export($reflectionClass);
  }
}
```

When executed, the code in Listing 7-1 will show something like the following:

```
Class [ <user> class userClass ] {
  @@ reflector.php 3-5

  - Constants [0] {
  }

  - Static properties [0] {
  }

  - Static methods [0] {
  }

  - Properties [0] {
  }

  - Methods [1] {
    Method [ <user> public method userMethod ] {
      @@ reflector.php 4 - 4

      - Parameters [1] {
        Parameter #0 [ <optional> $userParameter = 'default' ]
      }
    }
  }
}
```

In Listing 7-1, you start actually using program metadata to make decisions. You learned about metadata in the previous chapter. Metadata can be further split into two different types:

- *Hard metadata* is metadata that is exposed by parsed code. It includes metadata like class names, methods, parameters, and so on.

- *Soft metadata* is any human-included data like a PHPDoc block, and in PHP, attributes.

While hard metadata is parsed by PHP and is guaranteed to be valid, soft metadata is prone to human error, and its structure is not governed by the PHP lexing process. Here's an example:

```
/**
This is soft metadata and its structure is not parsed by PHP
@see http://example.com/
*/
function mynameishardmetadata($myParamsToo) {}
```

The isUserDefined() method of ReflectionClass is an example of hard metadata being used to execute different code paths. In Listing 7-1, it is used to ignore any classes that are not user-defined.

The reflection API has a lot of is and has functions that can be used to create conditional execution. It also has functions that can be used to invoke methods. When the two are put together, you have the basis for a plug-in architecture.

Understanding the Reflection Plug-in Architecture

The reflection-based plug-in architecture doesn't really qualify as a pattern, as it's not actually a template; rather, it's a series of concepts that combine to form a program's architecture.

As you learned in earlier chapters, interfaces require any implementing class to declare all of the methods that are defined in the interface. This is ideal for rigid systems, but can begin to break down in larger, more complicated systems, where the two items interacting are themselves complex programs.

The reflection API plug-in approach is based on runtime-deterministic program capabilities; that is, it allows you to create interfacing methods that are optional and are detected at first use. These methods will be used only if they exist in the plug-in; otherwise, they will be ignored. This can help you to avoid implementing complex interfaces, and it allows for more flexible authoring.

For example, suppose you had the interface shown in Listing 7-2.

Listing 7-2. *A Rigid Interface*

```
interface IPlugin {
  function getMenuItems();
  function getArticles();
  function getSideBars();
}
class SomePlugin implements IPlugin {
  public function getMenuItems() {
    //We don't have any menu items
    return null;
  }
  public function getArticles() {
    //We don't have any articles
    return null;
  }
  public function getSideBars() {
    //We have a sidebar
    return array('SideBarItem');
  }
}
```

This doesn't make a lot of sense, because you've added function bodies for a bunch of methods you won't use in order to satisfy the interface. Imagine if there were hundreds of methods in your API. It just doesn't work.

Now, you might be thinking you could split each method into its own interface, but the same problem occurs. You have a class implementing hundreds of interfaces and hundreds of interface declarations. This isn't practical either. Is there a better way?

Some languages are event-driven and offer the ability to delegate methods to receive events from the host application, but PHP doesn't have native delegate support. As a result, a lot of frameworks have developed complicated sets of "hook" functions that require the plug-in to register its capabilities during some sort of initialization. This initialization and registration API makes it more difficult to create plug-ins, so fewer plug-ins are developed.

The reflection API offers a solution. In this approach, you use the get_declared_classes() function to get all the currently loaded classes and determine which implement a single-method IPlugin "marking" interface. This interface will be significantly simpler than the entire API that is available, but will contain a getName() function, which all plug-ins must have.

As an example, we will walk through the steps of building a very basic web page as a plug-in–based system. The page will contain a menu, sidebars, and articles. Via reflection, the application will detect which facilities each plug-in supports and will execute the appropriate method only if it's available. This example is extremely simple, and is not designed as an entire application, but it does demonstrate how to use reflection to load plug-ins.

First, create the interface that all plug-ins must follow, called IPlugin, as shown in Listing 7-3.

Listing 7-3. *Creating the IPlugin Interface*

```
interface IPlugin {
  public static function getName();
}
```

This interface is simple. It just defines a mandatory method that must be implemented by all plug-ins.

Next, you need to create a subroutine to detect all the currently included plug-ins. To do this, you just use get_declared_classes() and ReflectionClass, as shown in Listing 7-4.

Listing 7-4. *Finding Plug-ins with Reflection*

```
function findPlugins() {
  $plugins = array();
  foreach(get_declared_classes() as $class) {
    $reflectionClass = new ReflectionClass($class);
    if($reflectionClass->implementsInterface('IPlugin')) {
      $plugins[] = $reflectionClass;
    }
  }
  return $plugins;
}
```

The code in Listing 7-4 uses the implementsInterface() method of ReflectionClass to determine if the class implements IPlugin. This method does precisely what its name suggests: it checks if the class implements the interface. Unlike the instanceof operator (introduced in

Chapter 1), this method does not require an instance of the class to operate and is thus much more efficient.

You will also notice that you store instances of ReflectionClass and not instances of the classes or the names as strings. This is because creating a reflection class has some overhead, and you will need to determine if a plug-in has certain properties before invoking methods on the plug-in later. You might as well store it now, so that you don't need to execute the instantiation twice.

Now that you can locate your plug-ins, you need to create a mechanism that determines the subset of application functionality with which the plug-in will interact. A plug-in that contains menu items, for example, will have a method defined for adding entries to the menu, while a sidebar plug-in might not have such a method.

To determine if a class implements a method, you can use the hasMethod() method of the ReflectionClass. Listing 7-5 shows the menu-compiling function for this example.

Listing 7-5. *Determining Class Members for a Menu*

```
function computeMenu() {
  $menu = array();
  foreach(findPlugins() as $plugin) {
    if($plugin->hasMethod('getMenuItems')) {
      $reflectionMethod = $plugin->getMethod('getMenuItems');
      if($reflectionMethod->isStatic()) {
        $items = $reflectionMethod->invoke(null);
      } else {
        //If the method isn't static we need an instance
        $pluginInstance = $plugin->newInstance();
        $items = $reflectionMethod->invoke($pluginInstance);
      }
      $menu = array_merge($menu, $items);
    }
  }
  return $menu;
}
```

The code in Listing 7-5 may look a little complex at first, but it's really quite simple. The purpose of the computeMenu() function is to return an array of menu items. Assume for the moment that there is a menuItem class, and instances of the class will be stored in $menu as array entries.

Next, you use the findPlugins() function to locate all the plug-ins. Since you stored the ReflectionClass instances for each plug-in in the result array, you don't need to re-create those instances, and you can simply iterate the plug-ins to access the reflection information for each.

Your application now needs to determine if each plug-in has menu items. By design, creating menu items is optional for your plug-ins. You determine if the plug-in contains this capability by using the hasMethod() method of the ReflectionClass instance. If the method is located, then you will need to get a reflector for the method.

The getMethod() method of the ReflectionClass instance returns another reflector class: ReflectionMethod. Like ReflectionClass, ReflectionMethod allows you to access metadata, but this metadata is about the method, rather than the class. By getting a ReflectionMethod, you can introspect the method and determine its metadata.

Now that you have a ReflectionMethod instance, you need to determine if your API method should be called statically. If the method is static, you can just call invoke() without creating an instance of the plug-in. The invoke() method of ReflectionMethod has the following signature:

```
public mixed invoke(stdclass object, mixed args=null)
```

To invoke a static method, you must pass an implicit null as the first parameter to the invoke() method.

If, on the other hand, the method is non-static, you need to get an instance of the plug-in on which to invoke the method. To get an instance of a class from a ReflectionClass object, you call the newInstance() method. Then, assuming all went well constructing the instance, you can call the invoke() method of ReflectionMethod, passing it the instance returned by newInstance().

Whatever menu items were returned by each plug-in should then be merged into the $menu array. When all your plug-ins have completed processing, the entire $menu array is returned.

Using this same technique, you can continue to create facilities for articles and sidebars, as shown in Listing 7-6.

Listing 7-6. *Determining Class Members for Articles and Sidebars*

```
function computeArticles() {
  $articles = array();
  foreach(findPlugins() as $plugin) {
    if($plugin->hasMethod('getArticles')) {
      $reflectionMethod = $plugin->getMethod('getArticles');
      if($reflectionMethod->isStatic()) {
        $items = $reflectionMethod->invoke(null);
      } else {
        $pluginInstance = $plugin->newInstance();
        $items = $reflectionMethod->invoke($pluginInstance);
      }
      $articles = array_merge($articles, $items);
    }
  }
  return $articles;
}

function computeSidebars() {
  $sidebars = array();
  foreach(findPlugins() as $plugin) {
    if($plugin->hasMethod('getSidebars')) {
      $reflectionMethod = $plugin->getMethod('getSidebars');
      if($reflectionMethod->isStatic()) {
        $items = $reflectionMethod->invoke(null);
      } else {
        $pluginInstance = $plugin->newInstance();
        $items = $reflectionMethod->invoke($pluginInstance);
      }
```

```
      $sidebars = array_merge($sidebars, $items);
    }
  }
  return $sidebars;
}
```

Next, create a class that implements IPlugin, as shown in Listing 7-7. This plug-in class implements a menu item and an article, but does not implement a sidebar.

Listing 7-7. *Creating a Reflection Plug-in That Implements Some Optional Facilities (plugin.php)*

```php
<?php
class MyCoolPlugin implements IPlugin {
  public static function getName() { return 'MyCoolPlugin'; }
  public static function getMenuItems() {
    //Numeric indexed array of menu items
    return array(array(
              'description'=>'MyCoolPlugin',
              'link'=>'/MyCoolPlugin'
    ));
  }
  public static function getArticles() {
    //Numeric array of articles
    return array(array(
              'path'=>'/MyCoolPlugin',
              'title'=>'This is a really cool article',
              'text'=>'This article is cool because...'
    ));
  }
}
?>
```

This plug-in now provides some functionality. Listing 7-8 shows an extremely basic implementation involving this plug-in.

Listing 7-8. *Using the Plug-in*

```php
//First include your plug-ins;
require_once('/path/to/plugin.php');

$menu = computeMenu();
$sidebars = computeSidebars();
$articles = computeArticles();

//This could be a lot more complex
print_r($menu);
print_r($sidebars);
print_r($articles);
. . .
```

In Listing 7-8, you may replace the `print_r` calls with whatever way you wish to render the result data. This could be anything from `echo` calls to a full-blown template engine. In any case, the data is there, and it's loaded from plug-ins.

Currently, you need to include each plug-in file you wish to load. In Chapter 9, which introduces the Standard PHP Library (SPL), you will learn how to use class autoloading, so you no longer need to include your plug-ins manually. The result will be an extremely easy-to-manage, upload-and-go plug-in system.

Parsing Reflection-Based Documentation Data

In the previous chapter, I explained how doccomments are stored along with the program and promised to tell you how to access that data using reflection. Accessing the doccomment data is the easy part, and we'll get to that, but once you have the comment data, you will need to be able to parse it into a usable format. So, let's first look at how comments can be parsed.

Installing the Docblock Tokenizer

You can parse docblock comments by using the docblock tokenizer. However, installing the tokenizer can be tricky.

The instructions here assume you have a working `pecl` command and are using a Unix, Linux, or Mac OS X system. The installation should, however, work similarly on Windows systems.

Start by installing the docblock `pecl` extension. Execute the following command from an administrative account:

```
pecl install docblock
```

By the time this book is published, a stable version of the docblock package should be available. However, if it isn't, you will see a warning like the following:

```
Failed to download pecl/docblock within preferred state "stable", latest release
is version 0.2.0, stability "alpha", use "channel://pecl.php.net/docblock-0.2.0"
to install
```

In this case, use the full-channel URL the command returns to you, and rerun the `install` command in this form:

```
pecl install channel://pecl.php.net/docblock-0.2.0
```

If all went well, you now have the docblock tokenizer installed. You can confirm it is functioning correctly with the following command:

```
php -i |grep DocBlock
```

You should then see the following result (if it is functioning correctly):

```
DocBlock Tokenizer support => enabled
```

If you do not get this output, it is likely that you need to enable the extension in your php.ini file. To locate the php.ini file, execute the following command:

```
php -i |grep php.ini
```

You should get a result similar to this:

```
Configuration File (php.ini) Path => /etc/php5.1/cli/php.ini
```

You then need to add the following line to the php.ini file to enable the docblock extension:

```
extension=docblock.so;
```

Finally, reexecute the command to check that the docblock tokenizer is installed.

■**Note** Depending on your server distribution, there may be separate php.ini files for the command line and web server. Each will need the docblock extension enabled.

Once you have the docblock extension running, you can start parsing docblock comments using tokenizer-style parsing. However, first you need to actually get the documentation data to process from the reflection API.

Accessing Doccomment Data

Listing 7-9 demonstrates how to access doccomment data using reflection.

Listing 7-9. *Accessing Doccomments*

```
/**
 * This is a doccomment
 *
 * This doccomment documents the class demo
 */
class demo {}

$reflectionClass = new ReflectionClass('demo');
$docComment = $reflectionClass->getDocComment();

print($docComment);
```

When executed, the code in Listing 7-9 results in the following:

```
/**
 * This is a doccomment
 *
 * This doccomment documents the class demo
 */
```

Next, let's tokenize this data.

Tokenizing Doccomment Data

The docblock tokenizer `pecl` extension's primary method is `mixed docblock_tokenize($comment, $terseMode=false)`. The terse mode parameter controls whether nonsemantic tokens like the `commentstart` token are included in parsing. The function returns an array of tokens and their associated data.

The second function you will need is `docblock_token_name($token)`. This function takes a token identifier, which is the first index of each array entry that is returned from tokenization. The function transforms the numeric token ID into a human-readable string. Listing 7-10 demonstrates the tokenization process.

Listing 7-10. *Tokenizing Doccomments*

```
/**
 * This is a doccomment
 *
 * This doccomment documents the class demo
 */
class demo {}

$reflectionClass = new ReflectionClass('demo');
$docComment = $reflectionClass->getDocComment();

$tokens = docblock_tokenize($docComment,true);

foreach($tokens as $token) {
  echo $token[0] . '=';
  echo docblock_token_name($token[0]) . '=';
  print_r($token[1]);
  echo "\n";
}
```

The result of this code is as follows:

```
1=DOCBLOCK_NEWLINE=

2=DOCBLOCK_WHITESPACE=
36=DOCBLOCK_TEXT=This is a doccomment
1=DOCBLOCK_NEWLINE=

1=DOCBLOCK_NEWLINE=

2=DOCBLOCK_WHITESPACE=
36=DOCBLOCK_TEXT=This doccomment documents the class demo
1=DOCBLOCK_NEWLINE=
```

This result might look a little confusing, and rightly so—it's just a bunch of constants. But the data you need is there.

The result of tokenization is an array of arrays. Each entry array represents one part of the docblock. Each part is a token constant and its associated data. For the purposes of this tokenization, you are concerned only with tags and text.

Parsing the Tokens

Now you're ready to perform the parsing process. Listing 7-11 shows a simple parser.

Listing 7-11. *A Basic Docblock Parser*

```
/**
 * This is a doccomment comment
 *
 * This doccomment documents the class demo
 *
 * @author Kevin McArthur
 * @example This is a multiline example
 *   and this is more than valid
 * @example This is another separate example.
 */
class demo {}

$reflectionClass = new ReflectionClass('demo');
$docComment = $reflectionClass->getDocComment();

$tokens = docblock_tokenize($docComment,true);

$comments = array();
$tags = array();
$tagdata = array();
```

```php
foreach($tokens as $token) {
  //Switch on the token's code
  switch( $token[0] ) {
    case DOCBLOCK_TEXT: //Equiv to case 36:
      //If there is no tag found yet, text is a comment
      if(!isset($tagid)) {
        $comments[] = $token[1];
      } else {
        //If the tag already has data append to it.
        if(array_key_exists($tagid, $tagdata)) {
          //Pad the data with a space and concat
          $tagdata[$tagid] .= ' ' . trim($token[1]);
        } else {
          //If the tag doesn't exist, create it for the first time.
          $tagdata[$tagid] = trim($token[1]);
        }
      }
      break;
    case DOCBLOCK_TAG:
      //Assign a unique id to this tag.
      $tagid = uniqid();
      //Remember the mapping of unique id to tag name.
      $tags[$tagid] = trim($token[1], '@ ');
  }
}

//Join the array with unique id with the tag names
$compiled = array();
foreach($tagdata as $tagid => $data) {
  $tagName = $tags[$tagid];
  /*
    Create arrays where there are multiple tags
    of the same name.
  */
  if(array_key_exists($tagName, $compiled)) {
    if(!is_array($compiled[$tagName])) {
      $oldData = $compiled[$tagName];
      $compiled[$tagName] = array();
      $compiled[$tagName][] = $oldData;
    }
    $compiled[$tagName][] = $data;
  } else {
    $compiled[$tagName] = $data;
  }
}
print_r($comments);
print_r($compiled);
```

When run, this parser outputs the following:

```
Array
(
    [0] => This is a doccomment comment
    [1] => This doccomment documents the class demo
)
Array
(
    [author] => Kevin McArthur
    [example] => Array
        (
            [0] => This is a multiline example and this is more than valid
            [1] => This is another separate example.
        )

)
```

In this parsing process, you need to iterate the tokens produced by the tokenization function. During this iteration, you make a couple of assumptions. If a tag has not occurred yet, you assume that all text is a comment. Once a tag is found, all text is then associated with that tag until a new tag is found.

Note that text elements can occur more than once per tag and must be appended to the tag. Because tags can occur multiple times, you cannot just append the text. Instead, you need to assign a tag a unique ID to differentiate it from other tags that happen to have the same name. Later, you combine both the tags and their unique IDs, producing arrays when there are multiple tags.

You could stop here and format the output. But then, you have not really associated the rest of the program metadata with the comments or created a package that is easy to use. Those goals require extending the reflection API to add the parsed doccomments to the reflection classes, as explained next.

Extending the Reflection API

Reflection API classes are like all OOP classes—they can be derived from and extended. In this section, you will learn how to overload the reflection API to support advanced documentation parsing as part of the reflection API itself. Once you have successfully extended the reflection API, you will be able to create an extremely powerful metadata system.

Integrating the Parser with the Reflection API

To start, let's integrate the docblock parser from the previous listing with the reflection API. You do this by extending the core Reflection class and adding the parser as a static method. Listing 7-12 shows this extension. Place this and all subsequent reflection classes in a common include file called DocumentingReflection.php.

Listing 7-12. *Integrating the Doccomment Parser (DocumentingReflection.php)*

```php
class DocumentingReflection extends Reflection {

  public static function ParseDocComment($docComment) {

    $returnData = $comments = $tags = array();
    $tagNames = $tagData = array();

    $tokens = docblock_tokenize($docComment,true);
    foreach($tokens as $token) {

      switch( $token[0] ) {

        case DOCBLOCK_TEXT:

          if(!isset($tagId)) {
            $comments[] = $token[1];
          } else {
            if(array_key_exists($tagId, $tagData)) {
              $tagData[$tagId] .= ' ' . trim($token[1]);
            } else {
              $tagData[$tagId] = trim($token[1]);
            }
          }
          break;

        case DOCBLOCK_TAG:

          $tagId = uniqid();
          $tagNames[$tagId] = trim($token[1], '@ ');
          break;

      }
    }

    foreach($tagData as $tagId => $data) {

      $tagName = $tagNames[$tagId];
      if(array_key_exists($tagName, $tags)) {
        if(!is_array($tags[$tagName])) {
          $backupData = $tags[$tagName];
          $tags[$tagName] = array();
          $tags[$tagName][] = $backupData;
        }
        $tags[$tagName][] = $data;
```

```
    } else {
      $tags[$tagName] = $data;
    }

  }

  $returnData['comments'] = $comments;
  $returnData['tags'] = $tags;
  $returnData['tokens'] = $tokens;

  return $returnData;
  }
}
```

Now you have defined the static function `ParseDocComment`. This is where you will add additional processing logic, such as handling in-line tags. But before you get to that, you need to extend some of the other reflection classes.

Extending Reflection Classes

The next class you will extend is the `ReflectionMethod` class. This is because it is the most generalized reflector implementor that still contains a `getDocComment()` method. You also need to extend the `ReflectionParameter` class, but you need to get the data from the associated method, and thus the method class extension must logically come first. Listing 7-13 shows a very basic reflection extension that integrates `ParseDocComment` with the `ReflectionMethod` class to create a `DocumentingReflectionMethod` class.

Listing 7-13. *Creating the DocumentingReflectionMethod Class (DocumentingReflection.php)*

```
class DocumentingReflectionMethod extends ReflectionMethod {

  protected $_comments, $_tags, $_tokens, $_declaringClass;

  public function __construct($object, $method) {
    parent::__construct($object, $method);

    $docComment = $this->getDocComment();
    $this->_declaringClass = $object;

    $parsedComment = DocumentingReflection::ParseDocComment($docComment);

    $this->_comments = $parsedComment['comments'];
    $this->_tags = $parsedComment['tags'];
    $this->_tokens = $parsedComment['tokens'];

  }
```

```php
    public function printDocTokens() {
      foreach($this->_tokens as $token) {
        echo $token[0] . '=';
        echo docblock_token_name($token[0]) . '=';
        print_r($token[1]);
        echo "\n";
      }
    }

    public function getParsedTags() {
      return $this->_tags;
    }

    public function getParsedComments() {
      return $this->_comments;
    }

}
```

The `DocumentingReflectionMethod` class extends from `ReflectionMethod`, inheriting all the abilities of `ReflectionMethod`. Then it initializes the base class by calling `parent::__construct`. This parent construction must be done as the first line in the overridden constructor; otherwise, you may get errors or, even worse, code that crashes without any error explanation.

After the base class is initialized, the documentation extensions go into effect. The class calls the static method you previously defined to parse the doccomment, passing in its own doccomment, and storing its results in several protected member variables. Finally, several accessor methods are added to allow you to see that it's all working.

With all the code in Listings 7-12 and 7-13 in `DocumentingReflection.php`, you can test the results so far. Create another file named `test.php` and add the code shown in Listing 7-14.

Listing 7-14. *Testing the DocmentingReflection Classes (test.php)*

```php
require_once('DocumentingReflection.php');

class demo {

  /**
   * This method is for demonstration purposes.
   *
   * It takes a single parameter and returns it.
   *
   * @param mixed $param1 A variable to return.
   * @returns mixed The input variable is returned.
   */
  public function demoMethod($param1) {
    return $param1;
  }
```

```
}

$reflector = new DocumentingReflectionMethod('demo', 'demoMethod');
$reflector->printDocTokens();
print_r($reflector->getParsedTags());
print_r($reflector->getParsedComments());
```

The script in Listing 7-14 should result in the following output:

```
1=DOCBLOCK_NEWLINE=
1=DOCBLOCK_NEWLINE=

2=DOCBLOCK_WHITESPACE=
36=DOCBLOCK_TEXT=This method is for demonstration purposes.
1=DOCBLOCK_NEWLINE=

1=DOCBLOCK_NEWLINE=

2=DOCBLOCK_WHITESPACE=
36=DOCBLOCK_TEXT=It takes a single parameter and returns it.
1=DOCBLOCK_NEWLINE=

1=DOCBLOCK_NEWLINE=

2=DOCBLOCK_WHITESPACE=
5=DOCBLOCK_TAG=@param
36=DOCBLOCK_TEXT= mixed $param1 A variable to return.
1=DOCBLOCK_NEWLINE=

2=DOCBLOCK_WHITESPACE=
5=DOCBLOCK_TAG=@returns
36=DOCBLOCK_TEXT= mixed The input variable is returned.
1=DOCBLOCK_NEWLINE=

Array
(
    [param] => mixed $param1 A variable to return.
    [returns] => mixed The input variable is returned.
)
Array
(
    [0] => This method is for demonstration purposes.
    [1] => It takes a single parameter and returns it.
)
```

Next, you need to create an extension class for ReflectionParameter. Since there is no doccomment associated with parameters, you will need to obtain the parameter data from the param tags of the associated methods' doccomments. To do this, you must customize ReflectionParameter to fetch the data from the method, as follows.

```
public void ReflectionParameter::__construct(mixed function, mixed parameter)
```

Notice that the function parameter is of mixed type. This parameter may be passed a numeric array consisting of a class name string or object instance and a method name string.

The code for extending ReflectionParameter is shown in Listing 7-15.

Listing 7-15. *Extending ReflectionParameter (DocumentingReflection.php)*

```php
class DocumentingReflectionParameter extends ReflectionParameter {
  protected $_reflectionMethod, $_reflectionClass, $_comment, $_type;

  public function __construct($method, $parameter) {
    parent::__construct($method, $parameter);

    $this->_comment = '';
    $this->_type = 'undefined';

    $this->_reflectionMethod =
              new DocumentingReflectionMethod($method[0], $method[1]);

    $tags = $this->_reflectionMethod->getParsedTags();

    if(array_key_exists('param', $tags)) {
      $params = $tags['param'];

      if(is_array($params)) {
        foreach($params as $param) {
          if($this->_isParamTag($this->getName(), $param)) {
            $paramFound = $param;
          }
        }
      } else {
        if($this->_isParamTag($this->getName(), $params)) {
          $paramFound = $params;
        }
      }
      if(isset($paramFound)) {
        $tokens = preg_split("/[\s\t]+/", $paramFound, 3);
        $this->_comment = $tokens[2];
        $this->_type = $tokens[0];
      }
    }
  }
}
```

```php
    public function getDeclaringFunction() {
      return $this->_reflectionMethod;
    }

    public function getComment() {
      return $this->_comment;
    }

    public function getType() {
      return $this->_type;
    }

    private function _isParamTag($paramName, $paramData) {
      $paramSplit = preg_split("/[\s\t]+/", $paramData, 3);
      $explodedName = trim($paramSplit[1], ' $,.');
      if($explodedName == $paramName) {
        return true;
      } else {
        return false;
      }
    }

}
```

This class is a lot more complicated than the previous classes. Most of the comment processing for this class is done in the constructor.

First, you construct the class and call the parent methods. Default values are assigned for cases where there is no documentation associated. Then processing begins.

Using the information passed to the constructor, a DocumentingReflectionMethod is instantiated. This class will give you access to the documentation information via the getParsedTags() method. Next, it checks for the presence of 'param' in the $tags array. If it's there, it determines whether the entry is an array or a single string value and processes accordingly.

During this process, the private member function _isParamTag() is called to determine if the parameter is the one described by the tag. The function determines this by splitting the param tag into three parts. The split is based on a regular expression that divides the string into tokens, separating them where there are one or more of tabs or spaces. The third parameter to the function limits string splitting to three times. This will produce an array with the type, variable name, and the comment.

The variable name entry is checked against the ReflectionParameter class's own name. If there is a match, the tag currently being tested is known to belong to the parameter.

Once the correct tag is found, the data is split up and stored in the protected member variables _comment and _type. This data can be later accessed by get functions.

You can now experiment with this class, as shown in Listing 7-16.

Listing 7-16. *Experimenting with DocumentingReflection (Experiment.php)*

```
require_once('DocumentingReflection.php');

class demo {

  /**
   * @param string $param this is the comment
   */
  public function demoMethod($param='test') {}

}

$refparam = new DocumentingReflectionParameter(
             array('demo', 'demoMethod'),
             'param'
           );

var_dump($refparam->getComment());
var_dump($refparam->getType());
```

You should see the following output:

```
string(19) "this is the comment"
string(6) "string"
```

Now, normally you don't access parameters by providing that much information. Let's modify the DocumentingReflectionMethod class to override the getParameters() function, making it return DocumentingReflectionParmeter[] instead of ReflectionParameter[]. Include the code in Listing 7-17 in the DocumentingReflectionMethod class.

Listing 7-17. *Overriding getParameters (DocumentingReflection.php)*

```
public function getParameters() {
  $parameters = array();

  if(is_object($this->_declaringClass)) {
    $class = get_class($this->_declaringClass);
  } else if(is_string($this->_declaringClass)) {
    $class = $this->_declaringClass;
  }
```

```
    foreach(parent::getParameters() as $parameter) {
      $parameters[] = new DocumentingReflectionParameter(
                    array($class, $this->getName()),
                    $parameter->getName()
                );
    }

    return $parameters;
  }
```

This method first determines the declaring class that was stored at construction and checks if it is an object or a string. Since you need a string for the next step, determine the object's type with get_class().

Following that, the parent's getParameters() method is called. This will get you an array of ReflectionParameter objects, but not DocumentingReflectionParameter objects. The whole purpose of this function is to invoke the extended documenting form rather than the native form.

To test the getParameters() override, run the code in Listing 7-18.

Listing 7-18. *Using getParameters (test2.php)*

```
require_once('DocumentingReflection.php');

class demo {

  /**
   * @param mixed $param1 The first comment.
   * @param string $param2 The second comment.
   */
  public function demoMethod($param1, $param2) {}

}

$reflector = new DocumentingReflectionMethod('demo', 'demoMethod');
foreach($reflector->getParameters() as $param) {
  echo $param->getName() . ' ';
  echo $param->getType() . ' ';
  echo $param->getComment();
  echo "\n";
}
```

```
param1 mixed The first comment.
param2 string The second comment.
```

So, now you have the methods and parameters worked out. What about classes? DocumentingReflectionClass is the next class you need to create. Create this class as shown in Listing 7-19. and place the code in your DocumentingReflection.php file.

Listing 7-19. *Creating the DocumentingReflectionClass (DocumentingReflection.php)*

```php
class DocumentingReflectionClass extends ReflectionClass {

  protected $_comments, $_tags, $_tokens;

  public function __construct($class) {

    parent::__construct($class);

    $docComment = $this->getDocComment();
    $parsedComment = DocumentingReflection::ParseDocComment($docComment);

    $this->_comments = $parsedComment['comments'];
    $this->_tags = $parsedComment['tags'];
    $this->_tokens = $parsedComment['tokens'];

  }

  public function getMethods() {
    $methods = array();

    foreach(parent::getMethods() as $method) {
      $methods[] = new DocumentingReflectionMethod(
                    $this->getName(), $method->getName()
                  );
    }

    return $methods;
  }

  public function printDocTokens() {
    foreach($this->_tokens as $token) {
      echo $token[0] . '=';
      echo docblock_token_name($token[0]) . '=';
      print_r($token[1]);
      echo "\n";
    }
  }

  public function getParsedTags() {
    return $this->_tags;
  }

  public function getParsedComments() {
    return $this->_comments;
  }

}
```

By now, this should be getting repetitive. Dozens of functions in these classes need to be overridden, and I've included only the most critical few in processing an OOP tree. Any function in the API that returns a `Reflection*` class natively should be converted to a `DocumentingReflection*` class and translated, just as `getParameters()` and `getMethods()` were translated.

Updating the Parser to Handle In-Line Tags

Now we need to return to the original documentation parser. The parser you created earlier in the chapter does not respect any of the in-line PHPDoc tags. As an example, Listing 7-20 shows a parser capable of processing the in-line `link` tag.

Listing 7-20. *Processing In-Line Link Tags (DocumentingReflection.php)*

```php
public static function ParseDocComment($docComment) {

  $returnData = $comments = $tags = array();
  $tagNames = $tagData = array();

  $tokens = docblock_tokenize($docComment,true);

  foreach($tokens as $token) {
    switch( $token[0] ) {

      case DOCBLOCK_INLINETAG:
        $inlineTag = trim($token[1], ' @{}');
        break;

      case DOCBLOCK_ENDINLINETAG:
        switch($inlineTag) {
          case 'link':
            $inlineTagContents = preg_split("/[\s\t]+/", trim($inlineTagData), 2);
            $data = '<a href="'. $inlineTagContents[0];
            $data .= '">'. $inlineTagContents[1] .'</a>';
          break;
        }

        if(array_key_exists($tagId, $tagData)) {
          $tagData[$tagId] .= ' ' . $data;
        } else {
          $tagData[$tagId] = $data;
        }

        unset($inlineTag, $inlineTagData, $inlineTagContents);
        break;

      case DOCBLOCK_INLINETAGCONTENTS:
        $addData = trim($token[1], ' }');
```

```php
        if(isset($inlineTagData)) {
          $inlineTagData .= ' ' . $addData;
        } else {
          $inlineTagData = $addData;
        }

        unset($addData);
        break;

      case DOCBLOCK_TEXT:
        if(!isset($tagId)) {
          $comments[] = $token[1];
        } else {
          if(array_key_exists($tagId, $tagData)) {
            $tagData[$tagId] .= ' ' . trim($token[1]);
          } else {
            $tagData[$tagId] = trim($token[1]);
          }
        }
        break;

      case DOCBLOCK_TAG:
        $tagId = uniqid();
        $tagNames[$tagId] = trim($token[1], '@ ');
        break;
    }
  }

  foreach($tagData as $tagId => $data) {
    $tagName = $tagNames[$tagId];
    if(array_key_exists($tagName, $tags)) {
      if(!is_array($tags[$tagName])) {
        $backupData = $tags[$tagName];
        $tags[$tagName] = array();
        $tags[$tagName][] = $backupData;
      }
      $tags[$tagName][] = $data;
    } else {
      $tags[$tagName] = $data;
    }
  }

  $returnData['comments'] = $comments;
  $returnData['tags'] = $tags;
  $returnData['tokens'] = $tokens;

  return $returnData;
}
```

The code in Listing 7-21 demonstrates how to use the getMethods() method as well and the processing of the in-line link tag.

Listing 7-21. *Using getMethods() and Processing the In-Line Link Tag (test3.php)*

```php
require_once('DocumentingReflection.php');

class demo {

  /**
   * This is the first test method
   *
   * @param mixed $param1 The first comment {@link
   *    http://www.apress.com See the website}
   * @param string $param2 The second comment.
   */
  public function demoMethod($param1, $param2) {}

  /**
   * This is the second test method
   *
   * @param mixed $param1 The first comment of the second method
   * @param string $param2 The second comment of the second method
   */
  public function demoMethod2($param1, $param2) {}

}

$reflector = new DocumentingReflectionClass('demo');
foreach($reflector->getMethods() as $method) {
  echo $method->getName() . "\n";
  echo print_r($method->getParsedComments(),1);
  foreach($method->getParameters() as $param) {
    echo "\t". $param->getName() . ' ';
    echo $param->getType() . ' ';
    echo $param->getComment();
    echo "\n";
  }
  echo "\n\n";
}
```

This code has the following output:

```
demoMethod
Array
(
    [0] => This is the first test method
)

        param1 mixed The first comment <a href="http://www.apress.com">See the
                    website</a>
        param2 string The second comment.


demoMethod2
Array
(
    [0] => This is the second test method
)

        param1 mixed The first comment of the second method
        param2 string The second comment of the second method
```

Adding Attributes

Attributes are programming language elements that are used to add programmatically accessible metadata to your application, most commonly to communicate with another program that may be working in conjunction with your code. Although attributes can be very complex, the simplest attributes declare that some action can be done with a class.

PHP does not natively support attributes. However, in the same way that you added reflection abilities to parse documentation, you can add attributes.

The easiest way to add an attribute to a class is to just define another PHPDoc tag, such as @attribute, and then extend your Reflection* classes to expose this tag as a collection. If this extension is done correctly, you could then write classes that look at attributes of the classes and methods and make a programmatic decision.

As an example, I'll demonstrate how to add an attribute for a web services application to mark a class or some methods as safe to expose via a web service. To start, add a method to get attributes (tags named attribute) in the DocumentingReflectionMethod class, as shown in Listing 7-22.

Listing 7-22. *Adding the getAttributes Method to DocumentingReflectionMethod (DocumentingReflection.php)*

```php
public function getAttributes() {

    if(array_key_exists('attribute', $this->_tags)) {

        $rawAttributes = $this->_tags['attribute'];
        $attributes = array();
```

```php
    //If only a single attribute
    if(is_string($rawAttributes)) {
      $rawAttributes = array($rawAttributes);
    }

    foreach($rawAttributes as $attribute) {
      //Parse attribute
      $tmp = explode(' ',$attribute, 2);
      $type = $tmp[0];
      $data = isset($tmp[1])?$tmp[1]:null;

      /*
         Create an attribute class instance by taking
         the attribute name and adding the string
         'Attribute' to the end. Thus an attribute
         WebServiceMethod becomes a class
         WebServiceMethodAttribute
      */
      $rc = new ReflectionClass($type . 'Attribute');
      $instance = $rc->newInstance($data);

      //Associate the ReflectionMethod with the attribute
      $instance->setMethod($this);

      $attributes[] = $instance;
      unset($instance, $rc, $type, $data, $tmp);
    }

    return $attributes;

  }

  //Return an empty array if there are no attributes
  return array();

}
```

Next, as shown in Listing 7-23, create two new classes for your Attribute types: an abstract class called Attribute and a specialization of that class called WebServiceMethodAttribute.

Listing 7-23. *Adding Classes for Attribute Types (Attributes.php)*

```php
<?PHP

abstract class Attribute {

  protected $method;
```

```php
  function setMethod(ReflectionMethod $method) {
    $this->method = $method;
  }

  function getMethod() {
    return $this->method;
  }

}

class WebServiceMethodAttribute extends Attribute {

  protected $data;

  function __construct($data) {
    $this->data = $data;
  }

  function getData() {
    return $this->data;
  }

}

?>
```

Finally, create a demonstration class and use reflection to examine its attributes, as shown in Listing 7-24.

Listing 7-24. *Testing the Attributes (Testing.php)*

```php
<?php

require_once('DocumentingReflection.php');
require_once('Attributes.php');

class demo {

  /**
   * Add two numbers together
   *
   * @param int $a The first number to add
   * @param int $b The second number to add
   * @attribute WebServiceMethod Some Extra Info
   */
  public function add($a, $b) { return $a+$b; }
```

```
    /**
     * Divide two numbers
     *
     * @param int $a The value
     * @param int $b The divisor
     */
    public function divide($a, $b) { return $a+$b; }

}

$reflector = new DocumentingReflectionClass('demo');
foreach($reflector->getMethods() as $method) {
  foreach($method->getAttributes() as $attribute) {
    if($attribute InstanceOf WebServiceMethodAttribute) {
      //If the code gets here, this method is safe to expose

      //Get the class name
      $class = $attribute->getMethod()->getDeclaringClass()->getName();

      //Get the method name
      $method = $attribute->getMethod()->getName();

      //Get any data passed to the right of the attribute name
      $data = $attribute->getData();

      //Add the method to your web service (not included)
      //$service->add(array($class, $method));
    }
  }
}
```

The result of this code is that only the add($a,$b) method is exposed because it has the WebServiceMethod attribute. You can take this concept and expand on it, using the getData() method to pass parameters.

Just the Facts

In this chapter, you learned about the reflection API structure and created a reference for your-self by reflecting on the Reflection extension.

The reflection API's get_declared_classes() and isUserDefined() methods can be combined to automatically find classes you declared.

Using reflection-based capability determination, you can create applications that auto-matically load available plug-ins. This approach uses the methods implementsInterface(), hasMethod(), newInstance(), and invoke() (to invoke methods both statically and nonstatically).

Using reflection, you can access and parse docblock comments. This chapter's example used the docblock tokenizer `pecl` extension to perform the parsing. Using docblock tags and some algorithms, you can parse the data into usable arrays.

By extending the reflection API, you can integrate a docblock parser with the reflection classes to create documenting reflection classes that interpret the data provided in PHPDoc comments. Similarly, you can add reflection attributes.

CHAPTER 8

■■■

Testing, Deployment, and Continuous Integration

In the course of development for any reasonably complex application, you will encounter bugs, logic errors, and collaboration headaches. How you handle these issues can make the difference between a successful development cycle with happy developers and an overdue, overbudget application with an employee-turnover problem.

There is no silver bullet that prevents these problems, but a series of tools can help you better manage your projects and track your project's progress in real time. These tools, when combined, form a programming technique called *continuous integration*.

Any continuous integration project includes four main components: revision control, unit testing, deployment, and debugging. Typically, when working with PHP, the tools used for these four areas are Subversion, PHPUnit, Phing, and Xdebug, respectively. To tie them all together, you can use the continuous integration server, Xinc.

Subversion for Version Control

Subversion (often abbreviated as SVN) is a version control system that lets you keep track of the changes you make to your application files. If you are a PHP developer, you will likely already be familiar with revision control, maybe in the form of the Concurrent Versions System (CVS), which predates Subversion and is still widely used.

Subversion can help prevent a common scenario that occurs when two or more developers work on the same file. Without revision control, one developer downloads the source file (typically from an FTP server), makes modifications, and then uploads the file, overwriting the original copy. If another developer downloads the same source file while it is being worked on, makes some other changes, and then uploads the file, she ends up undoing the first developer's work.

With Subversion, this scenario can no longer occur. Instead of downloading a file, a developer *checks out* the current version of the file, makes changes, and then *commits* those changes. During the commit process, Subversion checks to see if any other users have changed the file since it was downloaded. If it has been modified, Subversion then attempts to merge any changes so that the resulting file contains both sets of changes. This works fine if the changes do not affect the same portion of the file. However, if the same code is changed, a *conflict* will be raised, and the last committer is responsible for integrating her changes with those that came before. In this way, no work is ever lost, and the project stays internally consistent.

Installing Subversion

Subversion can be installed from package management on almost any distribution of Linux. With Debian/Ubuntu style package management, the following command will install Subversion:

```
> apt-get install subversion subversion-tools
```

This will provide all the tools you need to create a local Subversion repository. A *repository* is a version-controlled directory of files and folders. You can create multiple repositories, typically for multiple projects, and these tools will allow you to administer them on your server.

■**Note** Subversion is also designed to work remotely via the Apache web server. For this function, you need to additionally install the `libapache2-svn` package, which provides the necessary bindings between Apache and Subversion. Then you should take extra care to secure the server properly. If you chose to use Apache with Subversion, I strongly suggest that you deploy Secure Sockets Layer (SSL) client-side certificates, as explained in Chapter 21.

Setting Up Subversion

Administering a Subversion repository is actually quite simple. First, find a suitable location on your server to store your repositories; I suggest /usr/local/svn, but any location will do. Next, use the svnadmin create command to create a repository in this directory:

```
> svnadmin create myfirstrepo
```

You will now see a new directory (/usr/local/svn/myfirstrepo), which contains all the files and databases needed to manage your project.

The next step is to get a working checkout of your repository. A *checkout* is a workspace for Subversion, where you will add files and make changes. It is important to never make changes directly to the files within your repository directory. To create a checkout, go to a new directory— I suggest your home directory—and issue the svn checkout command:

```
> cd ~
> svn checkout file:///usr/local/svn/myfirstrepo
Checked out revision 0.
```

■**Caution** Do not call `svn checkout` within the repository containing directory /usr/local/svn/.

You will now see your repository directory. If you have an existing project, you can use the svn import command to bring those files under revision control:

```
> svn import ~/existingproject file:///usr/local/svn/myfirstrepo
```

You will be asked for a commit message. These messages are critical for determining who changed what and why. For the initial import, just specify `Initial Import of <Project>` and save the file.

Tip You can change the editor Subversion uses for commit messages by setting the `EDITOR` environment variable. For example, `export EDITOR=pico` changes the editor to Pico on a Bash shell.

Your project is now under revision control, but your checkout, having been created before the import, is now out-of-date and does not reflect the import. This is by design; all checkouts must be manually updated with the `svn update` command:

```
> svn update
A    index.html
Updated to revision 1.
```

Tip Regularly updating Subversion before changing files will reduce the number of merges you will need to do.

From now on when you change the files, you change them in a checkout. In fact, you can back up your original files, because you shouldn't need to work with them again.

You will notice that each directory in your checkout contains a `.svn` directory. In some circumstances, such as when you're creating a release of your application, you may wish to obtain a copy without these directories. To get a copy of your project that does not have these working directories included, use the `svn export` command:

```
> svn export file:///usr/local/svn/myfirstrepo ~/exportdirectory
A    /home/user/exportdirectory
A    /home/user/exportdirectory/index.html
Exported revision 1.
```

To add new files to your repository, use the `svn add` command. Adding files is a local modification, which, unlike importing files, is not saved to the repository until you explicitly save the change with an svn commit command (discussed next):

```
> echo test > newfile.txt
> svn add newfile.txt
A         newfile.txt
> svn commit
Adding          newfile.txt
Transmitting file data .
Committed revision 2.
```

Committing Changes and Resolving Conflicts

Now that the files are under revision control, you can change them as required. When you want to save your changes to the repository, you need to commit them. To determine if you have any changes to commit, use the svn status command:

```
> echo changed > newfile.txt
> svn status
M      newfile.txt
```

This example shows that newfile.txt has been changed. The M beside the file indicates that all local file changes have been merged with changes from the repository. Therefore, the changes should be committed.

If you don't like your changes, you can restore the old file with the svn revert command:

```
> svn revert newfile.txt
Reverted 'newfile.txt'
> cat newfile.txt
test
```

Next, to simulate another developer working on the project, create a second checkout in your home directory.

```
> svn co file:///usr/local/svn/myfirstrepo ~/myfirstrepo2
A    /home/user/myfirstrepo2/newfile.txt
A    /home/user/myfirstrepo2/index.html
Checked out revision 2.
```

Then add some content to newfile.txt in the myfirstrepo2 directory:

```
> echo newdata >> newfile.txt
>  svn commit
Sending        newfile.txt
Transmitting file data .
Committed revision 3.
```

Return to the myfirstrepo directory, and *do not* choose to update it. Open newfile.txt, and you will notice that the changes from the other checkout have not yet been reflected in this file. Now make a similar, but different, change to the same line of the file in this checkout, and try to commit it. You will get an out-of-date error, indicating someone else has changed the file. You must always have the latest version of the file to commit changes. Running an update now will result in a conflicted state, because you have changed the same line in both checkouts:

```
> echo alternativedata >> newfile.txt
> svn commit
Sending        newfile.txt
svn: Commit failed (details follow):
svn: Out of date: 'newfile.txt' in transaction '3-1'
> svn update
C    newfile.txt
Updated to revision 3.
```

Notice the C beside `newfile.txt`. This indicates a conflict. If you run `ls` on the directory, you will see that three new files have been created:

```
> ls -1
index.html
newfile.txt
newfile.txt.mine
newfile.txt.r2
newfile.txt.r3
```

These files represent the conflict. The r2 file is the original file, the r3 file contains the modification that was made in `myfirstrepo2`, and the `.mine` file is the local change. The `.txt` file has also been changed and now contains both changes, to make resolving the conflict easier.

```
> cat newfile.txt
test
<<<<<<< .mine
alternativedata
=======
newdata
>>>>>>> .r3
```

Your job now is to make `newfile.txt` contain both change sets. Start by removing the <<<, >>>, and === lines, and then add or remove changes to the file so that the result you want is achieved. In more complex merges, you may wish to reject certain changes or rework both if there is functional overlap. In this case, however, you want to keep the `newdata` change as well as the local change. Your final file should look like this:

```
> cat newfile.txt
test
newdata
alternativedata
```

Next, you need to tell Subversion that you have resolved the conflict with the `svn resolved` command:

```
> svn resolved newfile.txt
Resolved conflicted state of 'newfile.txt'
```

This deletes the three extra files. They have served their purpose by helping you to resolve the conflict, and now are no longer needed.

The final step is to commit your resolved changes by calling `svn commit`:

```
svn commit
Sending        newfile.txt
Transmitting file data .
Committed revision 4.
```

As you can see, using this process, developers are prevented from simply overwriting each other's code.

Enabling Subversion Access

The next step is to enable Subversion access via Apache. To do this, create a virtual host on your Apache web server (for details on creating a virtual host, see Chapter 14).

Once you have created a virtual host, simply add a <Location> tag to your configuration file, following this format:

```
<Location /svn/myfirstrepo>
  DAV svn
  SVNPath /usr/local/svn/myfirstrepo
</Location>
```

You can now check out your files from other client locations using http://yoursite.com/svn/myfirstrepo in place of file:///usr/local/svn/myfirstrepo, which works only on the local server.

■**Caution** Note that the <Location> tag form shown here contains absolutely no security. Before exposing any real code, be sure that you have proper authentication and SSL security measures in place. See Chapter 21 for SSL client certificate setup instructions.

PHPUnit for Unit Testing

PHPUnit lets you create unit tests for your application. In short, PHP unit testing involves writing PHP scripts specifically to test other PHP scripts. This type of testing is referred to as *unit* testing because the test apparatus is designed to test individual code units, like classes and methods, one at a time. PHPUnit is an elegant solution to writing these tests, and it follows an object-oriented development approach.

Installing PHPUnit

Installing PHPUnit is done through PEAR and is fairly straightforward. First use PEAR to "discover" the pear.phpunit.de channel:

```
> pear channel-discover pear.phpunit.de
Adding Channel "pear.phpunit.de" succeeded
Discovery of channel "pear.phpunit.de" succeeded
```

Next, install PHPUnit and any dependencies it needs:

```
> pear install --alldeps phpunit/PHPUnit
downloading PHPUnit-3.1.9.tgz . . .
Starting to download PHPUnit-3.1.9.tgz (116,945 bytes)
......................done: 116,945 bytes
install ok: channel://pear.phpunit.de/PHPUnit-3.1.9
```

Depending on your system's PEAR layout, the PHPUnit source files should be found in /usr/share/php/PHPUnit.

Creating Your First Unit Test

To get started creating your unit tests, you need to set up a directory structure. There is no particular convention as to where to place your tests. Some developers keep their test files in the same directory as the code being tested. Others create a separate tests directory and mirror the code directory structure, which helps keep testing code separate. In this example, you will use the latter approach.

First, clean up your Subversion file:

```
> svn rm index.html newfile.txt

D          index.html
D          newfile.txt
> svn commit

Deleting        index.html
Deleting        newfile.txt

Committed revision 5.
```

■**Note** Using svn rm will remove the file from the repository as well as the checkout upon svn commit. A standard rm will not remove the file from the repository, and the file will be restored the next time you use svn update.

Now create two directories, one for code and one for your tests:

```
> svn mkdir code tests
A          code
A          tests
```

In the code directory, create a Demo class that does something easily tested—addition and subtraction—as shown in Listing 8-1.

Listing 8-1. *A Demo Class (./code/Demo.php)*

```php
<?php
class Demo {
  public function sum($a,$b) {
    return $a+$b;
  }
  public function subtract($a,$b) {
    return $a-$b;
  }
}
```

Next, create a unit test, as shown in Listing 8-2.

Listing 8-2. *A Unit Test (./tests/DemoTest.php)*

```php
<?php
require_once('PHPUnit/Framework.php');
require_once(dirname(__FILE__). '/../code/Demo.php');

class DemoTest extends PHPUnit_Framework_TestCase {
  public function testSum() {
      $demo = new Demo();
      $this->assertEquals(4,$demo->sum(2,2));
      $this->assertNotEquals(3,$demo->sum(1,1));
   }
}
```

Now, in the `tests` directory, run your test using the `phpunit` test runner:

```
> phpunit DemoTest
PHPUnit 3.1.9 by Sebastian Bergmann.
.
Time: 0 seconds
OK (1 test)
```

As you can see, the test runner reports that your test ran correctly.

Understanding PHPUnit

Now that you know where to put unit tests and how to call them from the command line, you might be wondering what a `PHPUnit_Framework_TestCase` is and how the `testSum()` method works.

PHPUnit tests typically follow a naming convention where the test class is named the same as the class being tested followed by the word `Test`, and the file it's located in has the same name as the test class with a `.php` extension. The test class name should be descriptive of the component or functionality being tested. For example, a class that tests user authentication (the `Authentication` class) should be called `AuthenticationTest` and stored in `AuthenticationTest.php`.

Tests—or more specifically, test cases—are simply classes that inherit from `PHPUnit_Framework_TestCase`. This test class provides access to all the different types of assertions and is responsible for running all the test methods against the target class.

In our example, when the test runner is passed the `DemoTest` class, it calls each of the testing methods one at a time, collecting information along the way. Inside each method, you define a set of assumptions about what the code being tested will do. These assumptions need to be translated into an assertion. If you expect that the `sum()` of 2 and 2 will always be 4, then you would write an assertion that the function result is equal to 4.

Without changing `DemoTest`, modify the `Demo` class so that its `sum()` method no longer returns a valid result; changing the + operator to - will do the trick. Once the `Demo` class is changed, you should get a result like the following when you run your unit test again:

```
> phpunit DemoTest
PHPUnit 3.1.9 by Sebastian Bergmann.
F
Time: 0 seconds
There was 1 failure:
1) testSum(DemoTest)
Failed asserting that <integer:0> matches expected value <integer:4>.
/home/user/myfirstrepo/tests/DemoTest.php:12

FAILURES!
Tests: 1, Failures: 1.
```

The test failed because the sum() method no longer passes your equality assertion that 2 + 2 = 4.

You can choose from literally dozens of assertions. In the example, you used assertEquals and assertNotEquals, both of which take two items to compare. There are also assertions like assertSame for objects, assertTrue or assertFalse for Booleans, and setExpectedException for exceptions. For a reference list and exact syntax details, see the PHPUnit manual at http://www.phpunit.de.

When writing unit tests, you will need to set up your objects, as when you assigned $demo = new Demo() in the previous test. This can become tedious if you are always doing the same setup for each test. Fortunately, PHPUnit provides two methods, called setUp() and tearDown(), which allow you to define a common configuration for every test. Listing 8-3 shows the same test, split into setUp() and tearDown() methods.

Listing 8-3. *A Test Split into setUp and tearDown Methods (./tests/DemoTest.php)*

```php
<?php
require_once('PHPUnit/Framework.php');
require_once(dirname(__FILE__). '/../code/Demo.php');

class DemoTest extends PHPUnit_Framework_TestCase {
  public function setUp() {
    $this->demo = new Demo();
  }

  public function testSum() {
    $this->assertEquals(4,$this->demo->sum(2,2));
  }

  public function testSubstract() {
    $this->assertEquals(0,$this->demo->subtract(2,2));
  }

  public function tearDown() {
    unset($this->demo);
  }
}
```

The setUp() and tearDown() methods are called with each test and on a clean instance of the test class, so your setup code will not persist between tests and can be expected not to leak state between each test.

You can also create a test suite that runs multiple test cases, as shown in Listing 8-4.

Listing 8-4. *A Suite of Tests*

```php
<?php
require_once 'PHPUnit/Framework.php';
require_once 'PHPUnit/TextUI/TestRunner.php';

require_once 'DemoTest.php';

class AllTests {
  public static function main() {
    PHPUnit_TextUI_TestRunner::run(self::suite());
  }

  public static function suite() {
    $suite = new PHPUnit_Framework_TestSuite('Zend Framework - Zend');
    $suite->addTestSuite('DemoTest');
    return $suite;
  }
}
```

To execute the suite, just use the AllTests command:

```
> phpunit AllTests
PHPUnit 3.1.9 by Sebastian Bergmann.
..
Time: 0 seconds
OK (2 tests)
```

Now that you have a couple of unit tests and a utility class, create an index.php document to use your Demo class, as shown in Listing 8-5.

Listing 8-5. *Using the Demo Class (code/index.php)*

```php
<?php
require_once('Demo.php');

$demo = new Demo();
echo "Two plus Two = ". $demo->sum(2,2);
```

Next, run svn status, and then add any files or folders that are denoted with a ?. Finally, run svn commit. You now have a complete web site under unit testing and revision control. The next step is to automate the deployment of these files.

Phing for Deployment

Phing (a recursive acronym, for Phing Is Not GNU make) is a way of automating the deployment of your PHP applications. It lets you run unit tests in an automated manner and perform common tasks like copying files between folders.

Installing Phing

First, you need to install Phing, which you can do through PEAR:

```
> pear channel-discover pear.phing.info

Adding Channel "pear.phing.info" succeeded
Discovery of channel "pear.phing.info" succeeded

> pear install phing/phing
phing/phing can optionally use package
"pear/VersionControl_SVN" (version >= 0.3.0alpha1)
Starting to download phing-2.3.0beta1.tgz (397,990 bytes)
.....................done: 397,990 bytes
install ok: channel://pear.phing.info/phing-2.3.0beta1
```

At this point, Phing is installed. Since you're working with Subversion, and Phing optionally supports Subversion, you should get the PEAR VersionControl_SVN package, too. You could try to use pear install pear/VersionControl_SVN, but since it is an alpha package, you will probably get an error like the following:

```
> pear install pear/VersionControl_SVN

Failed to download pear/VersionControl_SVN within preferred state "stable",
latest release is version 0.3.1, stability "alpha", use
"channel://pear.php.net/VersionControl_SVN-0.3.1" to install
Cannot initialize 'pear/VersionControl_SVN', invalid or missing package file
Package "pear/VersionControl_SVN" is not valid
install failed
```

So, instead, you must install it using the full-channel URI:

```
> pear install channel://pear.php.net/VersionControl_SVN-0.3.1

downloading VersionControl_SVN-0.3.1.tgz ...
Starting to download VersionControl_SVN-0.3.1.tgz (33,483 bytes)
.........done: 33,483 bytes
install ok: channel://pear.php.net/VersionControl_SVN-0.3.1
```

Now, with the PEAR packages installed, it's time to write your first build file.

Writing a Phing Deployment Script

Phing uses a simple XML configuration file format, which takes information about the project and allows you to define groups of actions, called *targets*. As an example, you will create a basic Phing deployment script that defines four targets:

- get will export the latest files from your Subversion repository.

- test will execute your unit tests.

- try will copy files to a nonproduction web site for functional testing.

- deploy will copy the files to a production web site.

By default, the phing binary looks for an XML file called build.xml when it is called on the command line. Listing 8-6 shows a simple build.xml file.

Listing 8-6. *A Phing Build File (build.xml)*

```xml
<?xml version="1.0"?>
<project name="MyFirstPhingProject" basedir="." default="try">

  <fileset dir="./code" id="codefiles">
    <include name="**" />
  </fileset>

  <target name="get">
    <svnupdate
      svnpath="file:///usr/local/svn/myfirstrepo"
      todir="."
    />
  </target>

  <target name="test" depends="get">
    <phpunit haltonfailure="true" printsummary="true">
      <batchtest>
        <fileset dir="./tests">
          <include name="*Test.php" />
        </fileset>
      </batchtest>
    </phpunit>
  </target>

  <target name="try" depends="test">
    <copy
      todir="/usr/local/www/beta.example.com/document_root"
      overwrite="true"
```

```
  >
    <fileset refid="codefiles" />
  </copy>
</target>

<target name="deploy" depends="try">
  <copy
    todir="/usr/local/www/www.example.com/document_root"
    overwrite="true"
  >
    <fileset refid="codefiles" />
  </copy>
</target>
```

```
</project>
```

The first part of the file is the `<project>` element. This defines the name of the project, where the source files are located, and the default target to call if Phing is invoked without any arguments.

Next, you define a set of files with the `<fileset>` element and give it an `id` alias for use later. You use ** to indicate a recursive include; a single * would not be recursive. This creates a sort of array of code files that will be used by copy commands later.

Then you create the set of four targets: `get`, `test`, `try`, and `deploy`. These targets have various dependencies, which will be called automatically before the target is run. For example, if you were to call `phing deploy`, all the targets would be called, because Phing would walk the entire dependency tree back to the `get` target.

The `get` target uses the `<svnupdate>` element to ensure that the checkout is up-to-date. This element is provided by the PEAR package `VersionControl_SVN`.

■**Caution** The `<svnupdate>` element is experimental. If you encounter an issue with the Subversion checkout not updating properly, use `<exec command="svn update" />` instead.

PHPUnit is invoked in the `test` target. At the time of writing, Phing does not support PHPUnit test suites, and will instead compile its own test counters and other information when you use the `<batchtest>` element. It does this by using a `fileset` to locate all files ending in `Test.php`. Your `DemoTest.php` file will be found and run. If any tests fail, the target will fail, and as a result, the tasks `try` and `deploy` will not occur, as they depend on `test`. The `printsummary` attribute will give you some extra information about the test success when you run the `phing` command.

Next, you need to define copy commands for `try` and `deploy`. These should reference only the code files and copy them to your web root directories.

To use your Phing build file, simply type `phing` at the command line. Since `try` is the default, you will see `get`, `test`, and then `try` run, in that order. The output should look something like the following:

```
phing
```

```
Buildfile: /home/user/myfirstrepo/build.xml

MyFirstPhingProject > get:

[svnupdate] Updating SVN repository at '.'

MyFirstPhingProject > test:

  [phpunit] Tests run: 2, Failures: 0, Errors: 0, Time elapsed: 0.00035 sec

MyFirstPhingProject > try:

    [copy] Copying 2 files to /usr/local/www/beta.example.com/document_root

BUILD FINISHED

Total time: 0.2601 seconds
```

To call a specific target, simply call phing `<target>`. Here's how to call deploy:

```
> phing deploy
//… all of above plus…
MyFirstPhingProject > deploy:
    [copy] Copying 2 files to /usr/local/www/www.book.lan/document_root
```

At this point, you have a Phing deployment system. You could stop here, and you would have a respectable deployment solution. However, you still need to call phing manually when you want to get, test, and try—common development actions that will become tedious quickly. Fortunately these, too, can be automated.

■**Note** Phing can be configured to produce PEAR packages, encode your projects, generate code-coverage reports, and more. See http://www.phing.info for more information.

Xinc, the Continuous Integration Server

Xinc is a way to continuously integrate a PHP project. Essentially, Xinc monitors a Subversion repository for changes, and when changes are detected, automatically calls Phing.

Installing Xinc

Installing Xinc 1.0 is trivial. First download the binary package from http://code.google.com/p/xinc/, and then install it, as follows:

```
> wget http://xinc.googlecode.com/files/xinc-1.0.tar.gz
> tar zxf xinc-1.0.tar.gz
> ./install.sh
```

The install program will ask you about your PHP environment and create installation directories.

Next, Xinc needs a working directory for your project. I suggest `/usr/local/www/projects/myfirstrepo`. Check out a copy of your repository there and execute `phing try` to ensure that the project can be integrated properly.

Creating the Xinc Configuration File

With Xinc installed, you next need to create the Xinc configuration file, `config.xml`, as shown in Listing 8-7. Place this file in `/etc/xinc`.

Listing 8-7. *A Xinc Configuration File (/etc/xinc/config.xml)*

```
<?xml version="1.0"?>
<projects>
  <project name="MyFirstXincProject" interval="60">
    <modificationsets>
      <svn directory="/usr/local/www/projects/myfirstrepo" />
    </modificationsets>
    <builder
      type="phing"
      buildfile="/usr/local/www/projects/myfirstrepo/build.xml"
      workingdirectory="/usr/local/www/projects/myfirstrepo/"
      target="try"
    />
    <publishers>
      <email
        to="user@example.com"
        subject="Build Failed"
        message="Someone committed something that doesn't pass unit tests."
        publishonfailure="true"
      />
    </publishers>
  </project>
</projects>
```

The configuration file is fairly self-explanatory. Each project is checked for changes at a given interval—60 seconds in this case. Within the `<project>` element is a `<modificationsets>` element, which refers to the files you want to watch for modification. This directory must be a Subversion *checkout* and not the repository itself.

The `<builder>` element controls the execution of your Phing build script. In this example, Phing is being automatically configured to publish the files with the `try` target. Xinc optionally offers the ability to separate build and publication steps for the actual deployment, but with your Phing `build.xml`, this functionality is not required.

That said, Xinc offers an option to call publishers on both the success and failure of the build process. In this case, when the build fails, you want to receive an e-mail alerting you to the broken build. You could also configure a host of other actions, such as calling another Phing target using `publishonsuccess` or `publishonfailure`.

Starting Xinc

With your `config.xml` in place in `/etc/xinc`, you can start Xinc:

```
> /etc/init.d/xinc start
```

To test that Xinc is working correctly, make a change to your repository and commit. Within a minute, it should show up on your testing site, or you should receive an e-mail message about failing unit tests.

You now have a fully integrated build, test, and deployment system.

Xdebug for Debugging

Debugging is one of the more complicated parts of PHP development. Many people use `echo` statements and print out values, while others use frameworks that provide logging components. Xdebug is the next level of this concept. It allows you to examine even more detail about a PHP application while it is running. Beyond debugging, Xdebug also has a number of profiling options that can help you determine where your code is running slowly.

Installing Xdebug

Xdebug for PHP is most easily distributed through PECL and installation is fairly straightforward:

```
> pecl install xdebug

…compiling…

Build process completed successfully
Installing '/usr/lib/php5/20060613+lfs/xdebug.so'
install ok: channel://pecl.php.net/xdebug-2.0.1
configuration option "php_ini" is not set to php.ini location
You should add "extension=xdebug.so" to php.ini
```

At this point, Xdebug has been compiled but it is not active. The instructions on the screen here are slightly confusing and not quite accurate. In your `php.ini` file, you will need to add the following line:

```
zend_extension=/usr/lib/php5/20060613+lfs/xdebug.so
```

■**Caution** Despite Xdebug's postinstallation message, you must add `zend_extension`, not `extension`, to the `php.ini` file.

Remember that you may have separate `php.ini` files for both the CLI PHP binary and your web server. An easy way to see if you have successfully installed Xdebug is as follows:

```
> php -v
PHP 5.?.? (cli) (built: Jul 17 2007 18:14:23)
Copyright (c) 1997-2007 The PHP Group
Zend Engine v2.2.0, Copyright (c) 1998-2007 Zend Technologies
    with Xdebug v2.0.2-dev, Copyright (c) 2002-2007, by Derick Rethans
```

If you see with Xdebug in the PHP CLI version, confirm that it also shows up in `phpinfo()` when used on your web server. You will need to restart Apache to pick up the change to the PHP environment.

Tracing with Xdebug

Much of the Xdebug functionality is in the form of extra debugging statements that you can use to get extra information about your application. For example, you can find out what class, method, or function called the current context, and from which file and line that call originated. For example, Listing 8-8 demonstrates a simple call trace.

Listing 8-8. *Using Xdebug to Trace Call Stacks*

```php
<?php
class MyClass {
  public function myCaller($other) {
    $other->myCallee();
  }
}

class MyOther {
  public function myCallee() {
    printf("%s", xdebug_call_class());
    printf("::%s",    xdebug_call_function());
    printf(" in %s", xdebug_call_file());
    printf(":%s\n",    xdebug_call_line());
  }
}

$a = new MyClass();
$b = new MyOther();

$a->myCaller($b);
```

This example outputs the following:

```
MyClass::myCaller in /path/to/xdebug.php:4
```

You could also call the `xdebug_get_function_stack()` method, which returns an array of information about the function calls up to this point. This function is similar to the standard `debug_backtrace()` PHP function.

If you need to determine all the functions and methods that are called between two points in a script, such as when execution enters another component, you can use Xdebug function traces. These traces record all the calls to a file for later review. Start and stop a function trace as follows:

void `xdebug_start_trace(string filename [, int options])`: This function begins tracing function calls. The `options` value is a bitmask that allows you to append trace files using the `XDEBUG_TRACE_APPEND` constant, create a computerized output format with `XDEBUG_TRACE_COMPUTERIZED`, or even create an HTML format table trace with `XDEBUG_TRACE_HTML`.

void `xdebug_stop_trace()`: When you want the trace to stop, call this function. If you do not call `stop`, the trace will end automatically when execution finishes.

Listing 8-9 shows how to trace a method call. This example modifies the previous one by wrapping the final call in tracing statements.

Listing 8-9. *Tracing with xdebug_start_trace*

```
xdebug_start_trace('trace');
$a->myCaller($b);
xdebug_stop_trace();
```

```
TRACE START [16:53:57]
    0.0010      57964    -> MyClass->myCaller() /code/xdebug.php:21
    0.0011      58104      -> MyOther->myCallee() /code/xdebug.php:4
    0.0011      58104       -> xdebug_call_class() /code/xdebug.php:10
    0.0011      58128       -> printf() /code/xdebug.php:10
    0.0014      58196       -> xdebug_call_function() /code/xdebug.php:11
    0.0015      58196       -> printf() /code/xdebug.php:11
    0.0016      58196       -> xdebug_call_file() /code/xdebug.php:12
    0.0016      58244       -> printf() /code/xdebug.php:12
    0.0017      58244       -> xdebug_call_line() /code/xdebug.php:13
    0.0017      58244       -> printf() /code/xdebug.php:13
    0.0018      58244    -> xdebug_stop_trace() /code/xdebug.php:22
    0.0019      58244
TRACE END   [16:53:57]
```

Xdebug also allows you to get the current and peak memory utilization of a script and the time the script has taken since it started running.

Profiling with Xdebug

You can use the following functions to get profile information:

`int xdebug_memory_usage()`: This function returns the current memory usage at the time the function is called.

`int xdebug_peak_memory_usage()`: This function returns the greatest amount of memory the script has used from script startup until the time the function is called.

`float xdebug_time_index()`: This function returns the time in seconds since the script began running. It's very precise and will allow you to track down slow sections of code.

Xdebug also ships with an application-wide profiler that saves information about which functions were called during execution and how many times each was called. To enable this profiler, add the following to your `php.ini` file:

```
xdebug.profiler_enable=1
xdebug.profiler_output_dir=/path/you/want/profile/file/placed
```

This enables the profiler to start saving information. To read the information, you will need an analyzer like KCacheGrind or WinCacheGrind.

■Caution Use the application-wide profiler feature only when necessary, as it will add significant overhead to your PHP scripts. Additionally, the profile files can use up significant amounts of disk space.

Checking Code Coverage with Xdebug

It is often useful to know how effective your library organization is. Theoretically, if only a fraction of the code in a given file is commonly executed, you may get some performance gain by breaking up the file into two or more files. However, as with all performance optimization, it is important not to get carried away. Code coverage can also help you identify if code never gets called and is simply dead or inaccessible.

The code-coverage functionality provided by Xdebug comes in the form of a function that tells you exactly which lines of a file have been run during any given execution, as well as functions to pause and get code coverage:

`void xdebug_start_code_coverage( [int options] )`: This function begins collecting code-coverage information. It has two options: `XDEBUG_CC_UNUSED` and `XDEBUG_CC_DEAD_CODE`, both of which can be used to determine if code is callable.

`void xdebug_stop_code_coverage( )`: This function pauses the collection of code-coverage data.

`array xdebug_get_code_coverage( )`: This function returns a multidimensional array, where the format is `$array[filename][line] = numberofcalls;`

Remote Debugging with Xdebug

Finally, Xdebug offers a way for integrated development environments (IDEs) to communicate with a running PHP script. It provides a communications channel that will let your IDE step through PHP scripts and analyze them. Every environment is different, so following the specific documentation for your IDE is crucial.

You can also use command-line debuggers, such as the official `debugclient` that is bundled with Xdebug. However, I strongly suggest a graphical approach to this type of debugging. The PDT project for Eclipse and ActiveState Komodo IDEs both support remote debugging with Xdebug.

When working with an attached debugger, the `xdebug_break()` command forces a breakpoint. Good places to use this function would be in an error-handler function or in a global exception `catch` block.

Just the Facts

In this chapter, you looked at some useful techniques that help you build, test, and manage PHP applications.

Subversion provides revision control. After you create a repository and checkouts, you can work with files under revision control.

PHP helps you perform unit testing with PHPUnit, following an object-oriented approach.

Phing automates your build and deployment steps. You can use it to create targets to update a Subversion checkout, run unit tests, copy files to a beta testing site, and deploy to production.

Xinc is a continuous integration server that can help you to monitor changes to the Subversion repository and continuously integrate your project with Phing build scripts. By combining Xinc, Phing, PHPUnit, and Subversion, you can create a comprehensive development environment that will help you solve common development process challenges.

Xdebug can provide you with some very useful debugging information, including code tracing, profiling, code coverage, and remote debugging.

PART 3

The Standard PHP Library (SPL)

■■■

CHAPTER 9

Introduction to SPL

The Standard PHP Library (SPL) is where PHP 5's object-oriented capabilities truly shine. It improves the language in five key ways: iterators, exceptions, array overloading, XML, and file and data handling. It also provides a few other useful items, such as the observer pattern, counting, helper functions for object identification, and iterator processing. Additionally, it offers advanced functionality for autoloading classes and interfaces. This chapter introduces you to this very important library, and in the following chapters, you will learn more about some of the advanced SPL classes.

SPL is enabled by default and is available on most PHP 5 systems. However, because SPL's features were dramatically expanded with the PHP 5.2 release, I recommend using that version or newer if you want to truly take advantage of this library.

SPL Fundamentals

The SPL is a series of Zend Engine 2 additions, internal classes, and a set of PHP examples. At the engine level, the SPL implements a set of six classes and interfaces that provide all the magic. These interfaces and the Exception class are special in that they are not really like a traditional interface. They have extra powers and allow the engine to hook into your code in a specific and special way. Here are brief descriptions of these elements:

ArrayAccess: The ArrayAccess interface allows you to create classes that can be treated as arrays. This ability is commonly provided by *indexers* in other languages.

Exception: The Exception class was introduced in Chapter 4. The SPL extension contains a series of enhancements and classifications for this built-in class.

Iterator: The Iterator interface makes your objects work with looping structures like foreach. This interface requires you to implement a series of methods that define which entries exist and the order in which they should be retrieved.

IteratorAggregate: The IteratorAggregate interface takes the Iterator concept a bit further and allows you to offload the methods required by the Iterator interface to another class. This lets you use some of the other SPL built-in iterator classes so you can gain iterator functionality without needing to implement Iterator's methods in your class directly.

Serializable: The Serializable interface hooks into the Serialize and Unserialize functions, as well as any other functionality, like sessions, that may automatically serialize your classes. Using this interface, you can ensure that your classes can be persisted and restored properly. Without it, storing object data in sessions can cause problems, especially where resource type variables are used.

Traversable: The Traversable interface is used by the Iterator and IteratorAggregate interfaces to determine if the class can be iterated with foreach. This is an internal interface and cannot be implemented by users; instead, you implement Iterator or IteratorAggregate.

In the rest of this chapter, we'll take a closer look at some of the SPL features, beginning with iterators.

Iterators

Iterators are classes that implement the Iterator interface. By implementing this interface, the class may be used in looping structures and can provide some advanced data-access patterns.

Iterator Interface

The Iterator interface is defined internally in C code, but if it were represented in PHP, it would look something like Listing 9-1.

Listing 9-1. *The Iterator Interface*

```
interface Iterator {
  public function current();
  public function key();
  public function next();
  public function rewind();
  public function valid();
}
```

■**Note** You do not need to declare Iterator or any other SPL interface yourself. These interfaces are automatically provided by PHP.

All iterable objects are responsible for keeping track of their current state. In a normal array, this would be called the array pointer. In your object, any type of variable could be used to track the current element. It is very important to remember the position of elements, as iteration requires stepping through elements one at a time.

Table 9-1 lists the methods in the Iterator interface.

Figure 9-1 shows the flow of the Iterator interface methods in a foreach loop.

Table 9-1. *Interator Interface Methods*

Method	Description
current()	Returns the value of the current element
key()	Returns the current key name or index
next()	Advances the array pointer forward one element
rewind()	Moves the pointer to the beginning of the array
valid()	Determines if there is a current element; called after calls to next() and rewind()

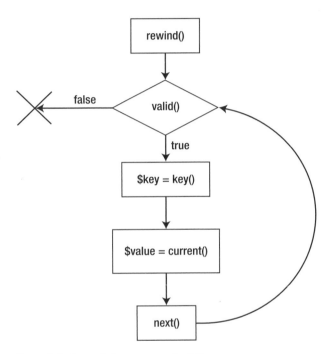

Figure 9-1. *foreach Iterator method flow*

Uses for iterators range from looping over objects to looping over database result sets, and even looping around files. In the next chapter, you will learn about the types of built-in iterator classes and their uses.

Iterator Helper Functions

Several useful convenience functions can be used with iterators:

iterator_to_array($iterator): This function can take any iterator and return an array containing all the data in the iterator. It can save you some verbose iteration and array-building loops when working with iterators.

iterator_count($iterator): This function returns exactly how many elements are in the iterator, thereby exercising the iterator.

■**Caution** The iterator_to_array($iterator) and iterator_count($iterator) functions can cause some spooky action if you call them on an iterator that does not have a defined ending point. This is because they require an internal exercise of the entire iterator. So if your iterator's valid() method will never return false, do not use these functions, or you will create an infinite loop.

---

iterator_apply(iterator, callback, [user data]): This function is used to apply a function to every element of an iterator, in the same way array_walk() is used on arrays. Listing 9-2 shows a simple iterator_apply() application.

Listing 9-2. *Using iterator_apply*

```
function print_entry($iterator) {
 print( $iterator->current() );
 return true;
}

$array = array(1,2,3);
$iterator = new ArrayIterator($array);
iterator_apply($iterator, 'print_entry', array($iterator));
```

This code outputs the following:

123

While the callback function returns true, the loop will continue executing. Once false is returned, the loop is exited.

Array Overloading

Array overloading is the process of using an object as an array. This means allowing data access through the [ ] array syntax. The ArrayAccess interface is at the core of this process and provides the required hooks to the Zend Engine.

ArrayAccess Interface

The ArrayAccess interface is described in Listing 9-3.

Listing 9-3. *The ArrayAccess Interface*

```
interface ArrayAccess {
  public function offsetExists($offset);
  public function offsetSet($offset, $value);
  public function offsetGet($offset);
  public function offsetUnset($offset);
}
```

Table 9-2 lists the methods in the ArrayAccess interface.

Table 9-2. *ArrayAccess Interface Methods*

Method	Description
offsetExists	Determines if a given offset exists in the array
offsetSet	Sets or replaces the data at a given offset
offsetGet	Returns the data at a given offset
offsetUnset	Nullifies data at a given offset

In the following chapters, you will be introduced to some of the advanced uses for array overloading.

Counting and ArrayAccess

When working with objects acting as arrays, it is often advantageous to allow them to be used exactly as an array would be used. However, by itself, an ArrayAccess implementer does not define a counting function and cannot be used with the count() function. This is because not all ArrayAccess objects are of a finite length.

Fortunately, there is a solution: the Countable interface. This interface is provided for just this purpose and defines a single method, as shown in Listing 9-4.

Listing 9-4. *The Countable Interface*

```
interface Countable {
  public function count();
}
```

When implemented, the Countable interface's count() method must return the valid number of elements in the Array object. Once Countable is implemented, the PHP count() function may be used as normal.

The Observer Pattern

The observer pattern is a very simple event system that includes two or more interacting classes. This pattern allows classes to observe the state of another class and to be notified when the observed class's state has changed.

In the observer pattern, the class that is being observed is called a *subject*, and the classes that are doing the observing are called *observers*. To represent these, SPL provides the SplSubject and SplObserver interfaces, as shown in Listings 9-5 and 9-6.

Listing 9-5. *The SplSubject Interface*

```
interface SplSubject {
  public function attach(SplObserver $observer);
  public function detach(SplObserver $observer);
  public function notify();
}
```

Listing 9-6. *The SplObserver Interface*

```
interface SplObserver {
  public function update(SplSubject $subject);
}
```

The idea is that the SplSubject class maintains a certain state, and when that state is changed, it calls notify(). When notify() is called, any SplObserver instances that were previously registered with attach() will have their update() methods invoked.

Listing 9-7 shows an example of using SplSubject and SplObserver.

Listing 9-7. *The Observer Pattern*

```
class DemoSubject implements SplSubject {

  private $observers, $value;

  public function __construct() {
    $this->observers = array();
  }

  public function attach(SplObserver $observer) {
    $this->observers[] = $observer;
  }

  public function detach(SplObserver $observer) {
    if($idx = array_search($observer,$this->observers,true)) {
      unset($this->observers[$idx]);
    }
  }

  public function notify() {
    foreach($this->observers as $observer) {
      $observer->update($this);
    }
  }
```

```
  public function setValue($value) {
    $this->value = $value;
    $this->notify();
  }

  public function getValue() {
    return $this->value;
  }

}

class DemoObserver implements SplObserver {

  public function update(SplSubject $subject) {
    echo 'The new value is '. $subject->getValue();
  }

}

$subject = new DemoSubject();
$observer = new DemoObserver();
$subject->attach($observer);
$subject->setValue(5);
```

Listing 9-7 generates the following output:

```
The new value is 5
```

The benefits of the observer pattern are that there may be many or no observers attached to the subscriber and you don't need to have prior knowledge of which classes will consume events from your subject class.

PHP 6 introduces the SplObjectStorage class, which improves the verbosity of this pattern. This class is similar to an array, except that it can store only unique objects and store only a reference to those objects. It offers a few benefits. One is that you cannot attach a class twice, as you can with the example in Listing 9-7, and because of this, you can prevent multiple update() calls to the same object. You can also remove objects from the collection without iterating/searching the collection, and this improves efficiency.

Since SplObjectStorage supports the Iterator interface, you can use it in foreach loops, just as a normal array can be used. Listing 9-8 shows the PHP 6 pattern using SplObjectStorage.

Listing 9-8. *SplObjectStorage and the Observer Pattern*

```
class DemoSubject implements SplSubject {

  private $observers, $value;
```

```php
  public function __construct() {
    $this->observers = new SplObjectStorage();
  }

  public function attach(SplObserver $observer) {
    $this->observers->attach($observer);
  }

  public function detach(SplObserver $observer) {
    $this->observers->detach($observer);
  }

  public function notify() {
    foreach($this->observers as $observer) {
      $observer->update($this);
    }
  }

  public function setValue($value) {
    $this->value = $value;
    $this->notify();
  }

  public function getValue() {
    return $this->value;
  }

}

class DemoObserver implements SplObserver {

  public function update(SplSubject $subject) {
    echo 'The new value is '. $subject->getValue();
  }

}

$subject = new DemoSubject();
$observer = new DemoObserver();
$subject->attach($observer);
$subject->setValue(5);
```

Listing 9-8 generates the following output:

```
The new value is 5
```

Serialization

The SPL's Serializable interface provides for some advanced serialization scenarios. The non-SPL serialization magic method's __sleep and __wakeup have a couple of issues that are addressed by the SPL interface.

The magic methods cannot serialize private variables from a base class. The __sleep function you implement must return an array of variable names to include in the serialized output. Because of where the serialization occurs, private members of the base class are restricted. Serializable lifts this restriction by allowing you to call serialize() on the parent class, returning the serialized private members of that class.

Listing 9-9 demonstrates a scenario that magic methods cannot handle.

Listing 9-9. *Magic Method Serialization*

```
error_reporting(E_ALL); //Ensure notices show

class Base {
  private $baseVar;

  public function __construct() {
    $this->baseVar = 'foo';
  }

}

class Extender extends Base {
  private $extenderVar;

  public function __construct() {
    parent::__construct();
    $this->extenderVar = 'bar';
  }

  public function __sleep() {
   return array('extenderVar', 'baseVar');
  }
}

$instance = new Extender();
$serialized = serialize($instance);
echo $serialized . "\n";
$restored = unserialize($serialized);
```

Running the code in Listing 9-9 results in the following notice:

```
Notice: serialize(): "baseVar" returned as member variable from
__sleep() but does not exist …

O:8:"Extender":2:{s:21:"ExtenderextenderVar";s:3:"bar";
s:7:"baseVar";N;}
```

To solve this problem and properly serialize the baseVar member, you need to use SPL's Serializable interface. The interface is simple, as shown in Listing 9-10.

Listing 9-10. *The Serializable Interface*

```
interface Serializable {
  public function serialize();
  public function unserialize( $serialized );
}
```

The serialize() method, when you implement it, requires that you return the serialized string representing the object; this is usually provided by using the serialize() function.

The unserialize() function will allow you to reconstruct the object. It takes the serialized string as an input.

Listing 9-11 shows the serialization of a private member of a base class.

Listing 9-11. *Serializing a Private Member in a Base Class*

```
error_reporting(E_ALL);

class Base implements Serializable {
  private $baseVar;

  public function __construct() {
    $this->baseVar = 'foo';
  }

  public function serialize() {
    return serialize($this->baseVar);
  }

  public function unserialize($serialized) {
    $this->baseVar = unserialize($serialized);
  }

  public function printMe() {
    echo $this->baseVar . "\n";
  }
}
```

```
class Extender extends Base {
  private $extenderVar;

  public function __construct() {
    parent::__construct();
    $this->extenderVar = 'bar';
  }

  public function serialize() {
   $baseSerialized = parent::serialize();
   return serialize(array($this->extenderVar, $baseSerialized));
  }

  public function unserialize( $serialized ) {
    $temp = unserialize($serialized);
    $this->extenderVar = $temp[0];
    parent::unserialize($temp[1]);
  }
}

$instance = new Extender();
$serialized = serialize($instance);
echo $serialized . "\n";
$restored = unserialize($serialized);
$restored->printMe();
```

Listing 9-11 has the following output:

```
C:8:"Extender":42:{a:2:{i:0;s:3:"bar";i:1;s:10:"s:3:"foo";";}}
foo
```

As you can see, the foo value of the base class was properly remembered and restored. The code in Listing 9-11 is very simple, but you can combine the code with functions like get_object_vars() to serialize every member of an object.

The Serializable interface offers a few other benefits. Unlike with the __wakeup magic method, which is called after the object is constructed, the unserialize() method is a constructor of sorts and will give you the opportunity to properly construct the object by storing construction input in the serialized data. This is distinct from __wakeup, which is called after the class is constructed and does not take any inputs.

The Serializable interface offers a lot of advanced serialization functionality and has the ability to create more robust serialization scenarios than the magic method approach.

SPL Autoloading

The __autoload($classname) magic function, if defined, allows you to dynamically load classes on their first use. This lets you retire your require_once statements. When declared, this function

is called every time an undefined class or interface is called. Listing 9-12 demonstrates the
__autoload($classname) method.

Listing 9-12. *The __autoload Magic Method*

```
function __autoload($class) {
  require_once($class . '.inc');
}
$test = new SomeClass(); //Calls autoload to find SomeClass
```

Now, this isn't SPL. However, SPL does take this concept to the next level, introducing the
ability to declare multiple autoload functions.

If you have a large application consisting of several different smaller applications or libraries,
each application may wish to declare an __autoload() function to find its files. The problem is
that you cannot simply declare two __autoload() functions globally without getting redeclara-
tion errors. Fortunately, the solution is simple.

The spl_autoload_register() function, provided by the SPL extension, gets rid of the magic
abilities of __autoload(), replacing them with its own type of magic. Instead of automatically
calling __autoload() once spl_autoload_register() has been called, calls to undefined classes
will end up calling, in order, all the functions registered with spl_autoload_register().

The spl_autoload_register() function takes two arguments: a function to add to the
autoload stack and whether to throw an exception if the loader cannot find the class. The first
argument is optional and will default to the spl_autoload() function, which automatically
searches the path for the lowercased class name, using either the .php or .inc extension, or any
other extensions registered with the spl_autoload_extensions() function. You can also register
a custom function to load the missing class.

Listing 9-13 shows the registration of the default methods, the configuration of file extensions for the default spl_autoload() function, and the registration of a custom loader.

Listing 9-13. *SPL Autoload*

```
spl_autoload_register(null,false);
spl_autoload_extensions('.php,.inc,.class,.interface');
function myLoader1($class) {
  //Do something to try to load the $class
}
function myLoader2($class) {
  //Maybe load the class from another path
}
spl_autoload_register('myLoader1',false);
spl_autoload_register('myLoader2',false);
$test = new SomeClass();
```

In Listing 9-13, the spl_autoload() function will search the include path for someclass.php,
someclass.inc, someclass.class, and someclass.interface. After it does not find the definition
in the path, it will invoke the myLoader() method to try to locate the class. If the class is not
defined after myLoader() is called, an exception about the class not being properly declared will
be thrown.

It is critical to remember that as soon as `spl_autoload_register()` is called, `__autoload()` functions elsewhere in the application may fail to be called. If this is not desired, a safer initial call to `spl_autoload_register()` would look like Listing 9-14.

Listing 9-14. *Safe spl_autoload_register Call*

```
if(false === spl_autoload_functions()) {
  if(function_exists('__autoload')) {
   spl_autoload_register('__autoload',false);
  }
}
//Continue to register autoload functions
```

The initialization in Listing 9-14 first calls the `spl_autoload_functions()` function, which returns either an array of registered functions or if, as in this case, the SPL autoload stack has not been initialized, the Boolean value `false`. Then you check to see if a function called `__autoload()` exists; if so, you register that function as the first function in the autoload stack and preserve its abilities. After that, you are free to continue registering autoload functions, as shown in Listing 9-13.

You can also call `spl_autoload_register()` to register a callback instead of providing a string name for the function. For example, providing an array like `array('class','method')` would allow you to use a method of an object.

Next, you can manually invoke the loader without actually attempting to utilize the class, by calling the `spl_autoload_call('className')` function. This function could be combined with the function `class_exists('className', false)` to attempt to load a class and gracefully fail if none of the autoloaders can find the class.

■**Note** The second parameter to `class_exists()` controls whether or not it attempts to invoke the autoloading mechanism. The function `spl_autoload_call()` is already integrated with `class_exists()` when used in autoloading mode.

Listing 9-15 shows an example of a clean-failure load attempt using both `spl_autoload_call()` and `class_exists()` in non-autoloading mode.

Listing 9-15. *Clean Loading*

```
//Try to load className.php
if(spl_autoload_call('className')
  && class_exists('className',false)
  ) {

  echo 'className was loaded';
```

```
    //Safe to instantiate className
    $instance = new className();

} else {

    //Not safe to instantiate className
    echo 'className was not found';

}
```

Object Identification

Sometimes it is advantageous to have a unique code for each instance of a class. For this purpose, SPL provides the spl_object_hash() function. Listing 9-16 shows its invocation.

Listing 9-16. *Invoking spl_object_hash*

```
class a {}
$instance = new a();
echo spl_object_hash($instance);
```

This code generates the following output:

```
c5e62b9f928ed0ca74013d3e85bbf0e9
```

Each hash is guaranteed to be unique for every object within the context of a single call. Repeated execution will likely result in the same hashes being generated but is not guaranteed to produce duplicate hashes. References to the same object in the same call are guaranteed to be identical, as shown in Listing 9-17.

Listing 9-17. *spl_object_hash and References*

```
class a {}
$instance = new a();
$reference = $instance;
echo spl_object_hash($instance) . "\n";
echo spl_object_hash($reference) . "\n";
```

Listing 9-17 generates the following output:

```
c5e62b9f928ed0ca74013d3e85bbf0e9
c5e62b9f928ed0ca74013d3e85bbf0e9
```

This data is similar to the comparison === operator; however, some uses may benefit from a hash code approach. For example, when registering objects in an array, the hash code may be used as the key for easier access.

Just the Facts

In this chapter, you were introduced to the SPL. The following chapters will build on this introduction.

Iterators can be used in looping structures. SPL provides the Iterator interface, along with some iterator helper functions, including iterator_to_array(), iterator_count(), and iterator_apply(). Array overloading allows you to treat objects as arrays.

SPL includes the Countable interface. You can use it to hook into the global count() function for your custom array-like objects.

Using the SPL observer pattern and the PHP 6-specific SplObjectStorage class, you can make certain objects monitor other objects for changes.

SPL autoloading is provided by the spl_autoload(), spl_autoload_register(), spl_autoload_functions(), spl_autoload_extensions(), and spl_autoload_call() functions.

Object identification is provided by the spl_object_hash() function. References to the same object in the same call are guaranteed to be identical.

In the following chapter, you will be introduced to some of the more advanced iterator patterns, so be sure to keep the lessons learned about iterators and their helper functions in mind.

CHAPTER 10

SPL Iterators

As you learned in the previous chapter, in order to control looping with the foreach statement, all objects must implement the Traversable interface. But, the Traversable interface is
an internal-only interface, so trying to implement it in your userland classes will simply result
in an error. To actually implement looping of your objects, you must implement Traversable
via the Iterator or IteratorAggregate interface.

For some uses, implementing Iterator might be enough, but when you need more functionality, you can choose from several extended iterator interfaces, which allow for seekable,
recursive, aggregated, or even cached access.

Along with providing the capability to iterate objects, the SPL also contains a number of
advanced iterator algorithms for filtering, searching, comparing, and integrating with the most
popular PHP data-access methods.

In this chapter, you will learn about the iteration interfaces and classes that the SPL provides.
The examples in this chapter are highly dependent on your PHP environment. If you plan to
use the SPL in your development, PHP version 5.2.1 or higher is recommended.

Iterator Interfaces and Iterators

The SPL iterator interfaces are designed to help you implement advanced iteration algorithms,
allowing you to create elegant data-access methods for your classes. These interfaces form the
basis for creating iterator classes. You could go ahead and create your own iterators from these
interfaces; however, the SPL extension defines an ever-growing number of built-in iterator
classes to tackle the most common iteration tasks. Let's look at the interfaces, and then review
some of the built-in classes.

Iterator Interfaces

The SPL provides five iterator interfaces: Traversable, Iterator, IteratorAggregate,
OuterIterator, and RecursiveIterator. These are described in the following sections.

Traversable

The Traversable interface isn't really an interface as much as it is an attribute. This is because
only internal classes—those written in C code—may implement Traversable directly. Any
userland class that needs to implement Traversable must do so by implementing one of the
userland interfaces that descend from Traversable.

Two base-level classes descend from Traversable and are accessible to your objects: Iterator and IteratorAggregate. By implementing one of these two interfaces, an object may be used with the foreach statement.

Iterator

The Iterator interface was introduced in the previous chapter. Its primary purpose is to allow a class to implement a basic iteration where it can be looped, keys accessed, and rewound. As a reminder, it contains five methods: rewind(), current(), key(), next(), and valid().

IteratorAggregate

The IteratorAggregate interface is used to offload the five iteration methods required by Iterator onto another class. This lets you make iteration external to the class and allows you to reuse common iteration methods instead of repeating them inside each iterable class you write.

The IteratorAggregate interface, if it were written in PHP, would have the following definition:

```
interface IteratorAggregate extends Traversable {
  function getIterator();
}
```

The getIterator() method, when implemented, must return an instance of a class that implements Iterator. Typically inside getIterator(), you will pass class information to the constructor of a specialized iteration class. This data might be an underlying array, or any other data that you can conceive of, as long as it is sufficient to control the five Iterator methods.

The SPL provides a few built-in iterators that are designed for use with the IteratorAggregate interface. Using these iterators will mean that you need to implement only one method and instantiate a single class to make your object iterable. Listing 10-1 shows the use of the ArrayIterator with the IteratorAggregate interface. ArrayIterator and the other built-in iterators are discussed in more detail in the "Iterators" section later in this chapter.

Listing 10-1. *Using the IteratorAggregate Interface*

```
class MyIterableClass implements IteratorAggregate {
  protected $arr;

  public function __construct() {
    $this->arr = array(1,2,3);
  }

  public function getIterator() {
    return new ArrayIterator($this->arr);
  }
}

foreach(new MyIterableClass() as $value) {
  echo $value . "\n";
}
```

```
1
2
3
```

> **Note** Instead of writing out a `foreach` loop to see the contents of your iterator, you could also use the function `iterator_to_array($iterator)`, as described in Chapter 9.

OuterIterator

Sometimes it is advantageous to enclose one or more iterators in another iterator, such as when you want to sequentially iterate several different iterators (which you can do with the `AppendIterator`, as discussed later in this chapter). For this purpose, you can use the `OuterIterator` interface.

The definition of the `OuterIterator` interface is as follows:

```
interface OuterIterator extends Iterator {
  function getInnerIterator();
}
```

This interface differs from the `IteratorAggregate` interface in that it extends the `Iterator` interface; thus, any class implementing it must also implement all the `Iterator`-defined methods.

The `getInnerIterator()` method should return the currently iterating iterator. For example, when two or more iterators are appended together and iterated one after the other, the `getInnerIterator()` method must return the first iterator, then the second, and so on, as the array pointer is increased by the `next()` method.

This interface forms the base interface for several more specialized iterators, including `AppendIterator`, `CachingIterator`, `FilterIterator`, `IteratorIterator`, `LimitIterator`, and `RecursiveIteratorIterator`.

RecursiveIterator

The `RecursiveIterator` interface is designed to allow for recursive iteration. This type of iterator interface can represent a tree data structure with nodes and leaves or parent and child elements. A directory is an example of a recursive structure.

The definition of the `RecursiveIterator` interface is as follows:

```
interface RecursiveIterator extends Iterator {
    function hasChildren();
    function getChildren();
}
```

All recursive functions (functions that call themselves) must have the ability to determine whether to continue recursing or to stop recursing and return to the top of the call stack. The `hasChildren()` method allows for this condition. If the iterator has children, the `getChildren()` method will be called, and it should return an iterator instance for the child elements.

Iterators

The SPL provides iterators that are capable of iterating iterators, filtering their data, caching their results, controlling pagination, and more.

ArrayIterator

The `ArrayIterator` is probably one of the most versatile iterators in the SPL package. It allows you to create an iterator from any PHP array. Listing 10-2 shows the creation and use of an iterator from an array.

Listing 10-2. *Using an ArrayIterator Iterator*

```
$arr = array('a','b','c');
$iterator = new ArrayIterator($arr);
foreach($iterator as $val) {
  echo $val;
}
```

abc

This might not seem terribly useful here, as you could have skipped the iterator creation entirely. However, it is important to understand how to manually get an iterator for an array, as many of the other SPL iterators require an iterator, not an array, to be passed to their constructors.

The `ArrayIterator` can also save you from needing to directly implement the `Iterator` interface's methods when working with `IteratorAggregate` classes. If your class uses an array as the underlying representation, you can simply return an `ArrayIterator` in `getIterator()`.

LimitIterator

The `LimitIterator` is one of the simpler iterators. It lets you do the iteration equivalent of SQL `LIMIT` and `OFFSET`, returning a set number of results and defining the index point at which that set will be taken. The `LimitIterator` implements the `OuterIterator` interface.

The `LimitIterator`'s constructor takes three parameters: an iterator, an offset, and a limit. Listing 10-3 shows a `LimitIterator` in use.

Listing 10-3. *Using a LimitIterator Iterator*

```
$arr = array(1,2,3,4,5,6,7,8,9);
$arrIterator = new ArrayIterator($arr);
$limitIterator = new LimitIterator($arrIterator, 3, 4);
foreach($limitIterator as $number) {
  echo $number;
}
```

```
4567
```

This iterator can be extremely useful for paginated display of a dataset.

AppendIterator

The `AppendIterator` allows you to sequentially iterate several different iterators. For example, if you wanted to iterate two or more arrays in a single loop, you would use the `AppendIterator`. Listing 10-4 shows how to use the `AppendIterator`.

Listing 10-4. *Using an AppendIterator Iterator*

```
$arrFirst = new ArrayIterator(array(1,2,3));
$arrSecond = new ArrayIterator(array(4,5,6));

$iterator = new AppendIterator();
$iterator->append($arrFirst);
$iterator->append($arrSecond);

foreach($iterator as $number) {
  echo $number;
}
```

```
123456
```

As you can see, the order in which the iterators are appended is the order in which they were iterated. Because an `AppendIterator` was used, only one loop was needed to iterate over both arrays.

This iterator is highly useful for aggregating data from multiple sources into a single iterator. You could use `array_merge()` to join arrays; however, using the iterator approach gives you the ability to use the features of any of the iterators described in this section in combination. Listing 10-5 shows how you would use the `LimitIterator`, `AppendIterator`, and `iterator_to_array()` to create an array consisting of the first two elements of each input array.

Listing 10-5. *Advanced Array Merging*

```
$arrFirst = new ArrayIterator(array(1,2,3));
$arrSecond = new ArrayIterator(array(4,5,6));

$iterator = new AppendIterator();
$iterator->append(new LimitIterator($arrFirst, 0, 2));
$iterator->append(new LimitIterator($arrSecond, 0, 2));
print_r(iterator_to_array($iterator, false));
```

```
Array
(
    [0] => 1
    [1] => 2
    [2] => 4
    [3] => 5
)
```

Note The PHP 5.2.1 and later $use_keys parameter to iterator_to_array() was used in Listing 10-5 to prevent the array keys from the first iterator being overwritten by the second. If you did not provide this parameter, the result would be array(0=>4,1=>5), because 0=>1 and 1=>2 are defined and then overwritten with the values from the second iterator.

FilterIterator

The FilterIterator class is an OuterIterator-based iterator. It is used to filter the data in an iterator and return any elements that are acceptable. For example, FilterIterator could be used in conjunction with DirectoryIterator to return a list of large files.

This class has one abstract method, accept(), which must be implemented. Because of this, the FilterIterator is usable only as a base class. The accept() method must return true or false for the current item in the iterator. If the return result is true, then that record will be included in the iteration. If it is false, it will be excluded from iteration.

Listing 10-6 demonstrates filtering with a FilterIterator.

Listing 10-6. *Using a FilterIterator Iterator*

```
class GreaterThanThreeFilterIterator extends FilterIterator {
        public function accept() {
                return ($this->current() > 3);
        }
}
$arr = new ArrayIterator(array(1,2,3,4,5,6));

$iterator = new GreaterThanThreeFilterIterator($arr);
print_r(iterator_to_array($iterator));
```

```
Array
(
    [3] => 4
    [4] => 5
    [5] => 6
)
```

The filter in Listing 10-6 rejects any entries that are not greater than three. You could also create a generic comparison filter by overriding the __construct() method and passing 3 as a parameter. Just remember that you also need to call the base class's constructor.

RegexIterator

The RegexIterator is an extended FilterIterator that allows you to use various regular expression patterns for matching and modifying an iterator's dataset.

The RegexIterator's most basic use is to match string keys or values to a pattern and return those keys that match. As an example, Listing 10-7 shows how to find all entries that start with the letter *a*.

Listing 10-7. *Using a Basic RegexIterator Iterator*

```
$arr = array('apple','avocado', 'orange', 'pineapple');
$arrIterator = new ArrayIterator($arr);

$iterator = new RegexIterator($arrIterator, '/^a/');
print_r(iterator_to_array($iterator));
```

```
Array
(
    [0] => apple
    [1] => avocado
)
```

The RegexIterator offers much more than the simple matching demonstrated in Listing 10-7, however. It has several other parameters that change the way that it works. The RegexIterator's constructor looks like this:

```
__construct ($iterator, $regex, $op_mode=0, $spl_flags=0, $preg_flags=0);
```

The first parameter of note is $op_mode, which controls the regular expression operation mode. This parameter defaults to RegexIterator::MATCH, but can also be one of the following:

GET_MATCH: In this mode, the current key in the iterator is passed as the third parameter to the preg_match() function. This will replace the current key with the &$matches data.

ALL_MATCHES: This option is the same as GET_MATCH but substitutes the function preg_match_all for preg_match.

SPLIT: This mode uses the preg_split function and works identically to GET_MATCH and ALL_MATCHES.

REPLACE: This option takes the current iterator value and performs a regular expression replacement, overwriting the value with the replaced string.

Listing 10-8 demonstrates the use of the GET_MATCH operational mode.

Listing 10-8. *Using the GET_MATCH $op_mode Parameter with RegexIterator*

```
$arr = array('apple','avocado', 'orange', 'pineapple');
$arrIterator = new ArrayIterator($arr);

$iterator = new RegexIterator(
                $arrIterator,
                '/^(a\w{3})\w*$/',
                RegexIterator::GET_MATCH
            );

print_r(iterator_to_array($iterator));
```

```
Array
(
    [0] => Array
        (
            [0] => apple
            [1] => appl
        )

    [1] => Array
        (
            [0] => avocado
            [1] => avoc
        )

)
```

The regular expression used in Listing 10-8 is fairly simple. It matches an entire word-based string starting with the letter *a* and consisting of three or more word characters. The pattern within the parentheses, (a/w{3}), controls which part of the string is used by GET_MATCH—in this case, the letter *a* and three word characters. The resulting array will contain the entire matched string at position 0, followed by any captured subpatterns.

The next RegexIterator parameter, $spl_flags, allows you to tell the iterator whether you want it to operate on the keys or on the values of the array. The default is to use values, however you can use the class constant USE_KEY for this parameter to enable key operation.

Listing 10-9 demonstrates how to use RegexIterator to filter out entries from an array where the array key is not numeric. The resulting array will have only numeric keys and their associated values.

Listing 10-9. *Using a RegexIterator to Extract Numeric Keys*

```
$arr = array(0=>'A', 1=>'B', 2=>'C', 3=>'D', 'nonnumeric'=>'useless');
$arrIterator = new ArrayIterator($arr);
```

```
$iterator = new RegexIterator(
               $arrIterator,
               '/^\d*$/',
               RegexIterator::MATCH,
               RegexIterator::USE_KEY
           );
print_r(iterator_to_array($iterator));
```

```
Array
(
    [0] => A
    [1] => B
    [2] => C
    [3] => D
)
```

The final RegexIterator parameter, $preg_flags, is used to pass any of the usual preg parameters to the underlying preg functions.

IteratorIterator

The IteratorIterator is actually one of the coolest iterators provided by SPL, though it's definitely hard at first to understand why.

The IteratorIterator is a nonspecific iterator type of iterator, which means that anything that implements Traversable can be iterated. This might not immediately seem useful, but various PHP extensions have classes that, for various good reasons, do not implement Iterator or IteratorAggregate but do implement Traversable.

One such example is the PHP Data Objects (PDO) extension. In PDO, the PDOStatement class implements only Traversable because it is a read-only collection, and because of this, the higher level iterators are not appropriate. The result of this read-only limitation is that to combine the result of a PDOStatement with any of the other iterators described in this chapter, you will need to use the IteratorIterator to wrap the PDOStatement.

■**Note** PDO is an extension you may already be familiar with, but if you need a refresher, it is covered very well in W. Jason Gilmore's book, *Beginning PHP and MySQL 5, Second Edition* (Apress, 2006; 1-59059-552-1).

Certain modifying iterators, like RegexIterator, may cause problems due to PDOStatement's read-only nature, and as such, they should not be used. That said, several useful iterators—like AppendIterator, FilterIterator, and LimitIterator—can be very useful when combined with PDOStatement result sets. Listing 10-10 shows how to use IteratorIterator and LimitIterator to limit a result set.

Listing 10-10. *Using IteratorIterator and PDOStatement*

```
$db = new PDO('pgsql:dbname=yourdb;user=youruser');
$pdoStatement = $db->query('SELECT * FROM table');

$iterator = new IteratorIterator($pdoStatement);
$limitIterator = new LimitIterator($iterator, 0, 10);
$tenRecordArray = iterator_to_array($limitIterator);
```

■**Note** Listing 10-10 is presented just for illustrative purposes. if you want to limit your result set to ten records, you should use the SQL LIMIT syntax in your SQL query instead.

CachingIterator

Caching iterators are used to perform one-ahead iteration. They are useful when you need to know, at a given point in the iteration cycle, information about the next element. For example, you could use this iterator to determine if the current element is the last element in a list. Using the recursive form, you could decide if a current node is a node or entry in a tree-like structure by finding out information about the next key.

SeekableIterator

The SeekableIterator is useful for creating nonsequential iteration. It allows you to jump to any point in the iterator without iterating all previous elements.

NoRewindIterator

The NoRewindIterator is designed for collections that cannot be rewound, or iterated more than once. This can be useful for iterators that perform a one-time operation during the iteration process, such as inserting a database record.

EmptyIterator

The EmptyIterator is a placeholder iterator and does nothing. It can be useful in certain cases where an abstract class requires a method to be implemented and return an iterator or when there is a comparison made between iterators.

InfiniteIterator

The InfiniteIterator is used to continually loop data. Once iteration has found the last element, the iterator is rewound and begins iterating from the first element again.

RecursiveArrayIterator

The RecursiveArrayIterator allows you to create an iterator for recursive array structures. This is an important iterator, as it allows for the operation of many of the more complicated iterators like RecursiveTreeIterator and RecursiveIteratorIterator. Listing 10-11 demonstrates using a RecursiveArrayIterator.

Listing 10-11. *Using a RecursiveArrayIterator Iterator*

```
$arr = array(
        0 => 'a';
        1 => array('a','b','c'),
        2 => 'b',
        3 => array('a','b','c'),
        4 => 'c'
);

$it = new RecursiveArrayIterator($arr);
print_r(iterator_to_array($it));
```

```
Array
(
    [0] => a
    [1] => Array
        (
            [0] => a
            [1] => b
            [2] => c
        )

    [2] => b
    [3] => Array
        (
            [0] => a
            [1] => b
            [2] => c
        )

    [4] => c
)
```

RecursiveIteratorIterator

The RecursiveIteratorIterator is actually one of the more useful iterators. It allows you to take a tree structure and flatten it into a single dimension. When the iterator finds a child iterator, it is traversed.

Observe the difference between the results of Listing 10-11 and Listing 10-12.

Listing 10-12. *Using a RecursiveIteratorIterator Iterator*

```
$arr = array(
        0 => 'a';
        1 => array('a','b','c'),
        2 => 'b',
        3 => array('a','b','c'),
        4 => 'c'
);

$arrayIterator = new RecursiveArrayIterator($arr);

$it = new RecursiveIteratorIterator($arrayIterator);

print_r(iterator_to_array($it, false));
```

```
Array
(
    [0] => a
    [1] => a
    [2] => b
    [3] => c
    [4] => b
    [5] => a
    [6] => b
    [7] => c
    [8] => c
)
```

As you can see, the result of Listing 10-12 is a single-dimensional array.

The signature of the RecursiveIteratorIterator's constructor is as follows:

```
__construct (RecursiveIterator $it, $mode=self::LEAVES_ONLY, $flags=0)
```

The $mode parameter can take one of three class constants: CHILD_FIRST, SELF_FIRST, or the default LEAVES_ONLY. This mode parameter controls whether the nodes are included in the tree and in what order. A directory structure, for example, would be best printed as a SELF_FIRST tree, but when searching for files, LEAVES_ONLY would make more sense.

The $flags parameter can be set to CATCH_GET_CHILDREN, which is used to catch any exception when trying to call the child iterators and to just proceed to the next element when an exception is thrown.

RecursiveTreeIterator

The RecursiveTreeIterator is not a built-in iterator, but is a sample iterator that is provided with the SPL extension in the examples directory, /ext/spl/examples/recursivetreeiterator.inc.

Once included, this iterator will allow you to visualize a tree, as demonstrated in Listing 10-13.

> ■**Note** If your PHP installation is from package management, you can still use the files in the examples directory by downloading the PHP source distribution for your PHP version. You do not need to compile/reinstall PHP for these examples to function properly.

Listing 10-13. *Using the Sample RecursiveTreeIterator Iterator*

```
require_once('/path/to/php-src/ext/spl/examples/recursivetreeiterator.inc');

$arr = array(
        0 => 'a';
        1 => array('a','b','c'),
        2 => 'b',
        3 => array('a','b','c'),
        4 => 'c'
);

$arrayIterator = new RecursiveArrayIterator($arr);

$it = new RecursiveTreeIterator($arrayIterator);

print_r(iterator_to_array($it, false));
```

```
Array
(
    [0] => |-a
    [1] => |-Array
    [2] => | |-a
    [3] => | |-b
    [4] => | \-c
    [5] => |-b
    [6] => |-Array
    [7] => | |-a
    [8] => | |-b
    [9] => | \-c
    [10] => \-c
)
```

RecursiveTreeIterator, like all the included sample iterators, is designed to be extended. There is no requirement that the tree iterator must output text-based delimiters. It is possible to construct an iterator that outputs an HTML tree.

ParentIterator

The ParentIterator is an extended FilterIterator that can filter out nonparent elements from a RecursiveIterator, to find only keys that have children. Listing 10-14 demonstrates the use of a ParentIterator.

Listing 10-14. *Using a ParentIterator Iterator*

```
$arr = array(
        0 => 'a';
        1 => array('a','b','c'),
        2 => 'b',
        3 => array('a','b','c'),
        4 => 'c'
);

$arrayIterator = new RecursiveArrayIterator($arr);

$it = new ParentIterator($arrayIterator);

print_r(iterator_to_array($it, false));
```

```
Array
(
    [0] => Array
        (
            [0] => a
            [1] => b
            [2] => c
        )

    [1] => Array
        (
            [0] => a
            [1] => b
            [2] => c
        )

)
```

DualIterator

The DualIterator offers simultaneous iteration over two iterators. This iterator has a fairly complex constructor that takes two iterators and flags. The flags control whether the current and key properties return the left-hand or right-hand side iterator values, or if they should return both values as an array.

This iterator also provides a static compareIterators($lhs, $rhs, $identical=false) method that can compare two iterators for equality or identicalness.

During iteration, the iterator provides two methods that allow you to access the right-hand and left-hand iterators: getLHS() and getRHS(). It also offers two methods that compare these values: areEqual() and areIdentical().

Listing 10-15 demonstrates using the DualIterator.

Listing 10-15. *Using a DualIterator Iterator*

```
require_once('/path/to/php-src/ext/spl/examples/dualiterator.inc');

$arrayIterator1 = new ArrayIterator(array(true, false, true));
$arrayIterator2 = new ArrayIterator(array(1, 0, true));

$it = new DualIterator($arrayIterator1, $arrayIterator2);

foreach($it as $unused) {
        echo "Left: ". (($it->getLHS()->current())?'true':'false');
        echo " Right: ". (($it->getRHS()->current())?'true':'false');
        echo " Equal: ". (($it->areEqual())?'true':'false');
        echo " Identical: ". (($it->areIdentical())?'true':'false');
        echo "\n";
}

echo "\nIterators Equal:";
var_dump(DualIterator::compareIterators($arrayIterator1, $arrayIterator2, false));
echo "\nIterators Identical:";
var_dump(DualIterator::compareIterators($arrayIterator1, $arrayIterator2, true));
```

```
Left: true Right: true Equal: true Identical: false
Left: false Right: false Equal: true Identical: false
Left: true Right: true Equal: true Identical: true

Iterators Equal:bool(true)

Iterators Identical:bool(false)
```

You can also use the compareIterators() method to see if an iterator-returning method returned a valid iterator or an EmptyIterator by comparing the return value to a new EmptyIterator().

RecursiveFilterIterator

The RecursiveFilterIterator is the recursive form of the FilterIterator. It requires you to implement the abstract accept() method as before, but inside this method, you should access the currently iterating iterator using the $this->getInnerIterator() method.

RecursiveRegexIterator

The RecursiveRegexIterator is the recursive form of the RegexIterator. It has the same usage as RegexIterator, except that it must be given a RecursiveIterator to iterate.

RecursiveDualIterator

The RecursiveDualIterator allows you to concurrently iterate two RecursiveIterator iterators. It has the same basic usage as DualIterator. Once you obtain a left-hand or right-hand side iterator, you should call getInnerIterator().

RecursiveCachingIterator

The RecursiveCachingIterator performs one-ahead recursion on a RecursiveIterator and can be extremely useful for allowing you to determine if the current iterator entry is a leaf or a node.

SearchIterator

The SearchIterator iterator performs both a filter and a limit, and stops after it finds a matching element. It is presented as an abstract class, and you must implement accept(), just as with any other FilterIterator.

Real-World Iterator Implementations

At times, iterators can seem like an academic topic; however, they have many practical uses. As a PHP developer, you will find them in increasing frequency in nearly all your favorite PHP applications and frameworks. The following are some concrete examples that you may find useful in your applications.

Parsing XML with SimpleXML

The SimpleXML extension introduced in PHP 5 is a really efficient and easy way to access data in the XML format. It's not suitable for all applications, and it has its limitations. However, if you just need to read the structure, the SimpleXML iterator will make working with XML in PHP truly a pleasure.

SimpleXML is enabled by default and won't require any reconfiguration of PHP. To use the SimpleXML iterator, you will need to create a sample XML file, such as the one shown in Listing 10-16.

Listing 10-16. *A Sample XML File (test.xml)*

```
<library>
  <book>
    <name>Pro PHP</name>
    <author>Kevin McArthur</author>
  </book>
```

```
  <book>
    <name>Other Book</name>
  </book>
</library>
```

The `SimpleXMLIterator` is a `RecursiveIterator` that allows you to access all the nodes within an XML document. The example in Listing 10-17 uses the recursive nature of the iterator to create a listing of books and their elements in the `test.xml` file.

Listing 10-17. *Using the SimpleXML Iterator*

```
$it = new SimpleXMLIterator(file_get_contents('test.xml'));

foreach($it as $key=>$node) {
  echo $key . "\n";
  if($it->hasChildren()) {
    foreach($it->getChildren() as $element=>$value) {
      echo "\t". $element . ":" . $value ."\n";
    }
  }
}
```

```
book
        name:Pro PHP
        author:Kevin McArthur
book
        name:Other Book
```

The `hasChildren()` condition is not required, but is included for demonstration. Without `hasChildren()`, `getChildren()` will simply return no elements and the `foreach loop` would not be entered.

Accessing Flat-File Databases with DBA

The DBA extension provides access to many useful flat-file format databases, like the popular DB4 format. The DBA iterators are useful for accessing data exposed by the DBA extension. The following examples use the `.ini` file handler, but several other handlers are available. To build PHP with the DBA extension with `.ini` file and cdb drivers enabled, you must include the following in your PHP configure line:

```
--enable-dba --with-inifile
```

▐**Note** Many package-managed installations of PHP will include some support for DBA. Its presence, as well as the existence of specific drivers, is exposed via `phpinfo()`.

To follow the examples in this section, you will need to create an .ini file like the one shown in Listing 10-18.

Listing 10-18. *A Sample ini File (test.ini)*

```
[group1]
mykey=myvalue
```

DbaReader

DbaReader is the foundation iterator for the DBA iterators. Its constructor takes two parameters: a file and a handler. In the case of an .ini file, the handler parameter is inifile.

You can use the DbaReader iterator to read the sample .ini file in Listing 10-18 using the code shown in Listing 10-19.

Listing 10-19. *Using a DbaReader Iterator*

```
require_once('path/to/php-src/ext/spl/examples/dbareader.inc');
$it = new DbaReader('test.ini', 'inifile');
print_r(iterator_to_array($it,true));
```

```
Array
(
    [[group1]] =>
    [[group1]mykey] => myvalue
)
```

IniGroups

If you just want to determine the groups in an .ini file, you use the IniGroups iterator. This iterator is a type of KeyFilter iterator that will provide a list of .ini file groups. A demonstration is shown in Listing 10-20.

Listing 10-20. *Using an IniGroups Iterator*

```
require_once('path/to/php-src/ext/spl/examples/inigroups.inc');
$it = new IniGroups('test.ini', 'inifile');
print_r(iterator_to_array($it,true));
```

```
Array
(
    [group1] => group1
)
```

Just the Facts

This chapter covers SPL iterators, which can be an elegant solution to complex programming challenges.

To control looping of objects using foreach, your classes must implement the Traversable interface. You cannot directly implement Traversable; you must implement it through either the Iterator or IteratorAggregate interface. Iterator requires you to implement all the iteration methods. IteratorAggregate allows you to offload those methods to another class. As an example, you saw how to use the built-in ArrayIterator to iterate an array-based collection without implementing anything more than the getIterator() method described in IteratorAggregate. The SPL also includes more complicated iterator interfaces like RecursiveIterator, OuterIterator, and SeekableIterator.

The SPL provides a selection of iterator classes that implement the iterator interfaces and that solve common programming challenges. Of particular note are the ArrayIterator, LimitIterator, FilterIterator, and RegexIterator iterators, as well as their recursive forms.

The final section of this chapter presented examples of using iterators to solve common problems. The SimpleXMLIterator, included with the SimpleXML extension, is a RecursiveIterator that allows you to use XML files by looping through elements one at a time. The DbaReader and IniGroups iterators, included in the DBA extension, are useful for parsing files, such as .ini files.

■ ■ ■

CHAPTER 11

SPL File and Directory Handling

The SPL provides several classes and iterators that allow for object-oriented access of files and directories. In this chapter, you will learn about how the traditional file-access functions of PHP have been transitioned to object form.

Iteration plays an important role in working with files and folders. In this chapter, you will be introduced to several advanced iteration techniques for listing, searching, and filtering files and directories.

Finally, the SPL provides the ability to manipulate the content of files. It allows you to parse INI files, search using regular expressions, read comma-separated value (CSV) data, and so on. This chapter provides comprehensive examples of how to manipulate files in your applications.

File and Directory Information

The purpose of the SplFileInfo class is to provide object-oriented access to the properties of a file or directory. It is defined as shown in Listing 11-1.

Listing 11-1. *SplFileInfo Definition*

```
class SplFileInfo {
  function __construct($file_name) {}
  function getPath() {}
  function getFilename() {}
  function getFileInfo(string class_name = NULL) {}
  function getPathname() {}
  function getPathInfo(string class_name = NULL) {}
  function getPerms() {}
  function getInode() {}
  function getSize() {}
  function getOwner() {}
  function getGroup() {}
  function getATime() {}
```

```
    function getMTime() {}
    function getCTime() {}
    function getType() {}
    function isWritable() {}
    function isReadable() {}
    function isExecutable() {}
    function isFile() {}
    function isDir() {}
    function isLink() {}
    function __toString() {}
    function openFile($mode = 'r', $use_include_path = false, $context = NULL) {}
    function setFileClass(string class_name = "SplFileObject") {}
    function setInfoClass(string class_name = "SplFileInfo") {}
}
```

The typical usage of the SPLFileInfo class is to retrieve information about a file or folder. Listing 11-2 shows a basic invocation.

Listing 11-2. *Using SPLFileInfo*

```
$fileName = '/path/to/file/filename.php';

$fileInfo = new SPLFileInfo($fileName);

$fileProps = array();
$fileProps['path']          = $fileInfo->getPath();
$fileProps['filename']      = $fileInfo->getFilename();
$fileProps['pathname']      = $fileInfo->getPathname();
$fileProps['perms']         = $fileInfo->getPerms();
$fileProps['inode']         = $fileInfo->getInode();
$fileProps['size']          = $fileInfo->getSize();
$fileProps['owner']         = $fileInfo->getOwner();
$fileProps['group']         = $fileInfo->getGroup();
$fileProps['atime']         = $fileInfo->getATime();
$fileProps['mtime']         = $fileInfo->getMTime();
$fileProps['ctime']         = $fileInfo->getCTime();
$fileProps['type']          = $fileInfo->getType();
$fileProps['isWritable']    = $fileInfo->isWritable();
$fileProps['isReadable']    = $fileInfo->isReadable();
$fileProps['isExecutable']  = $fileInfo->isExecutable();
$fileProps['isFile']        = $fileInfo->isFile();
$fileProps['isDir']         = $fileInfo->isDir();
$fileProps['isLink']        = $fileInfo->isLink();

var_export($fileProps);
```

```
array (
  'path' => '/path/to/file',
  'filename' => 'filename.php',
  'pathname' => '/path/to/file/filename.php',
  'perms' => 33261,
  'inode' => 886570,
  'size' => 1131,
  'owner' => 1002,
  'group' => 1002,
  'atime' => 1167067832,
  'mtime' => 1167067771,
  'ctime' => 1167067771,
  'type' => 'file',
  'isWritable' => true,
  'isReadable' => true,
  'isExecutable' => true,
  'isFile' => true,
  'isDir' => false,
  'isLink' => false,
)
```

Using SPLFileInfo is pretty straightforward. Do be aware that if you do not provide a path and file name, then the pathname and path properties will omit the path. The path value is the same as calling dirname() on the construction parameter, and the pathname value is just a copy of the input parameter.

Note The perms mask can be decoded in standard bitwise manner. If you are unfamiliar with this, you can review an example in the fileperms() function documentation in the PHP manual, at http://www.php.net/fileperms.

The SPLFileInfo class supports extension through its provision of two key methods:

setInfoClass: This defaults to SPLFileInfo. If you extend the SPLFileInfo class, you will want to set this value to the name of your extended class.

setFileClass: This defaults to an SPLFileObject class. If you extend this class, you should set this value to ensure that your extended class is what is provided by consumers of SPLFileInfo.

These two functions have an effect on how the getFileInfo(), getPathInfo(), and openFile() methods operate. It may seem slightly unintuitive that SplFileInfo has a getFileInfo() method; however, since DirectoryIterator and SPLFileObject descend from SPLFileInfo, this method provides a way to access information about a specific file in an iterator or downcast a file object into an info object. The openFile() method will access the file and return an SPLFileInfo object, which can be used to perform operations within a file, as discussed in the "File Object Operations" section later in this chapter.

Iteration of Directories

Locating files and directories on disk used to be a somewhat tedious task involving the opendir() and readdir() functions. Fortunately, now we have the SPL, and instead of interpreting string values, we have a fully object-oriented interface for working with files. Iteration is a key part in working with directory structures in the SPL.

Listing Files and Directories

The most basic iterator is DirectoryIterator, which gives you access to a listing of the contents in a directory. The true power of the SPL starts to emerge when you meet the RecursiveDirectoryIterator and combine it with the advanced iterator patterns you learned about in the previous chapter, such as SearchIterator and FilterIterator.

DirectoryIterator

The definition of DirectoryIterator is shown in Listing 11-3.

Listing 11-3. *DirectoryIterator Definition*

```
class DirectoryIterator extends SplFileInfo implements Iterator {
  function __construct($path) {}
  function rewind() {}
  function valid() {}
  function key() {}
  function current() {}
  function next() {}
  function isDot() {}
  function isLink() {}
  function __toString() {}
}
```

The use of this iterator is like that of any other iterator, and it can be exercised with foreach. Its current() method returns an SplFileInfo object for the current entry in the directory.

Listing 11-4 shows a basic use of DirectoryIterator and SPLFileInfo's __toString() method.

Listing 11-4. *Using SplFileInfo and DirectoryIterator*

```
$pathName = '/path/to/iterate/';

foreach(new DirectoryIterator($pathName) as $fileInfo) {
  echo $fileInfo . "\n";
}
```

```
.
..
folder
file.ext
```

In addition to the typical SplFileInfo methods and the methods required by the Iterator interface, DirectoryIterator implements one other method: isDot(), which is used to determine if the current entry in the iterator is either the current (.) or parent (..) folders. This can be useful to ensure that you do not try to open these special entries.

RecursiveDirectoryIterator

It is often desirable to operate on a path hierarchy, rather than just a single directory at a time. For this purpose, you can use the RecursiveDirectoryIterator, which provides recursive iteration, as well as methods to determine if a path has child directories. Its definition is shown in Listing 11-5.

Listing 11-5. *RecursiveDirectoryIterator Definition*

```
class RecursiveDirectoryIterator
  extends DirectoryIterator implements RecursiveIterator
{

    const CURRENT_AS_FILEINFO   0x00000010;
    const KEY_AS_FILENAME       0x00000020;
    const NEW_CURRENT_AND_KEY   0x00000030;

    function __construct($path, $flags = 0) {}
    function key() {}
    function current() {}
    function hasChildren() {}
    function getChildren() {}
    function getSubPath() {}
    function getSubPathname() {}

}
```

__construct's flags parameter controls how the current and key values are returned. To visualize the operation of this iterator, you can use the RecursiveTreeIterator, as explained in the previous chapter. Listing 11-6 shows an example of a directory structure.

Listing 11-6. *Using RecursiveDirectoryIterator*

```
require_once('/path/to/php-src/ext/spl/examples/recursivetreeiterator.inc');

$pathName = '/path/to/php-src/ext/spl/examples';

$iterator = new RecursiveDirectoryIterator($pathName);
$treeIterator = new RecursiveTreeIterator($iterator);

foreach($treeIterator as $entry) {
        echo $entry . "\n";
}
```

```
|-/.../examples/tree.php
|-/.../examples/searchiterator.inc
|-/.../examples/tests
| |-/.../examples/tests/dualiterator_001.phpt
| \-/.../examples/tests/examples.inc
|-/.../examples/directorygraphiterator.inc
|-/.../examples/dbareader.inc
|-/.../examples/directoryfilterdots.inc
\-/.../examples/keyfilter.inc
```

Finding Files

So now that you've seen how to list files and directories, let's look at how to find files using FindFile and RegexFindFile.

FindFile

To locate files by file name, use the FindFile example iterator, as demonstrated in Listing 11-7.

Listing 11-7. *Searching for a File with FindFile*

```
require_once('/path/to/php-src/ext/spl/examples/findfile.inc');

$it = new FindFile('/path/to/php-src/', 'tree.php');

foreach($it as $entry) {
        echo $entry . "\n";
}
```

/path/to/php-src/ext/spl/examples/tree.php

You can also call getPathname() on the $entry SPLFileInfo object if you want to locate only the path.

RegexFindFile

You can also locate files using a regular expression search. The regular expression is matched on the entire path and file name, so your patterns should reflect that. Listing 11-8 demonstrates finding all files that have tree in their name.

Listing 11-8. *Using RegexFindFile*

```
require_once('/path/to/php-src/ext/spl/examples/findfile.inc');
require_once('/path/to/php-src/ext/spl/examples/regexfindfile.inc');

$it = new RegexFindFile('/path/to/php-src/ext/spl/examples/', '/tree/');
print_r(iterator_to_array($it));
```

```
Array
(
    /path/to/php-src/ext/spl/examples/class_tree.php] => SplFileInfo Object
        (
        )
...
)
```

To use this result set, you will most likely want to use the getFilename() method of SplFileInfo in a value-based loop.

Creating Custom File Filter Iterators

Creating your own filtering iterators is actually quite simple. All you need to do is create a class that inherits FilterIterator and implements accept().

The trick is in the constructor; you will presumably want to take a path and a predicate parameter. To create this constructor, you must receive two parameters, create a RecursiveDirectoryIterator for the path, and then create a RecursiveIteratorIterator to pass to the base FilterIterator class, as shown in Listing 11-9.

To operate, the FindFile iterator uses the RecursiveIteratorIterator to get a single-dimension list of all the files in all subfolders of the underlying RecursiveDirectoryIterator. In order to create your own filters, such as to find all files by file extension, you first need to flatten a recursive iterator. Flattening a recursive iterator involves walking the entire tree, and copying the current name of each step into a nonrecursive list. The flattening of a recursive iterator is an important part of Listing 11-9, as the filter may work with only a single dimension and not a tree.

■Note You can use a `RecursiveFilterIterator` for a custom file filter iterator if you want to have the results in a recursive format. For the example here, the results are presented as a nonrecursive list.

Listing 11-9. *Finding All Files of a Specific Type*

```
class FileExtensionFinder extends FilterIterator {

  protected $predicate, $path;

  public function __construct($path, $predicate) {
    $this->predicate = $predicate;
    $this->path = $path;

    $it = new RecursiveDirectoryIterator($path);
    $flatIterator = new RecursiveIteratorIterator($it);

    parent::__construct($flatIterator);

  }

  public function accept() {
    $pathInfo = pathinfo($this->current());
    $extension = $pathInfo['extension'];
    return ($extension == $this->predicate);
  }

}

$it = new FileExtensionFinder('/path/to/search/','php');

foreach($it as $entry) {
  echo $entry . "\n";
}
```

The accept() method for this class uses the PHP pathinfo function to determine the file's extension and accepts any current() entry with the proper file extension. Of course, you can create filters to search for large files or any other imaginable filtering task.

Creating a Plug-in Directory

It is often desirable to create a plug-in directory where, when files are added, they are loaded implicitly by the application.

To create a plug-in directory, in which all the code is invoked, you need to feed the results of a DirectoryIterator into the require_once function. Listing 11-10 shows how you could accomplish this.

Listing 11-10. *Creating a Plug-in Directory*

```
$dir = '/path/to/plugins';
$dirit = new DirectoryIterator($dir);

foreach($dirit as $file) {
  if(!$file->isDir()) { //Ignore directories, e.g., ./ and ../
    require_once($file);
  }
}
```

Instead of loading the files, you could integrate this example with the SPL autoload functionality, described in Chapter 9, and factor out any configuration requirements through the use of naming conventions. This could provide your application with a list of available plug-ins without any type of implicit installation.

■**Note** For the most part, you will generally want to use the SPL autoload functionality for loading classes when the name of the class is known.

Operating on a CVS Directory

Many of you probably have run into CVS version control in your projects. The CVS system creates a CVS directory and several associated files for every directory that is under revision control. Sometimes, you may need to perform operations on the contents of a CVS repository, either to modify permissions or extract information from a CVS checkout.

The NoCvsDirectory filter iterator is included with the SPL examples and provides a way to filter out these directories from a CVS checkout. You will find this class and an example of how to use it in nocvsdir.php inside the examples directory. You can find the examples directory at /ext/ spl/examples/ in the PHP source code.

Using Reflection with Directory Iterators

In Chapter 7, you learned about documenting with the reflection API. Using the SPL directory iterators, you can load all the files in a directory structure. Once they are loaded, you can use get_declared_classes() (discussed in Chapter 7) to create documentation for an entire application.

SPL File Object Operations

So far, I've talked about how to deal with file and directory names on the file system. The SplFileObject class takes this concept and allows you to operate on files themselves in a similar fashion.

The SplFileObject class consolidates the PHP file I/O functions like fopen, fread, and so on into a versatile, object-oriented interface. You can read and manipulate data using this class and an object-oriented approach as an alternative to the linear approach typically found in PHP applications.

SplFileObject is also an iterator and is seekable, which allows you to use the contents of files with the foreach loop.

File Iteration

First, let's look at basic line-by-line iteration. Create a CSV file like the one shown in Listing 11-11.

Listing 11-11. *Sample CSV File (pm.csv)*

```
"Prime Minister",From,To
"Stephen Joseph Harper",2006-02-06,
"Paul Edgar Philippe Martin",2003-12-12,2006-02-05
"Joseph Jacques Jean Chrétien",1993-11-04,2003-12-11
"Kim Campbell",1993-06-25,1993-11-03
"Martin Brian Mulroney",1984-09-17,1993-06-24
"John Napier Turner",1984-06-30,1984-09-16
"Pierre Elliott Trudeau",1980-03-03,1984-06-29
"Charles Joseph Clark",1979-06-04,1980-03-02
```

Now, you can iterate this data simply by using a foreach statement like the one shown in Listing 11-12.

Listing 11-12. *Line-by-Line Iteration*

```
$it = new SplFileObject('pm.csv');

foreach($it as $line) {
        echo $line;
}
```

So, that's pretty useful. But what if you want to actually read that CSV data in a loop and access each entry as an array?

CSV Operation

The CSV operation of SplFileObject is particularly useful as it allows you to interpret data as you parse it. Listing 11-13 shows CSV parsing operation.

Listing 11-13. *CSV Parsing*

```
$it = new SplFileObject('pm.csv');

while($array = $it->fgetcsv()) {
  var_export($array);
}
```

```
array (
  0 => 'Prime Minister',
  1 => 'From',
  2 => 'To',
)array (
  0 => 'Stephen Joseph Harper',
  1 => '2006-02-06',
  2 => '',
)
. . .
array (
  0 => '',
)
```

Listing 11-13 demonstrates parsing CSV records in numerical order, with a while loop. This is useful, but it could be more so. You can take this another step and create a CSVFileObject that is designed specifically for CSV operation. One thing you will have noticed from the example in Listing 11-13 is that the CSV headers were interpreted as data and the final line was interpreted as a blank array. Iterating a CSV file should take these two special cases into account.

First, create an Iterator class CSVFileObject that descends from SplFileInfo. In the constructor, call the parent SplFileInfo constructor, read the first line of the file, and assign an array mapping the CSV indexes to the column names. Next, implement the iterator methods. Listing 11-14 shows this CSV class.

Listing 11-14. *The CSVFileObject Class*

```
class CSVFileObject extends SPLFileInfo implements Iterator, SeekableIterator {

    protected $map, $fp, $currentLine;

  public function __construct( $filename,
                               $mode = 'r',
                               $use_include_path = false,
                               $context = NULL
                             )
{

    parent::__construct($filename);

    //Cannot pass an implicit null to fopen
    if(isset($context)) {
      $this->fp = fopen( $filename,
                         $mode,
                         $use_include_path,
                         $context
                       );
```

```php
  } else {
    $this->fp = fopen($filename, $mode, $use_include_path);
  }

  if(!$this->fp) {
    throw new Exception("Cannot read file");
  }

  //Get the column map
  $this->map = $this->fgetcsv();
  $this->currentLine = 0;
}

function fgetcsv($delimiter = ',', $enclosure = '"') {
  return fgetcsv($this->fp, 0, $delimiter, $enclosure);
}

function key() {
  return $this->currentLine;
}

function current() {
  /*
   * The fgetcsv method increments the file pointer
   * so you must first record the file pointer,
   * get the data, and return the file pointer.
   * Only the next() method should increment the
   * pointer during operation.
   */
  $fpLoc = ftell($this->fp);
  $data = $this->fgetcsv();
  fseek($this->fp, $fpLoc);
  return array_combine($this->map, $data);
}

function valid() {
  //Check for end-of-file
  if(feof($this->fp)) {
    return false;
  }

  /*
   * Again, need to prevent the file pointer
   * from being advanced. This check prevents
   * a blank line at the end of file returning
   * as a null value.
   */
```

```
    $fpLoc = ftell($this->fp);
    $data = $this->fgetcsv();
    fseek($this->fp, $fpLoc);
    return (is_array($data));
  }

  function next() {
    $this->currentLine++;
    //Bump the file pointer to the next line
    fgets($this->fp);
  }

  function rewind() {
    $this->currentLine = 0;

    //Reset the file pointer
    fseek($this->fp, 0);

    //Skip the column headers
    fgets($this->fp);
  }

  function seek($line) {
    $this->rewind();
    while($this->currentLine < $line && !$this->eof()) {
      $this->currentLine++;
      fgets($this->fp);
    }
  }

}
```

With this class in hand, you can now read the pm.csv file by using the code presented in Listing 11-15.

Listing 11-15. *Using CSVFileObject*

```
$it = new CSVFileObject('pm.csv');
var_dump(iterator_to_array($it));
```

```
array(8) {
  [0]=>
  array(3) {
    ["Prime Minister"]=>
    string(21) "Stephen Joseph Harper"
    ["From"]=>
    string(10) "2006-02-06"
```

```
    ["To"]=>
    string(0) ""
  }
  [1]=>
  array(3) {
    ["Prime Minister"]=>
    string(26) "Paul Edgar Philippe Martin"
    ["From"]=>
    string(10) "2003-12-12"
    ["To"]=>
    string(10) "2006-02-05"
  }
  . . .
}
```

Now the CSV data is converted to an array format with the keys being the CSV column headers. This can make CSV parsing cleaner and tie the data to the column names, rather than arbitrary array indexes. Also, the first record is no longer the headers, and the last record is the last line of CSV data in the file.

You could apply a filter iterator to this result set to create a searchable system.

Searching Files

Using the SPL file and directory facilities, you can put together a basic text-file search system. In this example, you will create two custom filter iterators: one based on SearchIterator, which searches the contents of a file for a substring match and stops as soon as a match is found, and another that invokes the search and sees if any results are returned. You will use a RecursiveDirectoryIterator and a RecursiveIteratorIterator to get the file names to test. Listing 11-16 shows a simple substring search using iterators.

Listing 11-16. *Substring Searching with Iterators*

```php
require_once('/path/to/php-src/ext/spl/examples/searchiterator.inc');

class InFileSearch extends SearchIterator {

  protected $search;

  public function __construct($it, $search) {
    parent::__construct($it);
    $this->search = $search;
  }

  //If the substring is found then accept
  public function accept() {
    return (strpos($this->current(), $this->search) !== FALSE);
  }
}
```

```
class FileContentFilter extends FilterIterator {

  protected $search;

  public function __construct($it, $search) {
    parent::__construct($it);
    $this->search = $search;
  }

  public function accept() {
    //Current holds a file name
    $fo = new SplFileObject($this->current());

    //Search within the file
    $file = new InFileSearch($fo, $this->search);

    //Accept if more than one line was found
    return (count(iterator_to_array($file)) > 0);
  }
}

//Create a recursive iterator for Directory Structure
$dir = new RecursiveDirectoryIterator('/path/to/php-src/ext/spl/examples/');

//Flatten the recursive iterator
$it = new RecursiveIteratorIterator($dir);

//Filter
$filter = new FileContentFilter($it, 'Kevin McArthur');

print_r(iterator_to_array($filter));
```

Just the Facts

This chapter introduced the SPL facilities for file I/O. These include the SplFileInfo object, directory iterators, and the SplFileObject class.

With SplFileInfo, you can get file names, sizes, and permissions. You can also integrate overloaded versions of this class.

Using DirectoryIterator, RecursiveDirectoryIterator, and other SPL iterators, you can perform iteration of directories. You can create iterators that display directory information, find files, filter information, load plug-ins, reflect on code, and so on.

Using SplFileObject, you can iterate over the contents of files. With an extended SplFileInfo class, such as CVSFileObject, you can operate on CSV data, using iterative means. By extending SplFileInfo, you can create an object similar to SplFileObject. You can utilize any of the standard SPL filtering and limiting iterators with a CSV file in this manner, which allows you to create a robust data-parsing system.

The final example in this chapter demonstrated how to create a basic substring file search engine using an iterative approach. This search facility combined directory iteration, flattening iterators, filtering, searching, and `SplFileObject` subfile iteration—putting together everything you learned about in this chapter.

In the next chapter, you will learn how to manipulate data, building on the lessons learned so far.

SPL Array Overloading

Array overloading is the process of using an object as an array. Some people coming from different language backgrounds may know this ability by another name: *indexers*.

The material in this chapter will help you learn how to create objects that can have their contents read and manipulated using the standard array syntax.

Introducing ArrayAccess

The ArrayAccess interface enables your objects to behave as arrays. It consists of four methods, as listed in Table 12-1.

Table 12-1. *ArrayAccess Methods*

Method	Description
offsetSet()	Sets an offset for array access. Takes two parameters: an offset to be used as the array index and a value to assign.
offsetGet()	Gets the associated value given a specified offset.
offsetExists()	Returns a Boolean value for a given offset to indicate whether (true) or not (false) a specific key has a value that may be fetched with offsetGet().
offsetUnset()	Removes an item from the collection. It is called when you use the unset statement or set an offset to null.

The code in Listing 12-1 shows a very simple form of implementing the ArrayAccess interface, and it is not even iterable. However, it does demonstrate how the array machinery works.

Listing 12-1. *Using ArrayAccess*

```
class MyArray implements ArrayAccess {

  protected $_arr;

  public function __construct() {
    $this->_arr = array();
  }
```

```
  public function offsetSet($offset, $value) {
    $this->_arr[$offset] = $value;
  }

  public function offsetGet($offset) {
    return $this->_arr[$offset];
  }

  public function offsetExists($offset) {
    return array_key_exists($offset, $this->_arr);
  }

  public function offsetUnset($offset) {
    unset($this->_arr[$offset]);
  }

}


$myArray = new MyArray();    // Create an object as an array
$myArray['first'] = 'test'; // offsetSet, set data by key
$demo = $myArray['first'];   // offsetGet, get data by key
unset($myArray['first']);    // offsetUnset, remove key
```

ArrayAccess is provided primarily because not all collections are based on a real array. Collections using the ArrayAccess interface may instead broker requests to a service-oriented architecture (SOA) back-end, or any other form of disconnected storage. This allows you to defer materialization of your underlying data until it is actually accessed.

However, for the vast majority of cases, you will likely use an array as the underlying representation. Then you will add methods to this class to work with this data. For this purpose, there is the built-in ArrayObject class, discussed next.

The ArrayAccess interface itself does not provide the ability to count the number of elements in the array. This is because not all ArrayAccess classes have a finite length. Those that do, however, can—and probably should—implement the Countable interface. This interface is extremely simple, containing only one method, count(), to return the number of elements.

Introducing ArrayObject

The ArrayObject class is an ArrayAccess implementer that also gives you iteration support, as well as quite a few useful methods for sorting and working with data, as listed in Table 12-2. ArrayObject also implements Countable for you. It is based on an Array internally, so it is limited to working with real, fully populated data, but it can serve as a useful base class for your applications.

Listing 12-2 demonstrates using ArrayObject.

Table 12-2. *ArrayObject Methods*

Method	Description
append($value)	Allows you to add another element to the end of the list. It is syntactically identical to using the [ ] array syntax.
asort()	Applies the PHP asort() function to the underlying array values.
ksort()	Sorts the array by key.
natcasesort()	Sorts using the natural-order algorithm, case-insensitively.
natsort()	Sorts using the natural-order algorithm, case-sensitively.
uasort($compare)	Can be used to create a custom sorting routine. The $compare function should be a function callback using the standard PHP callback syntax.
uksort($compare)	Same as uasort(), but operates on keys rather than values.
getArrayCopy()	Returns a copy of the underlying array.
exchangeArray($array)	Allows you to change the underlying array, substituting another. It can be used with getArrayCopy() to extract the information, modify it, and repopulate the ArrayObject.

Listing 12-2. *Using ArrayObject*

```
$myArray = new ArrayObject();
$myArray['first'] = 'test';
$demo = $myArray['first'];
unset($myArray['first']);
$numElements = count($myArray);
foreach($myArray as $key=>$value) {}
```

You can use ArrayObject in many more advanced ways, including initializing it with the values already contained within an array.

The ArrayObject class's constructor method is defined as follows:

```
__construct ($array, $flags=0, $iterator_class="ArrayIterator")
```

The flags parameter can be one of two class constants:

- The ArrayObject::ARRAY_AS_PROPS constant makes all elements of the array additionally become properties of the object.

- The ArrayObject::STD_PROP_LIST constant controls how properties are treated when using listing functionality like var_dump, foreach, and so on.

The iterator class parameter controls which type of iterator is returned within the IteratorAggregate implementation. This allows you to extend the object and provide your own iteration class instead of the default ArrayIterator.

So this could be useful, but it's hardly worth getting up off the couch for. The power of the ArrayObject object comes when you extend it. A common use for a web application is a shopping cart, so let's take a look at how to build a shopping cart collection.

Building an SPL Shopping Cart

All shopping carts are not created equal. Some just handle lists of items; others handle all kinds of advanced logic. By using an SPL class, you can include this logic, without needing to give up the ease of iteration and counting that you would have with a plain array.

In this example, you will create two classes: a generic Product class to encapsulate a single product and its attributes, and a shopping Cart class.

First, you need to define the properties of a product, as shown in Listing 12-3. For this example, you will have a part number, a price, and a description. The number of properties that you use is entirely up to you, so keep in mind that this example is extensible.

Listing 12-3. *A Product Class (Product.php)*

```php
class Product {

  protected $_partNumber, $_description, $_price;

  public function __construct($partNumber, $description, $price) {
    $this->_partNumber = $partNumber;
    $this->_description = $description;
    $this->_price = $price;
  }

  public function getPartNumber() {
    return $this->_partNumber;
  }

  public function getDescription() {
    return $this->_description;
  }

  public function getPrice() {
    return $this->_price;
  }

}
```

Next, extend ArrayObject to create a Cart class, as shown in Listing 12-4.

Listing 12-4. *Cart Object*

```php
require_once('Product.php');

class Cart extends ArrayObject {

  protected $_products;

  public function __construct() {
      $this->_products = array();

      /*
        Construct the underlying ArrayObject using
        $this->_products as the foundation array. This
        is important to ensure that the features
        of ArrayObject are available to your object.
      */
      parent::__construct($this->_products);
  }

}

$cart = new Cart();
$product = new Product('00231-A', 'Description', 1.99);

$cart[] = $product;

print_r($cart);
```

```
Cart Object
(
    [0] => Product Object
        (
            [_partNumber:protected] => 00231-A
            [_description:protected] => Description
            [_price:protected] => 1.99
        )

)
```

You now have a Cart object that behaves as an array. But you could have simply used an array for this. So what does this technique add? It lets you encapsulate other methods within this class. For example, you could add the ability to get a price total of all items that are currently in the cart. Listing 12-5 shows a method for this functionality that you can add to your Cart class.

Listing 12-5. *Adding a getCartTotal Method*

```
public function getCartTotal() {
  for(
    $i=$sum=0, $cnt = count($this);
    $i<$cnt;
    $sum += $this[$i++]->getPrice()
  );
  return $sum;
}
```

This method uses a single for loop to iterate over all the products in the cart by using $this as an array and calling getPrice() on each element. When this method is included in the Cart class, you can easily get the cart total, as shown in Listing 12-6.

Listing 12-6. *Summing the Cart*

```
$cart = new Cart();
$cart[] = new Product('00231-A', 'A', 1.99);
$cart[] = new Product('00231-B', 'B', 1.99);

echo $cart->getCartTotal();
```

```
3.98
```

For operation within a session environment, this $cart object can be added to the $_SESSION array, and it will be properly serialized/deserialized for you automatically.

Using this approach allows you to create an easily managed cart that encapsulates all cart functionality into a single class.

Using Objects As Keys

Normally, it is difficult to use an object as the key of an array in PHP. For example, suppose you try to run the following code:

```
class MyObject {}

$a = new MyObject();
$b = array($a=>'Test');
```

You will get the following warning, and the entry will be ignored.

```
Warning: Illegal offset type in yourfile.php on line .
```

The SPL has a solution to this problem. In Chapter 9, you were introduced to the spl_object_ hash() function. This function creates a unique identifier for any object instance and can allow you to store an object hash as a key in an array. Listing 12-7 shows an example of using spl_object_hash().

Listing 12-7. *Using spl_object_hash to Store Objects As Array Keys*

```
class MyObject {}

$a = new MyObject();
$b = array(spl_object_hash($a)=>'Test');

echo $b[spl_object_hash($a)];
```

```
Test
```

So that works, but it's not very convenient. You can do better with the ArrayAccess interface by making it do the object hashing for you. You will need to create two classes: a KeyObject class, which will serve as the object that will be stored in the key, and a CollectionObject class, which has custom ArrayAccess interface methods and will serve as your array. The customized ArrayAccess methods shown in Listing 12-8 will handle the hashing of the key and storing the objects within it.

Listing 12-8. *An Object-Keyed Collection*

```
class KeyObject {}

class CollectionObject implements ArrayAccess {

  protected $_keys, $_values;

  public function __construct() {
    $this->_keys = array();
    $this->_values = array();
  }

  public function offsetSet($key, $value) {
    $this->_keys[spl_object_hash($key)] = $key;
    $this->_values[spl_object_hash($key)] = $value;
  }

  public function offsetGet($key) {
    return $this->_values[spl_object_hash($key)];
  }
```

```php
  public function offsetExists($key) {
    return array_key_exists(spl_object_hash($key), $this->_values);
  }

  public function offsetUnset($key) {
    unset($this->_values[spl_object_hash($key)]);
    unset($this->_keys[spl_object_hash($key)]);
  }

}

$key = new KeyObject();
$collection = new CollectionObject();
$collection[$key] = 'test';

echo $collection[$key];
```

---

test

This collection works by storing the object's hash code as the index. When you provide an object to retrieve the value, it is hashed and used to look up the correct value.

To provide iteration support, you need to extend this class from ArrayIterator or implement the IteratorAggregate interface.

Note At the time of writing, it is currently illegal in PHP to return an object from key() in the Iterator interface. Because of this limitation, it is impossible to iterate this object returning object keys.

In addition to deriving your class from ArrayIterator, you will want to provide a method to return an object key given an object hash. Listing 12-9 shows this collection in completed form.

Listing 12-9. *Storing Complex Objects As Array Keys*

```php
class KeyObject {}

class CollectionObject extends ArrayIterator implements ArrayAccess {

  protected $_keys, $_values;

  public function __construct() {
    $this->_keys = array();
    $this->_values = array();
```

```php
    parent::__construct(&$this->_values);
  }

  public function offsetSet($key, $value) {
    $this->_keys[spl_object_hash($key)] = $key;
    $this->_values[spl_object_hash($key)] = $value;
  }

  public function offsetGet($key) {
    return $this->_values[spl_object_hash($key)];
  }

  public function offsetExists($key) {
    return array_key_exists(spl_object_hash($key), $this->_values);
  }

  public function offsetUnset($key) {
    unset($this->_values[spl_object_hash($key)]);
  }

  public function getKey($hash) {
    return $this->_keys[$hash];
  }

}

$key = new KeyObject();
$collection = new CollectionObject();
$collection[$key] = 'test';

foreach($collection as $k => $v) {
  print_r($collection->getKey($k));
  print_r($v);
}
```

```
KeyObject Object
(
)
test
```

■Note When calling the parent `ArrayIterator` constructor, be sure to pass the `$_values` array as a reference. This will ensure that future updates to the collection are reflected in the iterator.

Just the Facts

This chapter explained how to use objects as arrays. This is accomplished with the ArrayAccess interface and the four defined methods: offsetSet(), offsetGet(), offsetExists(), and offsetUnset(). The count() function can be interfaced through the Countable interface. This interface defines a single method, count(), which must return an integer representing the number of elements in a collection. Using the versatile ArrayObject class, you can create extensible collections.

As an example, these concepts were combined to create an elegant shopping cart solution using these SPL interfaces. This solution allowed you to add elements to the collection and also create methods on the collection, such as the ability to get a subtotal of all the items in the shopping cart.

As an advanced use of the ArrayAccess interface, you can create an Object class that will let you store complex objects as array keys.

CHAPTER 13

SPL Exceptions

The SPL provides a number of built-in exception base classes that are designed to handle everyday scenarios. In this chapter, you will learn about the base exception classes, when to apply them, and how to extend them for your own requirements.

Logic Exceptions

The SPL has two central classes of exceptions: LogicException and RuntimeException (discussed in the next section). The LogicException class descends from Exception directly, and does not add any additional methods.

```
class LogicException extends Exception
```

The purpose of this classification is to allow you to differentiate between compile-time logical exceptions and exceptions caused by bad data being passed to the application.

Invoking a logic exception is just like invoking a standard exception, except that it should be thrown only on the condition that the application is programmed incorrectly. This type of exception can be used to create a system for logging programming exceptions separately from those caused by runtime data.

To get started, Listing 13-1 shows how to invoke a logic exception and a typical scenario where you might correctly use a LogicException directly.

Listing 13-1. *Throwing LogicException*

```
class Lazy {
  protected $_loaded = false;
  protected $_name;

  public function materialize() {
    $this->_loaded = true;
    $this->_name = 'Kevin';
  }
```

```
  public function getName() {
    if(!$this->_loaded) {
      throw new LogicException('Call materialize() before accessing');
    }
    return $this->_name;
  }
}

$lazy = new Lazy();
echo $lazy->getName();
```

```
Fatal error: Uncaught exception 'LogicException' with message
'Call materialize() before accessing' in listing1.php:14
Stack trace:
#0 listing1.php(21): Lazy->getName()
#1 {main}
  thrown in listing1.php on line 14
```

Listing 13-1 is an example of a logical exception because it is caused entirely by bad programming (calling getName() before materialize()), rather than the result of runtime data.

Catching logic exceptions is very easy and also very useful. If your application has a central dispatch point—and I generally recommend this design pattern—then this can be implemented application-wide. You could also use the set_exception_handler() function from within each script if you do not use a central dispatch architecture.

■**Note** Central dispatch architecture is utilized by the Zend Framework, which is covered in Part 4 of this book.

Listing 13-2 shows a convenient method of catching LogicException exceptions and recording their details to a log file using the SplFileObject class (introduced in Chapter 11).

Listing 13-2. *Logging Logic Exceptions (Central Dispatch Architecture)*

```
$logfile = 'log.txt';

try {
  throw new LogicException("Demo");
} catch (LogicException $le) {
  $file = new SplFileObject($logfile,'a+');
  $file->fwrite($le->__toString());
}
```

The SplFileObject instance is created, and the open mode is a+ (append mode), creating the file if necessary and placing the file pointer at the end of the file. You can then fwrite() to the log. There is no need to close the file handle, as this will be done for you when the class is torn down.

The data that is written is the __toString() method of the exception, which returns some basic data, including the error message and call stack. For more complete data, use the var_export() function and set its second parameter, $return, to true.

```
exception 'LogicException' with message 'Demo' in
 listing2.php:7
Stack trace:
#0 {main}

-- var_export format -

LogicException::__set_state(array(
   'message' => 'Demo',
   'string' => '',
   'code' => 0,
   'file' => 'listing2.php',
   'line' => 7,
   'trace' =>
  array (
  ),
))
```

So now that you know what to do with unspecific logic errors, what do you do when something goes wrong at runtime? The answer is RuntimeException.

Runtime Exceptions

RuntimeException is LogicException's alter ego. It is designed to handle all things runtime.

```
class RuntimeException extends Exception
```

Like LogicException, RuntimeException is built upon by several specialization classes defined by the SPL, as explained in the following sections. What's left over becomes a standard RuntimeException. A good example of this is a banking scenario, wherein two concurrent actions cannot result in a negative account balance. Listing 13-3 shows this scenario.

Listing 13-3. *Throwing RuntimeException*

```
function purchase() {
  //Begin transaction and acquire lock

  //Check funds again to prevent race condition
  if(checkSufficientFunds()) {
    //Insert and commit transaction
```

```
  } else {
    //Abort transaction
    throw new RuntimeException("The account has insufficient funds.");
  }
}
```

Bad Function and Method Call Exceptions

BadFunctionCallException is designed to be thrown when a function call was illegal.

```
class BadFunctionCallException extends LogicException
```

This can occur in several scenarios. One of the more common is where too many parameters are passed to a function that accepts a variable number of arguments.

BadMethodCallException is the same as BadFunctionCallException, but is designed for use from a method context.

```
class BadMethodCallException extends BadFunctionCallException
```

Domain Exceptions

The DomainException class is designed to handle domain exceptions.

```
class DomainException extends LogicException
```

This calls for a bit of a math lesson. In researching this chapter, I found that many PHP programmers do not know what a domain is in a mathematical sense; in fact, I was one of them.

There are a lot of really complicated math-lingo explanations for what a domain is, but they involve a bunch of characters I can't find on my keyboard. The simple explanation is this: a domain is all the possible values for a function that will result in valid output from the function. Listing 13-4 shows an example.

Listing 13-4. *A Domain Function*

```
function mathy($x) {
  if($x==2) {
    throw new DomainException("X cannot be 2");
  }
  return (1 / ($x - 2));
}
```

In this case, the domain is any number that is not 2, because an input of 2 would result in a division-by-zero error. Thus, 2 is not in the domain of this function because it would result in an error.

What this means for you, as a programmer, is that any time you have a function that takes a certain valid set of values and you are provided with something invalid, you are supposed to throw a DomainException exception.

In my research, I found that this is commonly confused with the RangeException exception.

Range Exceptions

The RangeException class is designed to handle range exceptions.

```
class RangeException extends RuntimeException
```

Like the domain, the range of a function is a math term. Contrary to popular belief, it doesn't mean the valid range of any input for a function. For example, the code in Listing 13-5 is *semantically incorrect.*

Listing 13-5. *Improper Use of RangeException*

```
function mathy($x) {
  if ($x < 0) {
    throw new RangeException('$x must be 0 or greater');
  }
}
```

The range of a function has nothing to do with the inputs. Instead, that is the *domain* of the function and should be handled with DomainException.

The range of a function is the set of all possible values for its *result*—its output. So, RangeException is for throwing exceptions regarding the result of a function.

To understand where you might use RangeException, think of a temperature sensor. Its valid range when interfaced will be to return a value between –50 and +50 Celsius. If it starts returning a value outside this range, you know your sensor broke.

RangeException is a runtime exception, rather than a logical exception like DomainException, because it refers to result data. Listing 13-6 shows the proper use of RangeException.

Listing 13-6. *Proper Use of RangeException*

```
class Sensor {
  public static function getTemperature() {
    return 51;
  }
}

class Monitor {
  public static function watch() {
    $temp = Sensor::getTemperature();
    if(($temp < -50) || ($temp > 50)) {
      throw new RangeException('The sensor broke down.');
    }
  }
}

Monitor::watch();
```

```
Fatal error: Uncaught exception 'RangeException' with message
'The sensor broke down.' in listing6.php:14
Stack trace:
#0 listing6.php(19): Monitor::watch()
#1 {main}
  thrown in listing6.php on line 14
```

Invalid Argument Exceptions

The InvalidArgumentException exception is designed to be thrown when a function or method receives an argument that is invalid.

```
class InvalidArgumentException extends LogicException
```

This is distinct from a DomainException in that it does not deal with a set of values, but instead involves the mixing of incompatible types. For example, when calling a function that expects an integer, passing a string might be considered an invalid argument. Listing 13-7 demonstrates using InvalidArgumentException.

Listing 13-7. *Using InvalidArgumentException*

```
function sum($a, $b) {
  if(!is_numeric($a) || !is_numeric($b)) {
    throw new InvalidArgumentException("Invalid Argument");
  }
  return ($a+$b);
}

echo sum(1,2);
echo sum('a','b');
```

```
3
Fatal error: Uncaught exception 'InvalidArgumentException'
with message 'Invalid Argument' in listing7.php:6
Stack trace:
#0 listing7.php(12): sum('a', 'b')
#1 {main}
  thrown in listing7.php on line 6
```

Length Exceptions

LengthException should be thrown whenever a problem with length occurs.

```
class LengthException extends LogicException
```

This length may be the length of a string, too many or too few elements in an array, execution time limit, or even file size. Listing 13-8 shows an example of using LengthException.

Listing 13-8. *Using LengthException*

```
function printmax10($str) {
  if(strlen($str) > 10) {
    throw new LengthException("Input was too long");
  }
  echo $str;
}

printmax10('asdf');
printmax10('abcdefghijk');
```

```
asdf
Fatal error: Uncaught exception 'LengthException' with
message 'Input was too long' in listing8.php:6
Stack trace:
#0 listing8.php(12): printmax10('abcdefghijk')
#1 {main}
  thrown in listing8.php on line 6
```

Overflow Exceptions

The PHP language will automatically handle most overflow scenarios where an integer or buffer overflows. OverflowException is designed for arithmetical overflow scenarios or scenarios where a value is to be stored and the result would overflow the storage location.

```
class OverflowException extends RuntimeException
```

Listing 13-9 demonstrates a common SQL scenario.

Listing 13-9. *PostgreSQL Numeric Scale Overflow*

```
postgres=# create temporary table test (demo numeric(3,2));
CREATE TABLE
postgres=# insert into test values (333.99);
postgres-# ERROR:  numeric field overflow
DETAIL:  The absolute value is greater than or equal to
 10^2 for field with precision 3, scale 2.
postgres=# insert into test values (1.99);
postgres-# INSERT 0 1
```

In this example, any value over 9.99 will result in an overflow and produce an error. Thus, any function that inserts into this table must constrain its calculations to stay within this storage ability. If a function were to meet or exceed 10, the correct exception would be OverflowException, to prevent a SQL error from occurring downstream, as shown in Listing 13-10.

Listing 13-10. *Using OverflowException*

```
function sumThenInsertDemo($a, $b) {

  $sum = $a + $b;

  if ($sum >= 10) {
    throw new OverflowException("$a + $b will overflow storage");
  }

  $link = pg_connect(…);
  pg_query($link, 'insert into test values ('. $sum .')');

}
```

Underflow Exceptions

An arithmetical underflow occurs when any value is too small to maintain precision and the result of the function would result in a loss of accuracy. Underflows are handled with UnderflowException.

```
class UnderflowException extends RuntimeException
```

You may encounter an underflow when adding floats in PHP. PHP floating-point precision is highly dependent on the operating system, compilation settings, and processor on which the code is running. PHP floats will not give consistent operation. However, on many systems, it is possible to detect this underflow and write functions that are smart enough to detect it. Listing 13-11 shows an example of arithmetic underflow in PHP floating-point operations.

Listing 13-11. *Arithmetical Underflow in PHP*

```
echo (1-0.9) . "\n";
echo (1-0.99) . "\n";
echo (1-0.999) . "\n";
echo (1-0.9999) . "\n";
echo (1-0.99999) . "\n";
echo (1-0.999999) . "\n";
```

```
0.1
0.01
0.001
9.9999999999989E-05
9.9999999999545E-06
1.0000000000288E-06
```

As you can see, on my system, PHP can handle arithmetic up to three decimal points, after which, it goes into floating-point inebriation.

If you were writing a telephone billing system that deals in fractions of a cent, you would need to be wary of this effect. Otherwise, the results wouldn't be consistent, and the world would come to an end (OK, maybe not that extreme, but it would be bad).

Any function that will result in operations on high-precision floating points should throw an UnderflowException exception if it cannot reasonably complete the operation without a loss of precision. Listing 13-12 demonstrates using UnderflowException.

Listing 13-12. *Using UnderflowException*

```
function scale($a) {
  return strlen(strstr($a, '.'))-1;
}

function sum($a, $b) {
  if((scale($a) > 3) || (scale($b) > 3)) {
    throw new UnderflowException("Input scale exceeded");
  }
  return $a + $b;
}


echo sum(1,-0.9) . "\n";
echo sum(1,-0.99) . "\n";
echo sum(1,-0.999) . "\n";
echo sum(1,-0.9999) . "\n";
```

```
0.1
0.01
0.001

Fatal error: Uncaught exception 'UnderflowException'
 with message 'Input scale exceeded' in listing12.php:10
Stack trace:
#0 listing12.php(19): sum(1, -0.9999)
#1 {main}
  thrown in listing12.php on line 10
```

It is important that programmers understand the precision limits of the code they write and that they throw the proper underflow exceptions when the limits are reached. If you do not watch out for these effects, downstream damage can occur. Additionally, these types of errors can be exceedingly difficult to trace back to the offending routine.

Just the Facts

This chapter covered the following SPL exceptions:

- `LogicException` handles exceptions that are detectable at compile time—when the application is programmed incorrectly.

- `RuntimeException` handles exceptions that can be detected only at runtime.

- `BadFunctionCallException` handles exceptions due to illegal function calls.

- `BadMethodCallException` handles exceptions due to illegal method calls.

- `DomainException` handles domain exceptions. A *domain* is the set of all input values that are valid for a function.

- `RangeException` handles range exceptions. A *range* is the set of all output values that are valid for a function.

- `InvalidArgumentException` handles cases where a function or method receives an invalid argument.

- `LengthException` handles exceptions due to length, such as too many elements in an array.

- `OverflowException` handles exceptions due to overflow conditions—arithmetical overflow or overflow in the storage location.

- `UnderflowException` handles exceptions due to a value being too small to maintain precision, resulting in loss of accuracy. In PHP, this can occur when using floats.

PART 4

The Model-View-Controller (MVC) Pattern

CHAPTER 14

■ ■ ■

MVC Architecture

Model-View-Controller (MVC) is a design pattern that simplifies application development and maintenance. It achieves this by separating the application into three logical components:

Model: The model layer is responsible for the business logic of an application. It will encapsulate access to data stores and will provide a reusable class library. Typically, within the model, you will find facilities for database abstraction, e-mail delivery, validation, and authentication.

View: The view layer is typically what would be considered web design, or templating. It controls the look and feel of data and provides facilities to collect data from the user. Technologies exclusively found in the view are HTML, CSS, and JavaScript.

Controller: The controller layer glues everything together and merges the styling of the view with the functionality of the model. It is responsible for collecting input data from the view and deciding program execution. The controller will call model facilities and interpret the returning data so that it can be rendered by the view. It is also responsible for all application exception and flow control.

This chapter introduces the MVC pattern and its advantages. In the final section, you will create a minimal MVC framework to see how such a framework actually works.

Why Use MVC?

You might be wondering why MVC is so popular within web application development. While there are many compelling reasons to use an MVC framework—from cleanliness of code to ease of upgrading—the number one reason companies choose MVC development is the development workflow that it encourages.

In teams, MVC allows for efficient collaboration by splitting up responsibilities into three main roles:

Development: The developers are programmers working on the model. They will typically have skills related to PHP, database administration, algorithms, architecture, and data validation. This role will typically be responsible for the programming details (the "how") of an application, and will provide APIs and enforce policy for interacting with data.

Design: The designers handle the view and are responsible for how an application looks and feels. They will be highly skilled in technologies like HTML, CSS, JavaScript, and graphic design. Typically, this role will be responsible for interacting with both internal and external communication sources to determine realistic business rules for which an application will be developed or improved. Design usually leads to prototype development, creating mock-up designs showing ideal functionality.

Integration: The integration exists in the controller layer, which glues the work of designers and developers together. Integrators will typically have less experience than developers, and will be responsible for cutting up static templates and making the required regions dynamic. They are also responsible for brokering data from request sources. They will take request information from forms, pass the information to the model, interpret the results, and pass the information along to the view.

By providing division of responsibilities, the details of *how* are separated from the details of *why*, which allows the creative and technical disciplines to interact more easily.

In a typical workflow, first a designer will put together a static, stand-alone, prototype design based on the existing business requirements and how the application should behave. The designers will then pass the design to the developers for review.

Developers are responsible for ensuring that all of the requested functionality is feasible and fits with the company's security and privacy policies. If everything checks out, a development plan, including a mock-up API, will be created and passed to the integration role. If there are any issues with the prototype, the project will go back to the designer, and the process will continue again from the start.

Once the design prototype and the mock-up API are in place, the integration work begins. The integrators will dissect the prototype design and convert it into a template language like plain PHP, Smarty, and so on. This will enable the design to handle dynamic data, and will integrate the site URL structures for which the integrator role is solely responsible. Then a controller component is written to broker requests (forms, URL parameters, cookies, and so on) between the web server and the model information they are meant to manipulate. When a result is produced, the view will be retrieved and rendered, with the controller providing the values for any dynamic content.

Finally, when the mock-up API is fully implemented, the application can be handed off for testing. If the integrator wrote the controller to spec, and the model developers conformed to their API, then everything should work as expected.

As well as distributing responsibility between team members, the MVC architecture also offers several other key benefits. One is that it allows the presentation layer to be modified and updated at any time, as long as it does not break the contract with the controller. This means that copy editing or theme changes can be readily accomplished without changing the way the application works or sorting through a lot of PHP code.

The MVC architecture also provides a useful subdivision of the file structure. Each MVC framework has a different structure and layout, but with few exceptions, they all provide separate files for models, views, and controllers. This feature will reduce code conflicts and will save time that would otherwise be spent merging changes in your revision control system.

MVC Application Layout

The layout for MVC applications differs by framework; however, some concepts are common to all MVC frameworks. In the next chapter, you will learn about the specifics of the Zend Framework layout. The explanations in this section refer to the typical implementation of the MVC pattern in PHP.

From the Web Server

Unlike other PHP applications, MVC sites typically implement a centralized PHP script that handles all requests on a web site. So, instead of the browser going to */path/to/somefile*.php, the browser goes to */controller/action*. However, you won't find a folder named controller or a file named action. Instead, a URL rewriter like mod_rewrite is used to redirect *all* HTTP requests to a centralized script that is called the *bootstrap file*.

The bootstrap file is responsible for initializing the framework: loading files, reading configuration data, parsing the URL into actionable information, and populating the objects that encapsulate the request. Finally, it is responsible for initializing the controllers.

Actions and Controllers

After bootstrapping, a class called the front controller (FC) is instantiated and takes over. The front controller is typically a built-in class that is responsible for interpreting request variables and routing code execution to a user-defined class, which is called an action controller (AC). Usually, an action controller will implement a standard interface or descend from an abstract class, so that the front controller and action controller may interact using a common API.

The front controller will then invoke a method on the action controller specified by the URL. This method is called an *action*, and its name, like the action controller's name, is determined from the URL. The action is responsible for all the dirty work. In this method, you will instantiate model classes, parse view templates, and output the results.

Models

The models are typically the easy part. They usually don't follow any particular structure other than to exist in a common location, so that they may be automatically loaded by the framework. Models are simply utility classes that provide the required data manipulation and parsing functionality.

Views

The views are templates and can be written in any template language. The primary goal here is to not include any sort of processing logic or data manipulation in the view, and output only data that has been provided specifically by the controller. Typically, this means limiting yourself to displaying arrays, not data objects, when operating in the view.

The choice of templating language is your own, depending on whether it can be integrated with your framework. Personally, I find that plain PHP makes for the best templating language when working in MVC environments. FastTemplate and Smarty are viable second choices.

Criteria for Choosing an MVC Framework

Every MVC framework has certain advantages and certain downsides. You should consider five key factors when choosing a framework to use: architecture, documentation, community, support, and flexibility. I suggest that you sit down and score all the frameworks you are considering using these criteria, and then pick the most appropriate one for you.

Architecture of the MVC Framework

Every developer is different. What makes sense to one developer might be totally illogical to another. You should choose a framework that you understand. I have met far too many distressed developers using a complicated MVC framework because they have heard about all the benefits it may provide. I assure you that without an architectural understanding of your framework, it will hinder, not help, your development. Choose one that you are comfortable using.

You should also consider whether you want a framework that follows a linear function and callback style or an object-oriented approach. Personally, I prefer the latter because the concept of encapsulation really works wonders with model classes.

You will need to understand the framework's technical requirements and file structure, so that you can be sure it will work effectively with your deployment procedures. For example, some frameworks have very backward-compatible APIs, whereas others do not even attempt to maintain backward compatibility. There are valid arguments for both approaches. Choose the one that works for your organization.

MVC Framework Documentation

All frameworks come with documentation, and that's where the similarities end. Documentation can be as simple as an install file, or as complex as formal training courses.

When I look at a framework's documentation, I ask three key questions:

- Is it current? Documentation is useless if it's talking about a version that you are not using. Ensure that the version you download is the version that is documented.

- Is it clear? Is the documentation well written and easy to understand? If you can't understand what it is trying to say, move on.

- Is it complete? Is the documentation comprehensive? Does it cover everything in the framework or just the basics? All too often, you will get a combination of great introductory documentation and machine-generated advanced docs.

Good docs are essential to meeting deadlines and keeping costs down.

MVC Framework Community

The existence of community around an MVC framework is critical. You should look at what amount of participation is welcomed, and how long it takes members of the community to respond to a bug and produce a patch.

Community is also the number one factor managers will need to be concerned with, as it will heavily affect their ability to hire new staff members that are knowledgeable with the framework.

You should be able to communicate directly with the developers of your framework to report bugs, suggest features, and obtain fixes. However, the framework developers should *not* be considered technical support, which is an entirely separate, though related, topic.

The time between releases will give you an idea of how active the project is. This usually gives a good indication of the frequency of future updates. You will need to evaluate how fast your business can reasonably adapt to a changing framework. There are definite trade-offs between API stability and the introduction of new features, so your mileage may vary.

MVC Framework Support

As I noted in the previous section, the developers of your framework are not support. If you send them so much as a single e-mail with an "ignorance" question, you will be highly unlikely to receive future assistance that only they can provide. Consider this "crying wolf" to the development team.

So with that in mind, who can you ask when you have a support question? Some MVC frameworks are supported through a support-revenue model, where the framework is free, but support will cost you. Others offer no support at all; in those cases, you will need to find a knowledgeable third party.

Mailing lists and support chat channels will provide free support for a given framework. These sources can be highly useful, but may also prove highly unreliable compared with paid support. To get the best results from these sources, a share-and-share-alike attitude must be adopted—those with the most to offer should also get the most help.

Before beginning development with any particular framework, be sure you fully understand your support position. Getting stuck on problems for which you cannot quickly find the answer can be very costly.

MVC Framework Flexibility

How flexible is the MVC framework's implementation? Can you integrate your existing applications within the framework, and make sure it supports your databases?

Some frameworks are incredibly rigid and will place many restrictions on how you write and organize your code. They may dictate templating languages, and they may have very specific syntax that will incur a significant training cost.

Look for a flexible framework that imposes as few hard limits as possible.

Roll Your Own MVC Framework

It is generally recommended to choose from one of the publicly available frameworks, rather than creating your own. No matter how good a programmer you are, you will always flunk in the community department. However, to truly understand MVC, it helps to know how to write your own basic framework, so that's what you'll do now.

In this example, you will follow a layout similar to the Zend Framework, utilizing techniques you have learned in prior chapters and implementing a typical front controller/action routing system.

For this example, you will need a web server running Apache 2, PHP 5, mod_rewrite, and a database like PostgreSQL. The instructions in this chapter are for a Debian Linux installation, but they will work on all PHP-supported platforms.

■Note If you don't have a server with the required configuration, all the necessary applications can be downloaded to your desktop. Their installation is not complicated. Dive right in, and you'll more than likely be able to figure it out.

Setting Up a Virtual Host

First, you need to create a virtual host and a new site. Follow these steps:

1. Execute the following commands to create a virtual host:

   ```
   > mkdir -p /usr/local/www/yourdomain.com/document_root
   > cd /etc/apache2/sites-available
   ```

2. Edit a file called *yourdomain*.com.

   ```
   > pico -w yourdomain.com
   ```

3. Place the virtual host definition in the *yourdomain*.com file.

   ```
   <VirtualHost *>
           DocumentRoot /usr/local/www/yourdomain.com/document_root
           ServerName yourdomain.com
   </VirtualHost>
   ```

4. Execute the following commands to activate your site:

   ```
   > a2ensite yourdomain.com
   > /etc/init.d/apache2 reload
   ```

5. Make your browser access your site. You can do this by pointing the Domain Name System (DNS) for the domain at the server or by editing your hosts file. To edit your hosts file on Windows, locate the file at C:\WINDOWS\system32\drivers\etc\hosts. Open it in a text editor and add a new line. Type the IP address of your server, press Tab, and then type the name of the file (*yourdomain*.com) you just created. Save the file.

6. Open a new browser instance (if you have a browser open, it may need to be closed first to pick up the hosts file change) and browse to your new site. You should see an empty directory index.

You're now ready to start developing your very own MVC framework.

Creating an MVC Framework

At this point, you will need to start creating directories. I recommend the following layout:

```
> cd /usr/local/www/yourdomain.com
> mkdir document_root/images document_root/styles
> mkdir -p application/models application/views \
> application/controllers
> find
```

```
.
./document_root
./document_root/images
./document_root/styles
./application
./application/models
./application/views
./application/controllers
```

Next, create a placeholder for your bootstrap file, as shown in Listing 14-1.

Listing 14-1. *Creating the Bootstrap index.php*

```
> pico document_root/index.php
```

```
Hello, World!
```

At this point, reloading your browser should result in "Hello, World!" being shown. Navigate to http://*yourdomain*.com/nonexistent. You should get a 404 File Not Found error.

For this MVC framework to work, you need every single request to hit this index.php. To do this, you enlist mod_rewrite through an .htaccess file, as shown in Listing 14-2.

Listing 14-2. *Using mod_rewrite in an .htaccess File*

```
> pico document_root/.htaccess
```

```
RewriteEngine on
RewriteRule !\.(js|gif|jpg|png|css)$ index.php
```

Reload your browser, and you should see "Hello, World!" If you don't, you will need to ensure that your server has mod_rewrite available and does not restrict .htaccess overrides with a nonstandard allowOverrides directive.

Bootstrapping

The next stage in this process is to create a bootstrapping script in your index.php file. This file will be responsible for including files and initializing the front controller. Most MVC frameworks will use SPL autoloading mechanisms to load files, but for simplicity, you will just require_once for now. Create the file as shown in Listing 14-3.

Listing 14-3. *The Bootstrap Loader*

```
> pico -w document_root/index.php

<?php

//Require Components
require_once('../application/models/front.php');
require_once('../application/models/icontroller.php');
require_once('../application/models/view.php');


//Require Controllers
require_once('../application/controllers/index.php');

//Initialize the FrontController
$front = FrontController::getInstance();
$front->route();

echo $front->getBody();
```

■**Note** You do not need a closing ?> in Listing 14-3, as the end of file will close the tag automatically. It is not recommended to include closing tags, as newlines at the end of the file can result in premature output and may cause issues sending HTTP headers.

The Front Controller

The front controller's job is to parse the URL and to instantiate the controller and invoke the action method. This is a singleton class (see Listing 3-1 in Chapter 3), which is responsible for the application's program flow.

The theory of operation is that URLs follow the format /controller/action/key1/value1/ . . . . Once the URL has been parsed, you will use the reflection API (covered in Chapter 7) to invoke the action method on the IController implementing class.

To get started, first create the FrontController class, as shown in Listing 14-4.

Listing 14-4. *The FrontController Class*

```
> pico -w application/models/front.php

<?php

class FrontController {

  protected $_controller, $_action, $_params, $_body;
```

```php
  static $_instance;

  public static function getInstance() {
    if( ! (self::$_instance instanceof self) ) {
      self::$_instance = new self();
    }
    return self::$_instance;
  }

  private function __construct() {
    $request = $_SERVER['REQUEST_URI'];

    $splits = explode('/', trim($request,'/'));
    $this->_controller = !empty($splits[0])?$splits[0]:'index';
    $this->_action = !empty($splits[1])?$splits[1]:'index';
    if(!empty($splits[2])) {
      $keys = $values = array();
      for($idx=2, $cnt = count($splits); $idx<$cnt; $idx++) {
        if($idx % 2 == 0) {
          //Is even, is key
          $keys[] = $splits[$idx];
        } else {
          //Is odd, is value;
          $values[] = $splits[$idx];
        }
      }
      $this->_params = array_combine($keys, $values);
    }
  }

  public function route() {
    if(class_exists($this->getController())) {
      $rc = new ReflectionClass($this->getController());
      if($rc->implementsInterface('IController')) {
        if($rc->hasMethod($this->getAction())) {
          $controller = $rc->newInstance();
          $method = $rc->getMethod($this->getAction());
          $method->invoke($controller);
        } else {
          throw new Exception("Action");
        }
      } else {
        throw new Exception("Interface");
      }
    } else {
      throw new Exception("Controller");
    }
  }
```

```php
  public function getParams() {
    return $this->_params;
  }

  public function getController() {
    return $this->_controller;
  }

  public function getAction() {
    return $this->_action;
  }

  public function getBody() {
    return $this->_body;
  }

  public function setBody($body) {
    $this->_body = $body;
  }

}
```

The Controller

The controller is where you create your application code. It is just a normal class, except that it implements the IController "marker" interface that does not contain any methods. Create the IController interface as shown in Listing 14-5.

Listing 14-5. *The IController Interface*

```
> pico -w application/models/icontroller.php
```

```php
<?php

interface IController {}
```

Next, you will create a class to encapsulate your program logic. This class will be responsible for creating an instance of the view (which you'll define shortly), binding a variable to it, and calling the render method, which will return the parsed result.

Once the view is rendered, the controller sets the body of the FrontController and returns. Create this class as shown in Listing 14-6.

Listing 14-6. *A Default Controller*

```
> pico -w application/controllers/index.php
```

```php
<?php
```

```
class index implements IController {

  public function index() {
    $view = new View();
    $view->name = "Kevin";
    $result = $view->render('../views/index.php');

    $fc = FrontController::getInstance();
    $fc->setBody($result);
  }

}
```

The View

The view model is one of the more complex classes in an MVC framework. It is designed to create a scope for variables (such as $view->name in Listing 14-6) and include the file returning the parsed output.

This is achieved by including from within a method, and thus limiting the scope to that method, and by using the output buffering feature of PHP. The actual properties support is provided by the ArrayObject SPL class, using a blank starting array and the special flag ARRAY_AS_PROPS, which allows for easy creation of a property overloaded object.

Create the view model as shown in Listing 14-7.

■**Note** This class is called View and is a model. It provides view rendering functionality. The "view" is actually the template defined later on, and will be found in the views folder.

Listing 14-7. *The View Model Class*

```
> pico -w application/models/view.php

<?php
class View extends ArrayObject {
  public function __construct() {
    parent::__construct(array(), ArrayObject::ARRAY_AS_PROPS);
  }

  public function render($file) {
    ob_start();
    include(dirname(__FILE__) . '/' . $file);
    return ob_get_clean();
  }
}
```

Next, make a default view template, as shown in Listing 14-8.

Listing 14-8. *The Default View*

```
> pico application/views/index.php
```

```
Hello, <?php echo $this->name; ?>!
```

That's it. Reload your browser, and you should see "Hello, Kevin!"

URL Parameters

You're probably not named Kevin though, so let's integrate your name with this script. Because of encapsulation, to do this, you need to modify only the controller.

Replace your application/controllers/index.php file with the file shown in Listing 14-9.

Listing 14-9. *Using URL Parameters*

```
> pico -w application/controllers/index.php
```

```php
<?php

class index implements IController {
  public function index() {
    $fc = FrontController::getInstance();

    $params = $fc->getParams();

    $view = new View();
    $view->name = $params['name'];
    $result = $view->render('../views/index.php');

    $fc->setBody($result);
  }
}
```

Now change the URL to http://yourdomain.com/index/index/name/yourname =, and you should see "Hello, *yourname*!"

As you can see, creating an MVC framework is actually pretty basic. Well, this sample framework is so basic that it provides almost no functionality.

The frameworks you will find on the market have significant built-in features, such as database abstraction, data filtering and validation, and so on. In the next two chapters, you will learn about the built-in facilities a typical MVC framework provides.

Just the Facts

The MVC pattern is a design pattern that separates an application into three parts: the model, the view, and the controller. MVC is primarily designed to help with web application development workflow and allow teams to work together more efficiently by defining specific roles. These roles are developer, designer, and integrator. Developers are responsible for the model. Designers are responsible for the look and feel of the site. Integrators are in charge of putting it all together.

Most MVC frameworks follow similar concepts, providing classes for controllers and methods for actions. Views are templates, and can be created in plain PHP or a template language like Smarty.

There are a lot of considerations to bear in mind when choosing which framework is right for your project. The five key points are architecture, documentation, community, support, and flexibility.

The introduction to MVC in this chapter provides a basis for the next chapters, which discuss the specific implementation of the Zend Framework.

CHAPTER 15

Introduction to the Zend Framework

The Zend Framework is the result of a massive community effort to develop a standardized MVC framework for PHP. It is a truly open source project and is licensed under a BSD license, ensuring that everyone has the right to use it appropriately.

The Zend Framework follows the MVC architecture, but is far more robust and developed in its implementation. It provides facilities for most web development tasks and is extremely flexible in its operation.

This chapter introduces the Zend Framework and presents one method for development with the framework. This is by no means the only way, as the whole point of the Zend Framework is to create a flexible development environment that works for a wide range of developers.

Setting Up the Zend Framework

Getting started with the Zend Framework is fairly straightforward. You'll need to download and install it, and then configure your web server environment for the framework.

Installing the Zend Framework

Begin by visiting `http://framework.zend.com` and downloading the latest stable release. At the time of writing, the latest version is 1.0.3.

```
> wget http://framework.zend.com/releases/ZendFramework-1.0.3/ ➡
ZendFramework-1.0.3.tar.gz
```

■**Tip** You can download the Zend Framework directly to your server by copying the URL link from the web page and pasting it into the `wget` command.

You will need to pick a common location to place the framework libraries. This depends on how you organize your server. I use the following:

```
> mkdir /usr/share/php/ZendFramework
```

However, the directory is entirely up to you—all you need to do is remember where you put the framework files.

Next, extract the framework into this directory:

```
> tar xzf ZendFramework-1.0.3.tar.gz
```

You will now have a directory:

```
> drwx------   7 1005   513 ZendFramework-1.0.3
```

This will make the full path /usr/share/php/ZendFramework/ZendFramework-1.0.3/. You may notice, however, that the permissions are less than ideal. You have a couple of choices here: you can let the web server own the files, or you can protect them, so that modification is more difficult. I suggest the latter.

```
> cd ZendFramework-1.0.3
> chown root:root . -R
```

■**Note** On some systems, the root group is called wheel.

You will now have all framework files owned by the root user, but the web server won't be able to read them. You will need to set directories to chmod 755 (drwxr-xr-x) and files to chmod 644 (-rw-r--r--). The easiest way to do this is with the find command:

```
> find -type d -exec chmod 755 {} \;
> find -type f -exec chmod 644 {} \;
```

With the permissions correct and the framework set up, only the root user will be allowed to modify any of the framework files. This should give you some added security against your libraries being changed outside your main source location.

From this point on, you never upgrade to a newer version by replacing existing files. Instead, you follow this process and create a new directory each time.

Creating a Virtual Host

Now that the framework is installed, you will need to create a virtual host. This process is described in the previous chapter. The Zend Framework uses a very similar directory structure:

```
> cd /usr/local/www/yourdomain.com
> mkdir -p document_root/images document_root/styles
> mkdir -p application/models application/views/scripts/index \
> application/controllers
> find
```

```
.
./document_root
./document_root/images
./document_root/styles
./application
./application/models
./application/views
./application/views/scripts
./application/views/scripts/index
./application/controllers
```

Bootstrapping

Bootstrapping integrates your web server environment with the Zend Framework. It is where the web server will send every request for your site, and it will handle application dispatching.

The first step is to create your index.php (bootstrap) file and .htaccess file in document_root.

```
> cd document_root
> pico -w index.php

<?php
echo 'Rewrite working';

> pico -w .htaccess

RewriteEngine On

RewriteCond %{REQUEST_FILENAME} -s [OR]
RewriteCond %{REQUEST_FILENAME} -l [OR]
RewriteCond %{REQUEST_FILENAME} -d

RewriteRule ^.*$ - [NC,L]
RewriteRule ^.*$ /index.php [NC,L]
```

> **Note** An .htaccess file is a file that controls the Apache web server. If you are not operating with Apache, you will need to configure your server to send all requests to /index.php.

This script works by redirecting all requests that would have otherwise generated a 404 Not Found HTTP error to index.php. Technically, it checks if the request found a file, a symbolic link, or a directory and redirects when those conditions are not met.

Test your results by visiting http://yoursite.com/asdf to make sure that you see "Rewrite working." If you don't, you will need to troubleshoot mod_rewrite (see http://httpd.apache.org/docs/2.0/mod/mod_rewrite.html for documentation on mod_rewrite).

Assuming that all went well, the next step is to start building the index.php file for real. Clear the old file:

```
> echo > index.php
```

Then create a new index.php file and include the main Zend platform include file.

```
> pico -w index.php
```

```php
<?php
define('ZFW_VERSION','1.0.3');
define('ZFW_PREFIX','/usr/share/php/ZendFramework');
define('APP_PATH', realpath(dirname(__FILE__) . '/../'));

$paths = array(
  APP_PATH,
  APP_PATH . DIRECTORY_SEPARATOR . 'application' . DIRECTORY_SEPARATOR . 'models',
  ZFW_PREFIX . DIRECTORY_SEPARATOR . 'ZendFramework-'. ZFW_VERSION . ➥
DIRECTORY_SEPARATOR. 'library',
  get_include_path()
);

set_include_path(implode(PATH_SEPARATOR, $paths));

require_once('Zend/Loader.php');
```

Note The ZFW_VERSION constant defines which version of the framework your site will use.

At this point, if everything is working properly, reloading your page will show no errors and no content. If it's not working, your Zend Framework setup isn't quite right; the most likely culprit is file permissions.

Now you can continue to build the index.php file. From this point on, when you edit the file, you are *adding* content to the file, not replacing existing code.

Next, enable SPL autoloading of framework classes.

```
> pico -w index.php
```

```php
Zend_Loader::registerAutoload();
```

The final step is to enable exceptions. By default, the Zend Framework does not throw exceptions. This is a security measure, designed to keep confidential information from being displayed to the user unintentionally. However, this makes getting started with the framework much more difficult. To enable the throwing of exceptions, you must first get a reference to the front controller, and then call the throwExceptions() method, before finally calling run with your controller directory, as follows:

```
$front = Zend_Controller_Front::getInstance();
$front->throwExceptions(true);
$front->run(APP_PATH . '/application/controllers');
```

Before you launch your site, be sure to disable the throwing of exceptions, as it is an important security measure.

Completed, your bootstrap file should look like Listing 15-1.

Listing 15-1. *A Zend Framework Bootstrap File (index.php)*

```
<?php
define('ZFW_VERSION','1.0.3');
define('ZFW_PREFIX','/usr/share/php/ZendFramework');
define('APP_PATH', realpath(dirname(__FILE__) . '/../'));

$paths = array(
  APP_PATH,
  APP_PATH . DIRECTORY_SEPARATOR . 'application' . DIRECTORY_SEPARATOR . 'models',
  ZFW_PREFIX . DIRECTORY_SEPARATOR . 'ZendFramework-'. ZFW_VERSION . ➥
DIRECTORY_SEPARATOR. 'library',
  get_include_path()
);

set_include_path(implode(PATH_SEPARATOR, $paths));

require_once('Zend/Loader.php');

Zend_Loader::registerAutoload();

$front = Zend_Controller_Front::getInstance();
$front->throwExceptions(true);
$front->run(APP_PATH . '/application/controllers');
```

If you were to revisit your site now, you would see an exception that no index controller exists. To clear this exception, you need to create your first Zend Framework action controller.

Creating Controllers, Views, and Models

Since the Zend Framework is designed for MVC development, it expects those three components: a model, view, and controller. So, let's create those components, starting with the controller.

Adding an Index Controller

All controllers in the Zend Framework extend a common abstract class called Zend_Controller_Action and must have a class name ending in Controller. The default action that will be called is indexAction. The default controller file is named IndexController.php and should be placed within your application/controllers directory. Listing 15-2 shows your default controller, which should become /application/controllers/IndexController.php.

Listing 15-2. *The Default Controller (application/controllers/IndexController.php)*

```php
<?php
class IndexController extends Zend_Controller_Action {
  public function indexAction() {
  }
}
```

With your index controller created, your site should now show another exception.

```
'script 'index/index.phtml' not found in path
```

This is because you have no view defined for the index controller's index action.

Adding a View

In the previous chapter, you manually rendered your views by creating a view object, assigning variables, and calling a render() method. The Zend Framework has a default component called the *view renderer*, which handles two of these steps for you: automatically creating a view instance and rendering a view script. The view instance is stored in the controller instance as $this->view.

For your application, your first view template will be application/views/scripts/index/index.phtml, as shown in Listing 15-3. The directory index refers to the controller name, and the index.phtml file refers to the method name without the Action suffix.

Listing 15-3. *A Sample View (application/views/scripts/index/index.phtml)*

```html
<html>
  <body>
    <p>Welcome: <?php echo $this->name; ?></p>
  </body>
</html>
```

That's simple enough. Now, to use it, you need to refactor your indexAction method in IndexController.php and set the name variable, as shown in Listing 15-4.

Listing 15-4. *A View-Enabled Action (in IndexController.php)*

```php
public function indexAction() {
  $this->view->name = 'Kevin';
}
```

If you reload your page, you should see "Welcome: Kevin." You now have a working Zend Framework application!

Defining Models

The next step is to create data models that will provide some meaningful data to the application. The Zend Framework contains many useful classes that you can use for interacting with databases. You will create your data models using these base classes, but first you need a database.

Setting Up a Database

Which database you use is entirely up to you. The examples in this chapter use the PostgreSQL database, as it installs from package management on Debian Linux distributions. For your specific system, the location of binaries may not be in the path, and the location of pg_hba.conf may be different than shown.

First, you need to create a PostgreSQL user, to act as owner of the database, and section off your application's access from any other databases already running on your host. This is an interactive command and should be run as the postgres user. Be sure to use a custom password for your database.

```
> createuser -P
```

```
Enter name of role to add: demouser
Enter password for new role: demopass
Enter it again: demopass
Shall the new role be a superuser? (y/n) n
Shall the new role be allowed to create databases? (y/n) n
Shall the new role be allowed to create more new roles? (y/n) n
CREATE ROLE
```

Then create a database that is owned by the demouser user, is UTF-8 encoded, and is called demodb.

```
> createdb -O demouser -E utf-8 demodb
```

```
CREATE DATABASE
```

Next, in order to enable access to your new database, the PostgreSQL host-based authentication configuration (pg_hba.conf) must be edited so that your new user is given permission to connect to the database. The following line grants local (Unix socket) access on demodb to demouser using MD5 hashed passwords:

```
> pico -w /etc/postgresql/8.1/main/pg_hba.conf
```

```
local    demodb              demouser            md5
```

Now reload the postgresql daemon, using either an init script or the pg_ctl binary.

```
> /etc/init.d/postgresql reload
```

At this point, you should be able to connect to your database:

```
> psql -U demouser -W demodb
```

```
Password for user demouser:
Welcome to psql 8.X.X, the PostgreSQL interactive terminal.

Type:  \copyright for distribution terms
       \h for help with SQL commands
       \? for help with psql commands
       \g or terminate with semicolon to execute query
       \q to quit

demodb=>
```

Next, create a table. The first table you might create is one to store information about your customers:

```
demodb=> create table customers(customer_id serial, name varchar);
```

```
NOTICE:  CREATE TABLE will create implicit sequence
"customers_customer_id_seq" for serial column "customers.customer_id"
CREATE TABLE
```

Then create a record in the table:

```
demodb=> INSERT INTO customers (name) VALUES ('Kevin');
```

Finally, quit using the \q command:

```
demodb=> \q
```

Database in hand, you can now go about creating a model for your customers table, but first you must prepare the Zend Framework to use this database.

Configuring the Framework to Use the Database

To configure the Zend Framework for use with your database, edit the bootstrap index.php file:

```
> pico -w document_root/index.php
```

Add the code shown in Listing 15-5 *before* the line containing Zend_Controller_Front::run.

Listing 15-5. *Database Connection Information for Bootstrapping (in index.php)*

```
$params = array (
    'username' => 'demouser',
    'password' => 'demopass',
    'dbname'   => 'demodb'
);


$db = Zend_Db::factory('PDO_PGSQL', $params);


Zend_Db_Table::setDefaultAdapter($db);
```

The setDefaultAdapter() call ensures that any future attempt to connect to a database without explicit connection information will use this connection information. This allows any Zend_Db_Table instances to worry about the structure of the tables and not about where they need to connect. It also provides a convenient and centralized configuration point.

Creating the Customers Model, Controller, and View

Now you can create a Zend_Db_Table-derived model that will interact with your database table:

```
> pico application/models/Customers.php
```

Add the code shown in Listing 15-6.

Listing 15-6. *Customers Model (application/models/Customers.php)*

```
<?php
class Customers extends Zend_Db_Table {
  protected $_name = 'customers';
  protected $_primary = 'customer_id';
}
```

Next, in your controller directory, create a new action controller to list all your customers.

```
> pico -w application/controllers/CustomersController.php
```

Add the code shown in Listing 15-7.

Listing 15-7. *Customers Controller (application/controllers/CustomersController.php)*

```
<?php
class CustomersController extends Zend_Controller_Action {
  public function indexAction() {
    $table = new Customers();
    $this->view->customers = $table->fetchAll();
  }
}
```

The next step is to create the view for this information, as shown in Listing 15-8. Note that you will need to create a new directory to contain the views for the customers controller.

Listing 15-8. *Customers View (application/views/scripts/customers/index.phtml)*

```
<html>
  <body>
    <table>
      <thead>
        <th>ID</th>
        <th>Name</th>
      </thead>
      <tbody>
        <?php foreach($this->customers as $customer) { ?>
          <tr>
            <td><?php echo $customer->customer_id; ?></td>
            <td><?php echo $customer->name; ?></td>
          </tr>
        <?php } ?>
      </tbody>
    </table>
  </body>
</html>
```

Reloading the page should result in a stylish listing of the customers table.

You're now up and running with the Zend Framework, but you have not handled any input or done anything interactive yet.

Adding Functionality

The Zend Framework provides a set of functionality that is designed to make creating forms and working with input data easier. This functionality consists of three main parts:

- The request and response objects

- Action helpers and view helpers

- Input validation

Using the Request and Response Objects

The request object encapsulates all the HTTP data you could ever want to get your hands on, including all GET (query), POST, and cookie data. It also provides information parsed from the request URI, such as the controller and action names, as well as a special type of data called *parameters*, which can be set from the URL to make your sites more search engine-friendly than using query variables. Complementing the request object, the response object provides an encapsulated way to work with the output stream.

The Request Object

The following five request object methods all work the same and allow you to interact with the standard input streams:

```
getQuery($key = null, $default = null)
getPost($key = null, $default = null)
getCookie($key = null, $default = null)
getServer($key = null, $default = null)
getEnv($key = null, $default = null)
```

If you pass a null key parameter, you will get the entire array of information. If you pass a key, you will get the value for that key only. You can also pass a default value so that if there is no matching key, that value will be returned. In the case that no key is found and no default is passed, null will be returned.

If you need to access the HTTP request headers, you will use the getHeader() method by passing in the header name. Remember that HTTP headers are case-sensitive.

```
getHeader($header)
```

Parameters are a key part of any MVC implementation. They are an alternative to get variables and make your sites more attractive to search engines. To use parameters in a Zend Framework application, the URL is divided up like so:

```
http://example.com/controller/action/key1/value1/key2/value2 . . .
```

By using parameters, you can pass critical query information, such as a customer ID, to your scripts without using get information. Using parameters is one of the best ways to make sure that a search engine spider will fetch your dynamic content, as most spiders ignore query variables.

The getParam() method will also access query and post information if the requested key cannot be found in the URL parameters.

```
getParam($key, $default = null)
```

The getParams() method returns an array of all parameters, and query and post information.

```
getParams()
```

To determine the current HTTP request method—GET, POST, HEAD, and so on—you can use the following method:

```
getMethod()
```

Alternatively, you can use one of the is convenience functions:

```
isPost()
```

■**Tip** To obtain a reference to the current request object from within a controller/action context, you may call $this->getRequest() on the controller instance.

The Response Object

The response object contains methods that allow you to set headers and assign response bodies. Listing 15-9 demonstrates both setting a Content-Type header and assigning a request body in the context of a JavaScript Object Notation (JSON) serving action.

Listing 15-9. *A JSON Returning Action*

```
public function jsonAction() {
  //Don't render a template
  $this->getHelper('ViewRenderer')->setNoRender();

  //Set content type headers in the response object
  $this->getResponse()->setHeader('Content-Type', 'application/json');

  //Manually assign the response body, instead of rendering a template
  $json = '{"Name":"Kevin"}';
  $this->getResponse()->setBody($json);
}
```

Additionally, you might use setHttpResponseCode() to set the status code, such as when you want to create a 404 or 503 error page.

Using Built-in Action Helpers

Action helpers are reusable classes that add functionality to the controller—typically, functionality that would not be considered program logic. For example, the ability to redirect the user to another page is implemented as a helper in the Zend Framework.

You will learn how to create your own action helpers in Chapter 17. Here, let's look at a couple of the built-in action helpers.

The Redirector Helper

The Redirector helper does what its name implies: it allows you to redirect the user to a new page. It provides several methods, but the key one is goto().

```
void goto($action, $controller=null, $module=null, $params=array())
```

The goto() method performs the redirection and allows you to redirect to a specific action. The API provided is more desirable than using headers directly, as there are several factors that can affect a Zend Framework application's URL layout down the road.

To redirect a user to a new page, add an action method to your customers controller, as shown in Listing 15-10.

Listing 15-10. *Using the Redirector Helper (in CustomersController.php)*

```
public function redirectAction() {
  $this->getHelper('redirector')->goto('index');
}
```

When visited, at `/customers/redirect`, this action should forward you to the index action. You can access all helpers by their name using the `getHelper()` method of `Zend_Controller_Action`.

The FlashMessenger Helper

The FlashMessenger helper is designed to store messages from one request to the next. It allows you to add a message to be displayed on the next page, and it will handle all aspects of the session, including removing the message from the session after it has been displayed.

The use of the FlashMessenger helper is demonstrated in Listings 15-11 and 15-12.

Listing 15-11. *Using the FlashMessenger Helper (in CustomersController.php)*

```
public function redirectAction() {
  $this->getHelper('FlashMessenger')
      ->addMessage("This was set at the redirector");

  $this->getHelper('redirector')->goto('show');
}

public function showAction() {
  $this->view->messages = $this->getHelper('FlashMessenger')->getMessages();
}
```

Listing 15-12. *A Message View (application//view/scripts/customers/show.phtml)*

```
<?php foreach($this->messages as $message) { ?>
 <?php echo $message; ?><br />
<?php } ?>
```

If you visit `/customers/redirect`, you should be redirected to `/customers/show` and see your message. If you then reload the page, you will not see the message, because it was cleared from the session as soon as it was shown.

Using Built-in View Helpers

View helpers follow the same logic as action helpers, allowing you to create components that are reusable for your views. You'll learn about creating view helpers in Chapter 17. For now, let's look at the built-in helpers.

Many of the built-in view helpers assist with creating and binding forms to your views. The forms created with helpers can be slightly wordier than normal; however, they do useful things like output escaping, and they will make creating select drop-down lists from an array easier. They can also help to provide a more consistent final output.

Since your `customers` table is a single column, using a view helper will be easy. Create a new view as shown in Listing 15-13 and save it as `/application/views/scripts/customers/add.phtml`.

Listing 15-13. *Using View Helpers (application/views/scripts/customers/add.phtml)*

```
<form method="post" action="/customers/add">
  <?php echo $this->formText('name'); ?>
  <?php echo $this->formSubmit('submit'); ?>
</form>
```

This invokes two view helpers: formText and formSubmit. These views will resolve to create the following output HTML:

```
<form method="post" action="/customers/add">
  <input type="text" name="name" id="name" value="" />
  <input type="submit" name="submit" id="submit" value="submit" />
</form>
```

Next, add an empty action method to the controller class in CustomersController.php, as shown in Listing 15-14. Even without a method body, this method's mere presence will allow for the rendering of the view customers/add.phtml.

Listing 15-14. *Adding an Action Method (in CustomersController.php)*

```
public function addAction() {}
```

Next, visit http://example.com/customers/add, and you should see your form.

Before you start on any given form, it is usually useful to submit some good data and make sure it gets to your application correctly. Normally, you might use var_dump($_POST) or something similar to output all the form data. However, in the Zend Framework, you want to ensure that the data is getting through all the APIs properly. To do this, you will use Zend_Debug to display the post information parsed by the Zend_Request object. Modify the addAction() method as shown in Listing 15-15.

Listing 15-15. *Using Zend_Debug::dump (in CustomersController.php)*

```
public function addAction() {
      Zend_Debug::dump($this->getRequest()->getPost());
}
```

On submitting your form, you should see your form, as well as a result like this:

```
array(2) {
  ["name"] => string(4) "test"
  ["submit"] => string(6) "submit"
}
```

At this point, you know that your inputs are working and that the post action is going to the right action. You are now ready to process your form.

Validating Input

Before you can submit the posted information to your database, you must make sure that the information is valid so that your database remains consistent. The Zend_Db infrastructure will provide protection against SQL injection, so this validation layer is primarily to make sure the data is reasonable and is safe to be displayed on other pages.

Accepting user input in a Zend Framework application consists of two parts:

- Filtering, which involves the modification of data, to trim whitespace from the ends of strings or to strip HTML tags, for example

- Validation, which occurs after filtering and ensures that the data is reasonable, so that it won't cause issues like cross-site scripting

Both of these actions can be achieved separately with the Zend_Filter and Zend_Validate classes. However, they are more commonly used together through the Zend_Filter_Input class, which is designed to filter arrays of information, such as an entire form or set of URL parameters.

Using Zend_Filter_Input

To use Zend_Filter_Input, you need to first define two associative arrays: one for your filters and one for your validators. The keys in these arrays refer to the fields you wish to validate, whereas the values define the rules to apply. Listing 15-16 shows how to validate the customers form.

Listing 15-16. *Validating a Form (in CustomersController.php)*

```
public function addAction() {
  $request = $this->getRequest();

  //Determine if processing a post request
  if($request->isPost()) {

    //Filter tags from the name field
    $filters = array(
      'name' => 'StripTags'
    );

    //Validate name is not less than 1 character and not more than 64
    $validation = array(
      'name' => array (
        array('StringLength', 1, 64)
      )
    );

    //Initialize Zend_Filter_Input (ZFI) passing it the entire getPost() array
    $zfi = new Zend_Filter_Input($filters, $validation, $request->getPost());
```

```
    //If the validators passed this will be true
    if ($zfi->isValid()) {

        //Fetch the data from zfi directly and create an array for Zend_Db
        $clean = array();
        $clean['name'] = $zfi->name;

        //Create an instance of the customers table and insert the $clean row
        $customers = new Customers();
        $customers->insert($clean);

        //Redirect to the display page after adding
        $this->getHelper('redirector')->goto('index');

    } else {

        //The form didn't validate, get the messages from ZFI
        foreach($zfi->getMessages() as $field=>$messages) {

            //Put each ZFI message into the FlashMessenger so it shows on the form
            foreach($messages as $message) {
                $this->getHelper('FlashMessenger')
                    ->addMessage($field . ' : '. $message);
            }

        }

        //Redirect back to the input form, but with messages
        $this->getHelper('redirector')->goto('add');
    }
}

//Not a post request, check for flash messages and expose to the view
if($this->getHelper('FlashMessenger')->hasMessages()) {
    $this->view->messages = $this->getHelper('FlashMessenger')->getMessages();
}

//The view renderer will now automatically render the add.phtml template

}
```

You will also need to modify your add.phtml template. Add the code shown in Listing 15-17 to the top of the file.

Listing 15-17. *Modifying the Add View (in add.phtml)*

```
<?php if(isset($this->messages)) { ?>
  <?php foreach($this->messages as $message) { ?>
   <?php echo $message; ?><br />
  <?php } ?>
<?php } ?>
```

When you submit a blank value, it should fail to validate. If you enter an HTML tag, it should be filtered.

The arrays for validators and filters are where the real magic happens. The values demonstrated in the previous listings are extremely basic, but you can use significantly more complex validations. For validators, you may provide an array to apply multiple validators to a single field. For example, if you wanted to require that name contained only characters you could add the Alpha filter, as shown in Listing 15-18.

Listing 15-18. *Using Multiple Validators*

```
$validation = array(
  'name' => array (
    array('StringLength', 1, 64),
    'Alpha'
  )
);
```

You will notice that only the validator's name was used, not an array. This is because not all validators require parameters. The first format passes the values after the validator name to the validation class as constructor parameters. The second format doesn't have any parameters at all.

To find a list of built-in validation classes, locate the following path in your Zend Framework library installation:

```
/ZendFramework-1.0.3/library/Zend/Validate
```

Here, you will find a set of files that contain validation classes that you may use immediately. The parameters they take are defined by each class's __construct() method.

Similar to validators, filters can be chained. The following is the path to find information about filters:

```
ZendFramework-1.0.3/library/Zend/Filter
```

Take a look at the StripTags filter. You will notice that it takes a number of parameters, not the least of which is a list of allowed tags. I encourage you to experiment with different combinations of filters and validators to find a mix that works for your forms.

You may also notice that the error messages presented when a field fails to validate are rather terse, and you might want to change the default messages.

Using Metacommands

You can change the validation error messages through a special mechanism called a *metacommand*. Metacommands are used as another value in a validation or filtering record. These are special reserved words, or class constants that do something extra, such as setting the failure messages. For example, to set the validation messages for your name field, you would use the MESSAGES metacommand with a validation array, as shown in Listing 15-19.

Listing 15-19. *Controlling Error Messages*

```
$validation = array(
  'name' => array (
    array('StringLength', 1, 64),
    Zend_Filter_Input::MESSAGES => array(
      array(
        Zend_Validate_StringLength::TOO_SHORT => 'Name cannot be blank',
        Zend_Validate_StringLength::TOO_LONG => 'Name field is too long'
      )
    )
  )
);
```

The ALLOW_EMPTY metacommand allows a field to be submitted as blank. The field will still be required to be present in the input data array—this is called *presence*—but may have a value of ''. You might think of Zend Framework *presence* versus *empty* as the difference between null and '' in PHP. Listing 15-20 demonstrates using the ALLOW_EMPTY metacommand.

Listing 15-20. *Allowing Empty Fields*

```
$validation = array(
  'name' => array (
    'Alpha',
    Zend_Filter_Input::ALLOW_EMPTY => true
  )
);
```

This field may now contain zero or more alpha characters.
You may use several other metacommands:

- PRESENCE: Require a key to be present in the input array (Boolean).

- FIELDS: Don't use the input key as the field name; override and use this value instead.

- DEFAULT: Set a default value for the field if it is not *present*.

- BREAK_CHAIN: Instead of applying all validators to a field, stop after the first failure.

Just the Facts

In this chapter, you were introduced to the Zend Framework, including the setup and bootstrapping process. You downloaded the packages, fixed permissions, and generally configured your web server environment for the framework. Next, you learned about the elements in the MVC pattern as they apply to the Zend Framework.

The sample project in this chapter presented a very introductory view of how the Zend Framework can work with your development process. In the next chapters, you will learn how to use many of the other Zend Framework features, including module support and several of the built-in components, to control access to your applications, send mail, use sessions, log errors, and interact with web services.

CHAPTER 16

■■■

Advanced Zend Framework

In the previous chapter, you got up and running with a really basic Zend Framework application. It let you model a database, create a form, and validate data. The Zend Framework offers a lot more.

This chapter provides details about how the framework actually works and introduces some of its advanced features. You'll learn how to use its facilities for configuration, debugging, routing, caching, sending e-mail, creating PDF documents, and working with various web services.

Managing Configuration Files

Any reasonably complex application needs a set of configuration files. These files will hold information like the database credentials the site is operating with, domain configuration data, and other environment-related settings.

The Zend Framework, through the Zend_Config class, offers various ways of writing configuration data. We'll look at the following approaches here:

- Create a hierarchical array in your bootstrap file.

- Create an INI file. The framework even allows you to extend sections and override keys when working with INIs.

- Use an XML file.

The Array Approach

To add a configuration array in your bootstrap file, simply create a key/value array. You can nest arrays to create multiple-level hierarchies, too. When the Zend_Config class is instantiated with an array, it will transform the array keys into properties, allowing for a very clean interface. Listing 16-1 shows an example of using the array approach.

Listing 16-1. *Configuration Using an Array in the Bootstrap File (in index.php)*

```
$configArray = (
  'domain' => 'some.com',
  'database' => array(
    'name' => 'dbname',
    'password' => 'password'
  )
);
$config = new Zend_Config($configArray);

echo $config->database->name;
```

dbname

The INI Approach

The main difference between the INI approach and the array approach is that INI files may define override data, which is designed to be used under certain specific circumstances, such as when running from a staging or production server. This gives some useful flexibility, but alone would lead to cumbersome duplication; thus, the Zend Framework INI formats allow for sectional extension as well. Listing 16-2 shows an INI file that contains both production and staging configuration data.

Listing 16-2. *Configuration Using an INI File (Config.INI)*

```
[production]
domain = some.com
database.name = dbname
database.password = password

[staging : production]
domain = beta.some.com
database.name = stagingdb
```

In this example, staging extends from production and overrides two keys, but leaves a third password intact.

To tell Zend_Config which settings to use, the Zend_Config_Ini class is instantiated as follows:

```
$config = new Zend_Config_Ini('config.ini','staging');
echo $config->database->password;
```

password

The first argument points to the INI file, and the second argument indicates the section to use.

The XML Approach

The XML approach to configuration offers all the benefits of the INI methodology, but may allow for greater portability between applications. It also comes with the overhead of parsing an XML file. Listing 16-3 shows an example of an XML configuration file.

Listing 16-3. *Configuration Using an XML File (Config.xml)*

```xml
<?xml version="1.0"?>
<configdata>
  <production>
    <domain>some.com</domain>
    <database>
      <name>dbname</name>
      <password>password</password>
    </database>
  </production>
  <staging extends="production">
    <domain>beta.some.com</domain>
    <database>
      <name>dbname</name>
  </staging>
</configdata>
```

Accessing the XML configuration data works the same as with the INI file approach:

```php
$config = new Zend_Config_Xml('config.xml', 'staging');
echo $config->database->password;
```

```
password
```

I don't recommend using XML for configuration data, as the overhead of parsing an XML document is actually quite high. That said, you can use caching to neutralize this concern, as discussed in the "Caching" section later in this chapter.

Setting Site-Wide View Variables

By default, the framework will create a new Zend_View instance and register it with the view renderer for you automatically. However, in some circumstances, you may wish to customize the view. Customization of the view instance will allow you to set default application-wide variables, change the default path structure, and set various options. Listing 16-4 shows an example of registering a custom view.

Listing 16-4. *Registering a Custom View with the View Renderer*

```
$view = new Zend_View();
$view->siteWideProperty = 'value';
$viewRenderer =
Zend_Controller_Action_HelperBroker::getStaticHelper('ViewRenderer');
$viewRenderer->setView($view);
```

This is fairly straightforward, and you can do it during your bootstrapping process. Every view script now has access to the $this->siteWideProperty value, which can be extremely useful for setting paths to common locations, such as to your image, JavaScript, and CSS files.

Sharing Objects

The Zend_Registry component is designed to allow you to create objects and share them among the various framework classes. This approach is similar to using global variables, but is less likely to cause conflicts with other libraries you may be using in conjunction with the framework.

To store an object instance within Zend_Registry, you call the set() method and define a name for the entry:

```
Zend_Registry::set('handle', $instance);
```

To retrieve this object at a later time, simply call the get() method:

```
$instance = Zend_Registry::get('handle');
```

Error Handling

In the previous chapter, you created a framework bootstrap that threw exceptions. This is not the default behavior. You enabled it by calling throwExceptions(true) on the front controller instance.

By default, the framework looks for a controller called ErrorController whenever a problem is encountered, instead of throwing exceptions directly. It also sets a request parameter called error_handler with the request object. This parameter contains details about the error condition.

To properly handle errors in your sample application, create a new controller class named ErrorController and place it with your other controllers. In this controller, create a method called errorAction, which will be invoked by the framework when an error condition occurs.

At this point, you should have a controller that looks like this:

```
<?php
class ErrorController extends Zend_Controller_Action {

        public function errorAction() {
        }

}
```

You will also need to create a view called error.phtml and place it in a directory called error. The content of that view isn't particularly important yet.

Next, you will need to determine why the exception was thrown. The error information is contained in the request parameter 'error_handler' and can be fetched as shown in Listing 16-5.

Listing 16-5. *Fetching Error Information (ErrorController.php)*

```php
<?php
class ErrorController extends Zend_Controller_Action {

        public function errorAction() {
                $request = $this->getRequest();
                $errorHandler = $request->getParam('error_handler');

                Zend_Debug::dump($errorHandler);
        }
}
```

Finally set the throwExceptions() call in your bootstrap file to false, or simply remove the entire line to re-enable the default behavior.

Now, if you generate an error, such as by visiting a nonexistent URL, you will get pages of information about the error.

The error controller is not intended to catch all errors, like syntax errors, but it will do a reasonably good job of catching any exception that occurs within your action controller's execution.

Application Logging

Zend_Log allows your applications to generate and record information about their operation. This information can be integrated with error handling or used to generate debugging information about operational parameters.

Zend_Log has four architectural parts:

Logs: These are the responsible objects, where you will call methods to add messages to the log. They are responsible because they are where the other components tie in.

Writers: These allow you to record the data in a log to a variety of output formats— from files and streams to a database when integrated with Zend_Db. I recommend using files over recording events to a database, as database logging can make debugging a database connection failure much more difficult.

Formatters: These are used to take the Zend_Log data and turn it into a specific format. They are required because, by default, Zend_Log data is stored in an array format. Formatters take this array form and turn it into a string for logging.

Filters: These allow you to control which error messages will be logged by defining a priority threshold for your application. You may want to integrate the filter threshold with your Zend_Config file.

These four components work together to provide a very powerful set of logging options. To demonstrate the logging functionality, let's look at how you can integrate the ErrorController example from the previous section with Zend_Log. First, place the code shown in Listing 16-6 in your bootstrap file, at any location after the framework is loaded (registerAutoload()), but before your front controller is run(). This location is the same for any other additional functionality added to the bootstrap file.

Listing 16-6. *Creating a Logger (in index.php)*

```
//Create a log
$log = new Zend_Log();

//Filter out noise [optional]
$log->addFilter(new Zend_Log_Filter_Priority(Zend_Log::ERR));

//Create a writer
$logWriter = new Zend_Log_Writer_Stream(APP_PATH . '/application.log');

//Create a formatter [optional]
$logFormat = '%timestamp% %priorityName% %message%' . "\n";
$logWriter->setFormatter(new Zend_Log_Formatter_Simple($logFormat));

//Add the writer to the log
$log->addWriter($logWriter);

//Store it in the registry for easy access
Zend_Registry::set('log', $log);
```

Listing 16-6 creates an application.log file in the application's root folder. For this to work, the directory must be writable by the web server user, which may be www-data, nobody, or apache2, depending on your distribution. The log filters out any messages with a priority lower than ERR and formats the error message in a human-readable format. The formatter and filter are both optional steps.

Note Eight default message priorities ship with the Zend Framework: EMERG, ALERT, CRIT, ERR, WARN, NOTICE, INFO, and DEBUG.

At this point, your logger is set up, but you have yet to log any messages. Listing 16-7 demonstrates a possible integration between the ErrorController and this log.

Listing 16-7. *Logging with the ErrorController (ErrorController.php)*

```
class ErrorController extends Zend_Controller_Action {
  public function errorAction() {
    $request = $this->getRequest();
    $errorHandler = $request->getParam('error_handler');
```

```
    //Get the log instance
    $log = Zend_Registry::get('log');

    //Log an emergency message with the encountered exception
    $log->emerg($errorHandler['exception']->__toString());
  }
}
```

This integration logs the exception to a file instead of displaying it to the user. This will allow you to create a custom error page for your users, without losing any of that critical debugging error detail.

■**Tip** Logging a `uniqid()` along with your error message, and displaying the unique code to the user, can aid in production debugging by allowing you to correlate a user's experience with log-file information.

Caching

Caching is a critical part of any reasonably complex application. Whether you are caching static pages or just the result of a SQL query, it is critically important to the performance of your application that caching is sufficiently utilized.

The Zend Framework provides both block-level partial caching and entire-page caching. Deciding when to use each is very important, as caching certain requests will lead to significant headaches as well as significant security problems.

Caching Security Considerations

Here are some guidelines for safe caching:

- Cache data where the request's inputs will result in the same output with each page generation. For example, home pages are an excellent caching opportunity.

- Do not cache any data that is the product of input that may contain personal information. It may be used to create cross-domain scenarios that violate your users' privacy and create significant liability for your business.

- Be sure that caching the output of the page will not circumvent your security model and allow other users to read pages cached by a specific user. Take extreme caution when caching pages that require any sort of authentication to access, as circumvention possibilities are increased.

To better understand the security implications of caching, think of a web site with a member's area that contains a dashboard. You could create a scenario where when a user logs in, her dashboard is cached. When the next user logs in, he is presented with the cached page. The problem is the cache was the product of the first user's login, and you've just disclosed personal information to another user. Such caching scenarios are *extremely* common and have resulted in some very high-profile embarrassments for major organizations.

So now that you've been warned, what can caching do for you? In short, everything. The Zend Framework's caching solution is great because it allows you to cache not only full pages, but partial pages and even SQL queries.

Caching Techniques

The cache component has two key pieces: a front-end and a back-end. The front-end is responsible for deciding what and how to cache, and the back-end is responsible for storage of the cached information. Table 16-1 lists the available front-ends, and Table 16-2 lists the back-ends.

Table 16-1. *Zend_Cache Front-Ends*

Front-End	Description
Zend_Cache_Frontend_Core	A general-purpose caching front-end with both load($handle) and save($data) methods. This front-end defines the base class for all other front-ends, and as such, it defines a number of useful caching options, including caching (bool), lifetime (int seconds), logging (bool log to Zend_Log), write_control, automatic_ serialization, and automatic_cleaning_factor. They are fairly self-explanatory; see the Zend Framework reference for more details.
Zend_Cache_Frontend_Output	A caching front-end that captures all output between a $cache->start() and $cache->end() call. It is useful for caching partial blocks of output, when full-page caching is not appropriate.
Zend_Cache_Frontend_Function	Function caching allows you to save the result of a function as well as any content it might directly output. It has a single call(callback $function, array $params) function.
Zend_Cache_Frontend_Class	Class caching allows you to cache classes such that state is remembered between loads. It can be used to serialize/ deserialize objects and prevent you from having to go back to a database or configuration file to instantiate a class. To use this front-end, the option 'cachedEntity' must be set to a name or instance of a class. To call cached methods, simply call $cache->methodName(...).
Zend_Cache_Frontend_File	This is the same as the core front-end but with the extension that the cache will expire with the modification of a file. This allows you to cache items such as the parsing of an XML file indefinitely until the underlying file changes. To use this front-end, provide an option of 'master_file'=>'/path/to/file'.
Zend_Cache_Frontend_Page	This front-end caches an entire page and is quite simple to use. An option of 'regexps', which is an array of arrays, declares which pages should be cached. This front-end is demonstrated in Listing 16-8.

Table 16-2. *Zend_Cache Back-Ends*

Back-End	Description
Zend_Cache_Backend_File	The basic back-end, which saves cache objects to a file. You can set the cache file creation directory with the back-end option 'cache_dir'. The cache directory must be writable by the web server user.
Zend_Cache_Backend_Sqlite	A back-end that stores the cache items to a SQLite database file. Use the back-end option 'cache_db_complete_path'=>'/path/to/sqlitefile' to specify your database.
Zend_Cache_Backend_Memcached	A back-end that stores the cache into a memcached daemon. To enable it, you must provide the servers back-end option, which is an array of arrays with keys of host, port, and persistent. You can also enable on-the-fly compression with the compression back-end option set to Boolean true.
Zend_Cache_Backend_Apc	The APC cache back-end lets you use the APC extension to store cache data. You will need the APC extension, which is usually not standard on PHP installations. This back-end requires no extra options.
Zend_Cache_Backend_ZendPlatform	You can also use the Zend Platform for caching. This back-end requires no extra options.

The easiest type of caching to do is full-page caching. It's really simple, because you have no inputs and typically have really static content. To enable this type of caching, create a writable directory called cache in your application path and follow the example in Listing 16-8.

Listing 16-8. *Caching Your Front Page (in index.php)*

```
$cacheBackendOptions = array(
  'cache_dir' => APP_PATH . '/cache'
);

$cacheFrontendOptions = array(
  'regexps' => array(
    '^/$' => array() //use default caching options on front page
  )
);

$cache = Zend_Cache::factory(
                    'Page', //Use the page frontend
                    'File', //Use the file backend
                    $cacheFrontendOptions,
                    $cacheBackendOptions
              );
$cache->start();
```

The example in Listing 16-8 uses the page front-end and the file back-end to cache the entire output of the page. The page front-end takes an array with regular expressions specifying which pages to cache. Here, you used the default caching options, which say not to cache requests with variable information for gets, posts, cookies, sessions, and so on.

■**Caution** By default, the existence of cookies, sessions, and get and post variables will prevent caching! If you have cookies being sent, then your cache may appear not to work. A common problem you may encounter is the use of analytics tracking codes that set cookies that are otherwise outside your application.

To ensure that your cache is created when variables are present, you can use a variety of cache_with_*_variables and make_id_with_*_variables options. For example, if you wanted to cache the result of a GET request, you would use a cacheFrontendOptions array, as shown Listing 16-9.

Listing 16-9. *Caching GET Requests*

```
$cacheFrontendOptions = array(
  'debug_header' => true,
  'regexps' => array(
    '^/$' => array(
      'cache_with_get_variables' => true,
      'make_id_with_get_variables' => true
    )
  )
);
```

The option cache_with_get_variables says that it is OK to cache a page when get variables are present. The option make_id_with_get_variables says that each page cached must be cached separately for all of the page's inputs. Thus, two values for the same get variable result in two different cache files.

■**Caution** Enabling make_id_with_cookie_variables and make_id_with_session variables may have the result of creating a per-user cache. This could be less than desirable, depending on your caching scenarios. You can use the cache_with_*_variables option without using make_id_with_*_variables, but be careful, because doing so may expose user-specific data to other users. It is critical to always understand what data your cache will store.

You will also notice the debug_header option is set to true in Listing 16-9. This option makes the cached page output a header indicating that it has been cached, so that you can tell when your pages are being cached, which may aid in debugging.

Replacing get with post, cookie, session, or even files will result in distinct caching scenarios. Remember, though, that this type of caching is appropriate only where the page's output is always the same for the same input parameters.

Authorizing Users

The Zend_Auth component allows you to confirm a visitor's identity. This component combines sessions and database access to create a robust identity system. To understand Zend_Auth, it's best to see it in a complete example.

Listing 16-10 shows a complete authentication solution, integrated with forms processing, the FlashMessenger, and a database. The prerequisite for this example is a database table called users, with fields named email, password, and name. Create the IndexController.php file as shown in this listing.

Listing 16-10. *A Complete Zend_Auth Example (IndexController.php)*

```
//Builds on the Hello: name example
public function indexAction() {

  //Get a reference to Zend_Auth
  $auth = Zend_Auth::getInstance();

  //Check to see if the user is logged in
  if($auth->hasIdentity()) {
    //Get the user's identity and set view variable to name
    $identity = $auth->getIdentity();
    $this->view->name = $identity->name;
  } else {
    //No identity = Welcome: unknown.
    $this->view->name = 'unknown';
  }
}

public function loginAction() {
  if($this->getRequest()->isPost()) {

    //Filter tags from the fields
    $filters = array(
      'email' => 'StringTrim',
      'password' => 'StringTrim'
    );

    $validation = array(
      'email'=>array('emailAddress'),
      'password' => array (
        array('StringLength', 1, 64)
      )
    );
```

```
/*
   Initialize Zend_Filter_Input passing it the
   entire getPost() array
*/
$zfi = new Zend_Filter_Input(
                $filters,
                $validation,
                $this->getRequest()->getPost()
        );

//If the validators passed, this will be true
if ($zfi->isValid()) {

  $dbconfig = array(
    'host' => 'localhost',
    'username' => 'user',
    'password' => 'password',
    'dbname' => 'demo'
  );

  $db = Zend_Db::factory('PDO_PGSQL', $dbconfig);

  //Create a new Zend_Auth_Adapter
  $adapter = new Zend_Auth_Adapter_DbTable(
                $db,
                'users', //The name of the table
                'email', //The name of the 'identity' field
                'password', //The name of the 'credential' field
                'md5(?)' //SQL function to apply [optional]
              );

  //Set the identity and credential fields to validated values
  $adapter->setIdentity($zfi->email)
          ->setCredential($zfi->password);

  /*
     Get an instance of Zend_Auth and
     authenticate() using the adapter.
  */
  $auth = Zend_Auth::getInstance();
  $result = $auth->authenticate($adapter);

  //Check for authentication success
  if ($result->isValid()) {
```

```
        /*
            The next line stores the entire database row in the users
            Zend_Auth identity. Normally only the 'identity' column—
            in this case, the e-mail—is stored as a string. By
            storing the entire record, you can access the user's
            name and ID too.
        */
        $auth->getStorage()->write($adapter->getResultRowObject());


        //Redirect to /index/index when successfully logged in
        $this->getHelper('redirector')->goto('index','index');
      } else {
        //In this case, the authentication failed.
        $this->getHelper('FlashMessenger')
            ->addMessage(
                "The login credentials provided are not valid."
            );
        $this->getHelper('redirector')->goto('login');
      }
    } else {
      foreach($zfi->getMessages() as $field=>$messages) {
        foreach($messages as $message) {
          $this->getHelper('FlashMessenger')
              ->addMessage($field . ' : '. $message);
        }
      }
      $this->getHelper('redirector')->goto('login');
    }
  }
    $this->view->messages = $this->getHelper('FlashMessenger')
                                  ->getMessages();
}
```

You will also need a login.phtml view in /views/scripts/index/, as shown in Listing 16-11.

Listing 16-11. *The Login View (login.phtml)*

```
<?php foreach($this->messages as $message) { ?>
  <p>
    <strong>ERROR: </span><?php echo $this->escape($message); ?></strong>
  </p>
<?php } ?>

<form method="post">
  <p>Email Address:<br />
    <input type="text" name="email"/>
  </p>
```

```
<p>Password:<br />
  <input type="password" name="password"/>
</p>

<p>
  <input type="submit" name="submit" value="Submit">
</p>
</form>
```

To access your login form, visit `http://example.com/index/login`.

Using JSON with PHP

The `Zend_Json` class provides a simple encoder/decoder mechanism to convert variables between JSON and PHP. This component is fairly self-explanatory and is demonstrated in the context of a JSON action in Listing 16-12.

Listing 16-12. *Using Zend_Json*

```
public function jsonAction() {
  $this->getHelper('ViewRenderer')->setNoRender();

  //Simulate a JSON input value
  $jsonInput = '[0,1,2,3]';

  //Decode JSON to a PHP array
  $phpArray = Zend_Json::decode($jsonInput);

  //Do a PHP operation
  shuffle($phpArray);

  //Encode the data for output
  $jsonOutput = Zend_Json::encode($phpArray);

  //Get the response object and set content type HTTP header
  $response = $this->getResponse();
  $response->setHeader('Content-Type', 'application/json');

  //Make sure the JSON is the only output data
  $response->clearBody();
  //Set the response body to the JSON code
  $response->setBody($jsonOutput);
}
```

Normal operation of a JSON decode in PHP is to turn JSON objects into associative arrays. Since this is not always desirable, the Zend Framework provides an alternative decode syntax;

```
$phpObject = Zend_Json::decode('{"x":1}', Zend_Json::TYPE_OBJECT);
```

This produces a stdClass object, with a property for x. See Chapter 18 for coverage of Ajax, JSON, and the PHP JSON extension.

Customizing Routes

The previous chapter introduced the Zend Framework's front controller. This controller is fairly rigid in the URL format that controls routing. However, the designers of the Zend Framework realized that it is sometimes necessary to deviate from this typical structure—for example, to port an application with an existing structure or to create a multilingual site.

By using the rewrite router, you can add routes to the defaults or even override routes completely. Listing 16-13 shows how to integrate the rewrite router with your application, but without changing any functionality. Replace the following code in your bootstrap file from the previous chapter:

```
$front = Zend_Controller_Front::getInstance();
$front->throwExceptions(true);
$front->run(APP_PATH . '/application/controllers');
```

with the code shown in Listing 16-13.

Listing 16-13. *Bootstrapping the Rewrite Router (in index.php)*

```
$router = new Zend_Controller_Router_Rewrite();
$front = Zend_Controller_Front::getInstance();
$front->setRouter($router);
$front->run(APP_PATH . '/application/controllers');
```

At this point, the rewrite router is engaged but is not overriding any functionality. Call $router->addRoute() to add the override to the defaults. The format for a route is instantiated through the Zend_Controller_Router_Route class and is fairly straightforward. Listing 16-14 demonstrates a translation of the route /product/view/productId/1 into /product/view/1.

Listing 16-14. *Rewrite Routing*

```
$route = new Zend_Controller_Router_Route(
  '/product/view/:productId, array(
    'controller' => 'product',
    'action' => 'view',
    'productId' => false
  )
);
$router->addRoute('viewproduct', $route);
```

In this example, the controller and action are hard-set, and the productId parameter is optional and defaults to a Boolean value of false. From the action controller perspective, the productId value is still a parameter and is accessed as before. The only thing that has changed is the URL.

It is also important to realize that this approach does not replace the default routing rules. If you want to define an overall replacement to the routing system, the framework provides the `removeDefaultRoutes()` method for this purpose.

The class for instantiating the format for the route has this form:

`Zend_Controller_Router_Route($route, $defaults, $format)`

with the following parameters:

$route: Anything prefixed with a colon is a variable until terminated with a slash. There are three reserved variables: `:module`, `:controller`, and `:action`. These allow you to specify a mapping for which module, controller, and action should be called.

$defaults: The second parameter is an array of defaults. This is useful when you want a static URL but still need to map onto a controller and action. It is also useful to default parameters to `false` where they are optional.

$format: When a parameter is not optional, the final format array can be used to provide additional routing. The format is a key/value array, where the key is the parameter name and the value is a regular expression that the parameter must pass to match the route. This is not for validation of the data, as that can lead to unfortunate default routing, but instead to allow you to differentiate between two similar but different routes.

Consider the routes /product/view/ProPHP and /product/view/1. How would you write a route to map these two routes separately to viewByName and viewById actions? The format parameter provides this ability. The first route would be the last added, as routes in the framework take a first-matched, first-used approach. This route is shown in Listing 16-15.

Listing 16-15. *Format-Matching Route*

```
$route1 = new Zend_Controller_Router_Route(
  '/product/view/:productId',
  array(
    'controller'=>'product',
    'action'=>'viewById'
  ),
  array(
    'name' => '/[0-9]+/';
  )
);
```

Because this route will not be matched if there is anything but a number as the productId, the logic will fall through to the next route if the productId is actually a name. Then to catch the viewByName-destined request, add a route like that shown in Listing 16-16.

Listing 16-16. *Routing for a Name*

```
$route2 = new Zend_Controller_Router_Route(
  '/product/view/:name',
  array(
    'controller'=>'product',
    'action'=>'viewByName',
    'name'=>false
  ),
);
```

You will notice that this catchall route does not have a format and defaults the parameter to a value of false. Because the first route took out all the IDs, anything left must be a name and gets routed to viewByName instead. If you wanted to add a format regular expression, anything that did not match would end up not being routed properly.

■**Caution** The order in which routes are added is important and will control which route is called. Adding these routes in a backward order in the example here would result in the nullification of the numeric route.

Managing Sessions

Most readers will be familiar with working with sessions through the session_start() and $_SESSION methodology. The Zend Framework introduces a new Zend_Session class that makes working with sessions easier.

Zend_Session will handle starting the session for you, so you no longer need to call session_start(). It also features a namespace option that allows you to separate all session variables based on the component that is working with them. This lets you keep your variable names simple, but still ensure that they won't conflict with other parts of your application. Finally, the framework offers the ability to set a session expiry in a number of "hops," defined as the number of times a session is started. For example, if you want to pass data from one page, redirect, and load it on the next, you can set it to a single hop, and the information will be removed from the session automatically after it is read on the next page.

Using Zend_Session is demonstrated in Listing 16-17.

Listing 16-17. *Using Zend_Session (SessionController.php)*

```
public function OneAction() {
  $session = new Zend_Session_Namespace('AUniqueNamespace');
  $session->setExpirationHops(1);
  $session->key = 'value';

  $this->getHelper('redirector')->goto('two');
}
```

```
public function TwoAction() {
  $session = new Zend_Session_Namespace('AUniqueNamespace');
  $this->view->key = $session->key;
}
```

If you visit your /session/one action, it will set the session variable and forward to the /session/two location. If you reload on /session/two, the value will then become undefined, as the number of expiry hops has been reached.

It is often desirable to regenerate session IDs regularly. This helps reduce the likelihood that a session could be hijacked by a third party. For this, the Zend_Session class provides a static regenerateId() method that will re-create a new session ID and associate it with the client. By adding the following line to your bootstrap file, you can ensure that every page load results in a new session ID being identified.:

```
Zend_Session::regenerateId();
```

The framework is smart enough not to regenerate the ID when a session does not exist, and calling this method will not start a session that was not otherwise started.

Tip Zend_Session also has the ability to allow you to write your own storage back-end. This can allow you to create back-ends that work off memcached or a database and may improve your ability to cluster your session-based applications. For more information, see the Zend Framework reference manual at http://framework.zend.com.

Sending Mail

Most reasonably complex web applications need to generate all kinds of e-mail, for example to send notice of a posting or a product order, or even just a daily report. The Zend Framework offers an extensive mail-sending API.

The simplest implementation is sending a plain-text e-mail to a recipient via the local mail relay. Listing 16-18 demonstrates sending a one-line e-mail message.

Listing 16-18. *Sending Plain-Text Mail via the Local Relay*

```
$mail = new Zend_Mail();
$mail->addTo('user@example.com', 'Firstname Lastname');
$mail->setFrom('noreply@example.com', 'example.com messaging system');
$mail->setSubject('The subject');
$mail->setBodyText('The content');
$mail->send();
```

The next step is to upgrade from plain text to HTML e-mail. You have two options:

- If you want to send a multipart/alternative method (both plain text and HTML), *add* a setBodyHtml($html) call.

- If you want a single-part, text/HTML message, *replace* the existing setBodyText() call.

If you do not have a local mail server/mail relay and want to send mail via the Simple Mail Transfer Protocol (SMTP), the framework provides an interface for this. Listing 16-19 shows an example.

Listing 16-19. *Sending Mail via SMTP*

```
$transport = new Zend_Mail_Transport_Smtp(
  'mail.domain.com',
    array(
      'auth' => 'login',
      'username' => 'myusername',
      'password' => 'password'
    )
);
```

The auth parameter controls how authentication information is passed to the SMTP server. It can be can be plain, login, or cram-md5. To integrate the transport with the previous example, replace the final send() call in Listing 16-18 with send($transport).

You can also use Zend_Mail_Transport_Sendmail when you need to pass additional options to your sendmail-compatible mailer. Adding an -f option is often critical for correct delivery headers when sending mail with a sendmail interface.

■Note See the Zend Framework reference manual at http://framework.zend.com for more details about the advanced functionality that is available for sending mail.

Creating PDF Files

The Zend_Pdf component allows you to create or modify a PDF file in PHP code. It supports various image formats, fonts, and some basic drawing.

Creating a PDF from scratch is simple. Just create a new instance of Zend_Pdf:

```
$pdf = new Zend_Pdf();
```

If you want to modify a PDF, simply use the static load function:

```
$pdf = Zend_Pdf::load('/path/to/load/file.pdf');
```

To save a PDF, either new or modified, call save():

```
$pdf->save('/path/to/save/file.pdf');
```

To return a string containing the binary data, such as for output directly to a browser, call render():

```
$pdf->render();
```

All PDF documents have pages. You can retrieve pages, create new ones, and draw shapes, fonts, and images to them. When you load an existing PDF, a collection property called pages is created and populated with Zend_Pdf_Page objects in a numerical index, with zero being page one.

Creating New PDF Pages

You can create new pages in two ways:

- Create a new instance of Zend_Pdf_Page. This creates a page that is independent of a document.

- Use the $pdf->newPage() method. This creates an attached page.

The distinction between an independent and attached page is internal. It relates to the sharing of resources like fonts between multiple pages in the same document.

The framework offers four default page sizes: SIZE_ A4, A4_LANDSCAPE, LETTER, and LETTER_LANDSCAPE. Listing 16-20 demonstrates adding a new page to a PDF instance.

Listing 16-20. *Adding a Page to a PDF Instance*

```
$pdf->pages[] = new Zend_Pdf_Page(Zend_Pdf_Page::SIZE_LETTER);

//Alternatively
$pdf->pages[] = $pdf->newPage(Zend_Pdf_Page::SIZE_LETTER);

//Make a copy of page 1 and add it to the PDF
$pdf->pages[] = new Zend_Pdf_Page($pdf->pages[0]);
```

If you wish to remove a page, simply unset the array index in the pages collection.

Drawing on PDF Pages

The next step is drawing on a page. With PDFs, drawing coordinates start from the bottom left as 0,0 instead of the top left, as web developers will expect. For drawing in the y axis on a PDF page, you need to think of plus as minus and zero as the bottom.

You can draw shapes and lines, as well as fonts and images. All the drawing systems work on a graphics style system, which allows you to set line and fill colors, widths, and patterns. Listing 16-21 shows some of the options for PDF drawing.

Listing 16-21. *Drawing to a PDF (in IndexController.php)*

```
public function pdfAction() {
  //Disable the view renderer
  $this->getHelper('ViewRenderer')->setNoRender();

  //Get the response object and set content type http header
  $response = $this->getResponse();
  $response->setHeader('Content-Type', 'application/pdf');
```

```
//Create a new PDF and add a letter-sized page
$pdf = new Zend_Pdf();
$pdf->pages[] = $pdf->newPage(Zend_Pdf_Page::SIZE_LETTER);

//Get a reference to that page
$page = $pdf->pages[0];

//Create a graphics style and set options
$style = new Zend_Pdf_Style();

//Set the font color to black
$style->setLineColor(new Zend_Pdf_Color_Rgb(0,0,0));

//Load a font and add it to the style at size 12
$font = Zend_Pdf_Font::fontWithName(Zend_Pdf_Font::FONT_TIMES);
$style->setFont($font, 12);

//Apply the style
$page->setStyle($style);

//Draw text offset 100 x 100 from the top left of the page
$page->drawText('Your first dynamic PDF', 100, ($page->getHeight()-100));

/*
   Make sure there are no previous echoes or prior information
   to wreck the PDF output. You need a clean output buffer
   when outputting binary data.
*/
$response->clearBody();

//Output the PDF
$response->setBody($pdf->render());
}
```

Drawing images is slightly more complicated. Because PDF is a print format, PDF documents work on a 1:72 inches:points ratio system, which translates 1:1 with standard screen-resolution graphics. However, for print-resolution graphics, you must take the dots per inch (DPI) of the image into account when drawing. Listing 16-22 shows how to correctly draw an image based on a set image DPI.

Listing 16-22. *Drawing Images at a Specific DPI*

```
//Create an image object
$imageFile = dirname(__FILE__) . '/test.jpg';
$image = Zend_Pdf_Resource_ImageFactory::factory($imageFile);
```

```
//Set calculation variables
$dpi = 300; //The image DPI is important
$pointsPerInch = 72; //PDF standard points per inch is 72

//Calculate image width and height in points
$imageWidth = ($image->getPixelWidth() / $dpi) * $pointsPerInch;
$imageHeight = ($image->getPixelHeight() / $dpi) * $pointsPerInch;

//Set the drawing offset
$x = 100;
$y = ($page->getHeight()-150); //Find page top and go down 150 points

//Draw the image to the PDF (x1,y1,x2,y2) [bottom left coordinate system]
$page->drawImage($image, $x, ($y - $imageHeight), ($x + $imageWidth), $y);
```

Integrating with Web Services

The Zend Framework ships with a number of model classes that make integration with various web services quick and painless. Currently, it includes built-in facilities for Akismet, Amazon, Flickr, and Yahoo APIs.

As an example, let's focus on the Akismet service, which is used to determine if a comment to a web site is spam or legitimate. You will need an API key from WordPress.com to use this web service. Once you have your key, instantiation is fairly simple:

```
$akismet = new Zend_Service_Akismet($apiKey, 'http://your.com');
```

After you have an Akismet object, you can check if something is spam, report spam that got past the filter, and report ham (good comments) that were falsely flagged as spam.

To check if a comment is spam, you need to pass a certain amount of data about your commenter to Akismet. This includes HTTP headers, like the browser's user-agent, IP address, and so on. This information is used with the filter to determine if a comment is spam. The more data you pass, the more reliable a spam prediction you will get back.

This information is in the form of a *key=>value* array. Table 16-3 shows the keys that Akismet supports.

Table 16-3. *Akismet Keys*

Key	Data	Required
user_agent	$_SERVER['HTTP_USER_AGENT']	Yes
user_ip	$_SERVER['REMOTE_ADDR']	Yes
blog	URL to your main page	No
comment_author	First Last	No
comment_author_email	user@example.com	No
comment_author_url	A URL for the commenter	No

Table 16-3. *Akismet Keys*

Key	Data	Required
comment_content	The actual comment data	No
comment_type	The type of data provided, one of 'comment', 'trackback', 'pingback', '', or any other string.	No
permalink	The URL of the form page, not the main page	No
referrer	$_SERVER['HTTP_REFERER']	No
*	Any other information you feel like providing	No

After you have built your array of data, you can call the isSpam() method:

```
if( ! $akismet->isSpam($data)) { //data is clean }
```

If the filter misses data, you can also call submitSpam($data) so that the filter can learn how to block similar requests in the future. If the filter catches something that it shouldn't and returns a false positive, you can call submitHam($data) to help the filter learn not to block that information in the future. These two methods do not return a value.

Just the Facts

This chapter introduced several of the more advanced facilities the Zend Framework has to offer. Here is a summary:

- Zend_Config allows you to manage configuration files.

- With Zend_View, you can set site-wide view variables.

- Zend_Registry allows you to share objects among components.

- With the ErrorController, you can create an error handler that dumps out extensive amounts of debugging information. You can integrate this error information with a custom Zend_Log log file.

- By using Zend_Cache, you can increase the performance of your applications by applying effective caching. You must be careful how you implement caching, as it can be dangerous.

- You can create an authentication system using Zend_Auth and integrate it with a login controller.

- With Zend_Json you can create a JSON-emitting action.

- Zend_Controller_Router_Rewrite allows you to apply custom routes to make your URLs shorter and more specific.

- You can create a Zend_Session_Namespace and expire data after a specific number of "hops." To prevent session hijacking, you can use regenerateId().

- You can send e-mail with Zend_Mail.

- Zend_PDF allows you to create PDFs.

- Using Zend_Service, you can integrate with various web services. For example, with Zend_Service_Akismet, you can check blog comments for spammers using the Akismet service.

In the next chapter, you will learn about the internals of the Zend Framework and how to create your own plug-ins, helpers, and modules. You will also take lessons learned about authentication from this chapter, and combine them with access control, so you should have a firm grasp on Zend_Auth before proceeding.

CHAPTER 17

The Zend Framework Applied

In the previous chapters, you've seen a glimpse of some of the Zend Framework components and how to use them in your applications. In this chapter, you will get a better understanding of the Zend Framework's architecture, dispatch cycle, and plug-in architecture. You will also learn how to create your own reusable libraries and integrate them with Zend_Loader.

Near the end of this chapter, you will apply your knowledge and create a fully integrated authorization and access control system. Finally, you will learn about the Zend_Layout component, which allows you to create a site with a common look and feel throughout. After reading this chapter, you should have a sound understanding of how the Zend Framework works.

Module and Model Setup

In the previous chapters, you have created Zend Framework sites that follow a single controller/action hierarchy. This is typically all that is needed, but if you have a complex site, a third level can be added. This third level is called a *module* and allows you to build URLs that follow the /module/controller/action format.

Conventional Modular Directory Structure

This URL structure and its underlying framework layout are commonly known as the *Conventional Modular Directory Structure*. When working with a modular setup, your directory structure may look like Listing 17-1, assuming you have the two modules default and admin.

Listing 17-1. *A Modular Directory Structure*

```
.
./application
./application/modules
./application/modules/default
./application/modules/default/controllers
./application/modules/default/views
./application/modules/default/views/scripts
./application/modules/default/views/scripts/index
./application/modules/default/views/scripts/error
./application/modules/default/models
./application/modules/admin
```

```
./application/modules/admin/views
./application/modules/admin/views/scripts
./application/modules/admin/views/scripts/index
./application/modules/admin/models
./application/modules/admin/controllers
./document_root
```

To enable modular use, in your bootstrap file, simply point the front controller to your `modules` directory:

```
$front->addModuleDirectory(APP_PATH . '/application/modules');
```

The index module is called `'default'`, and requests for / will forward to /default/index/ index. That's all there is to using a modular setup with the framework.

Model Libraries and Zend_Loader

You will notice in the conventional setup that modules do not share `models` directories. This can help separate out component logic and make modules easier to share among applications; however, it can also lead to duplication.

Many framework developers find it useful to keep a reusable component library and to package it in a similar way to how the framework itself is packaged. The advantage to this versus application-level models is that you can share your library among applications and between modules. The downside is that you cannot make assumptions about the application environment, such as registry objects or bootstrap settings. Any settings of this nature that you wish to bind must be explicitly passed when your library is bootstrapped.

To add a model library, start by creating a directory called `library` somewhere global, such as /usr/share/php/YourPrefix. This `library` directory is what will be passed as an include path to the bootstrapping process.

The next part is to follow the naming convention very closely. Class names should all start with a common prefix, and then follow with camel-cased words separated by underscores (_) where you want a directory separation. For example, `YourPrefix_Tax_Calculator` would reside in `library/YourPrefix/Tax/Calculator.php`. If you don't wish to use this naming convention, perhaps because you want to integrate an existing library, you will not be able to access your library though the standard `Zend_Loader` autoloading mechanism.

Listing 17-2 shows how to create a library model.

Listing 17-2. *Creating a Library Model (/usr/share/php/YourPrefix/library/YourPrefix/Tax/ Calculator.php)*

```php
<?php
class YourPrefix_Tax_Calculator {
  public static function calculate($a) {
    return $a * 1.07;
  }
}
```

Once you have a library function, you need to add your library directory to the included paths in the application's bootstrap. Listing 17-3 demonstrates how to modify your bootstrap file.

Listing 17-3. *Bootstrapping a Custom Library (index.php)*

```php
<?php
define('ZFW_VERSION','1.0.2');
define('ZFW_PREFIX','/usr/share/php/ZendFramework');
define('YourPrefix_PREFIX','/usr/share/php/YourPrefix');
define('APP_PATH', realpath(dirname(__FILE__) . '/../'));

$paths = array(
  APP_PATH,
  ZFW_PREFIX . DIRECTORY_SEPARATOR . 'ZendFramework-' . ZFW_VERSION . ➡
DIRECTORY_SEPARATOR . 'library',
  YourPrefix_PREFIX . DIRECTORY_SEPARATOR . 'library',
  get_include_path()
);
set_include_path(implode(PATH_SEPARATOR, $paths));

require_once('Zend/Loader.php');
Zend_Loader::registerAutoload();

$tax = YourPrefix_Tax_Calculator::calculate(1);
```

This approach depends entirely on you closely following the Zend Framework standard class naming conventions. If you wanted to load a class like TaxCalculator without prefixes or underscores, you would need to write your own loader. This can be achieved by either extending Zend_Loader or by registering an additional spl_autoload function, as explained in Chapter 9.

The Request Cycle

Now that you have an understanding of modules and models, it's time to get into the gears of the Zend Framework and truly understand the steps the framework goes through when routing and dispatching your application. Figure 17-1 illustrates the complete flow of a Zend Framework application.

The first thing you'll notice is that after a request is received, routing begins. (Ignore the plug-in and helper brokers for now; they will be discussed in the next sections.) Routing is the process by which the framework takes the requested URL and matches it to the list of rules specified to the router. These rules allow the router to dissect the URL into a module, controller, action, and any number of defined parameters. All of this information is then stored in the Zend_ Request object and passed to the dispatching cycle.

Dispatching runs as a loop, allowing various mechanisms to reset the application and send it back to dispatch start, such as to forward an unauthorized user to a login screen. The dispatch process is handled by Zend_Controller_Dispatcher_Standard by default, which will instantiate your action controller and result in a call to init(). Next, it calls dispatch() on the action controller.

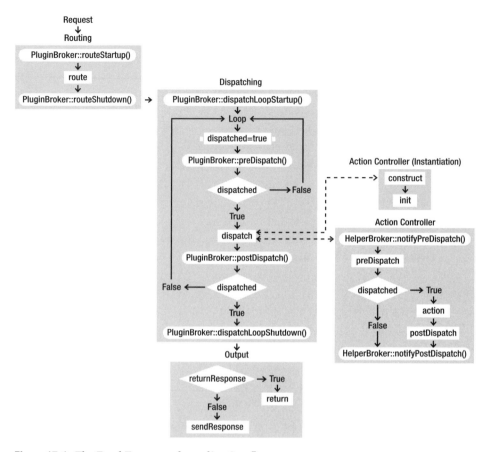

Figure 17-1. *The Zend Framework application flow*

Creating Plug-ins

As you may have noticed, the framework has a number of events that are fired on a class known as the PluginBroker, technically Zend_Controller_Plugin_Broker, which is a basic registration and notification class. These events allow you an opportunity to interact and disrupt the dispatching process. Typically, this disruption will be in the form of changing values in Zend_Request that will have effects down the road.

For example, a forwarding plug-in could set the controller and action request parameters at routeShutdown, and this would result in a totally different dispatch process. Another plug-in might append or remove content from the response body at dispatchLoopShutdown.

Writing your own plug-ins is fairly simple. First, all plug-ins must subclass Zend_Controller_Plugin_Abstract and may implement any of the PluginBroker methods shown in Figure 17-1. With the exception of dispatchLoopShutdown, all methods are passed the current Zend_Request object as their only parameter.

To get an idea of how this works, let's look at a simple example. Create a class in your library called YourPrefix_Controller_Plugin_Statistics, which will record each request's URI at routeStartup to a database. This plug-in is shown in Listing 17-4. This plug-in assumes that you have a table called stats with a column called uri.

Listing 17-4. *A Stats Logging Plug-in (YourPrefix_Controller_Plugin_Statistics)*

```
class YourPrefix_Controller_Plugin_Statistics extends
 Zend_Controller_Plugin_Abstract {
  public function routeStartup($request) {
    $uri = $request->getRequestUri();

    $dbconfig = array(
        'host' => 'localhost',
        'username' => 'user',
        'password' => 'password',
        'dbname' => 'demo'
    );

    $db = Zend_Db::factory('PDO_PGSQL', $dbconfig);

    $data = array(
      'uri' => $uri
    );

    $db->insert('stats', $data);

  }
}
```

To register the plug-in, you need to call `registerPlugin()` on the front controller:

```
$front->registerPlugin(new YourPrefix_Controller_Plugin_Statistics());
```

By using plug-ins, you can collect all sorts of information about your applications in a site-wide manner.

Creating Helpers

Helpers are classes that are designed to augment and integrate functionality for MVC components. The two main types of helpers are action helpers and view helpers.

Writing Action Helpers

Referring back to Figure 17-1, you will notice two more events that are called on the action `HelperBroker`: `notifyPreDispatch()` and `notifyPostDispatch()`. These two methods are translated to simply `preDispatch()` and `postDispatch()` for your action helpers and can give you the ability to work with action controller-specific events without registering a site-wide plug-in. This can enable load-on-use scenarios, which will be much more efficient if you have a large number of helpers.

The view renderer is a good example of built-in functionality that is deployed as an action helper. It uses the `Zend_Request::getActionName()` method as well as the `postDispatch()` event to determine and render a template specifically designed for an action.

The redirector helper doesn't implement either of the events, but uses its helper integration to provide a convenient interface for redirection.

If you wish to write your own action helper, simply subclass `Zend_Controller_Action_Helper_Abstract` and implement as many methods as you find useful. To register your action helper, call `addHelper()` on the `HelperBroker`:

```
Zend_Controller_Action_HelperBroker::addHelper(new YourHelperClass());
```

Alternatively, you can set a path where the `HelperBroker` can find all of your helpers with `addPath()`. For example, add all helper classes in the path that start with the class prefix `YourPrefix`:

```
Zend_Controller_Action_HelperBroker::addPath('/path/to/helpers', 'YourPrefix');
```

To access a helper from an action, call `$this->getHelper('YourHelperClass')` as you have done for previous examples involving `FlashMessenger`, `Redirector`, and `ViewRenderer`.

Writing View Helpers

You can also create your own view helpers, but you should take care to make sure that a helper is an appropriate choice. Ideally, view helpers should be used for repetitive tasks, and only as a way to gain convenience when working with common view data. They must not be used to circumvent processing in your actions, as that would significantly reduce the benefits of using an MVC framework and blur the line between what is a controller and what is a view.

To create your own view helper, create a class with a named prefix of `Zend_View_Helper_` and place it in `./views/helpers`. Listing 17-5 shows how to create a view helper that returns the current date.

Listing 17-5. *A Simple View Helper*

```php
<?php
class Zend_View_Helper_CurrentDate {
  public function currentDate() {
    return date("D M j");
  }
}
```

Inside a view, you can use your view helper by calling `$this->currentDate()`, as shown in Listing 17-6.

Listing 17-6. *A View Script Using a Custom Helper*

```html
<html>
  <body>
    <p>Current Date: <?php echo $this->currentDate(); ?></p>
  </body>
</html>
```

Implementing Access Control

Now that you have a handle on plug-ins, helpers, and the various parts of the request cycle, it's time to talk about access control. Zend_Acl is a powerful but decidedly confusing component that allows you to define the actions that a user is authorized to take on your web site.

While Zend_Acl can be used independently of plug-ins and helpers, it's far more powerful as a complete solution. It is a robust access system consisting of an inherited role assignment with both resource- and permission-level controls. Here, we'll look exclusively at resource-level control for simplicity.

For this example, you will create a basic subscription-area type web site where a specific controller is off-limits to guests but accessible to members. This controller will forward unauthenticated users to a login page. To achieve, this you will need a basic access control list (ACL), like the one shown in Listing 17-7.

Listing 17-7. *ACL Bootstrap (index.php)*

```
$acl = new Zend_Acl();

//Create guest role
$acl->addRole(new Zend_Acl_Role('guest'));

//Create members role, inheriting guest
$acl->addRole(new Zend_Acl_Role('member'), 'guest');

//Add a resource for the index controller
$acl->add(new Zend_Acl_Resource('index'));

//Add a resource for the articles controller
$acl->add(new Zend_Acl_Resource('articles'));

//Allow guest access to the index controller
$acl->allow('guest', 'index');

//Deny guest article access, but allow members
$acl->deny('guest', 'articles');
$acl->allow('member', 'articles');
```

Next, you will need to create an articles controller and a view for it, as shown in Listings 17-8 and 17-9.

Listing 17-8. *Articles Controller (ArticlesController.php.)*

```
<?php
class ArticlesController extends Zend_Controller_Action {
  public function indexAction() {}
}
```

Listing 17-9. *ArticlesController View (/view/scripts./articles/index.phtml)*

```
This is secret
```

Now for the fun part. In your library, create a plug-in called YourPrefix_Controller_Plugin_
Security and place it in /usr/share/php/YourPrefix/library/YourPrefix/Controller/Plugin/
Security.php. This plug-in should look like Listing 17-10.

Listing 17-10. *An ACL and Auth Combined Plug-in*

```
class YourPrefix_Controller_Plugin_Security
      extends Zend_Controller_Plugin_Abstract
{

  protected $_acl;

  //Take the bootstrapped ACL at plugin registration
  public function __construct($acl) {
    $this->_acl = $acl;
  }

  //Hook into the dispatchLoopStartup event
  public function dispatchLoopStartup($request) {

    //Get an instance of Zend_Auth and set the default role to guest.
    $auth = Zend_Auth::getInstance();
    $role = 'guest';

    //If the user is logged in, get their role identifier from db row
    if($auth->hasIdentity()) {
      $role = $auth->getIdentity()->role;
    }

    //The resource name is the controller name
    $resource = $request->getControllerName();

    //If the controller isn't under ACL, ignore access control
    if($this->_acl->has($resource)) {

      //Check role has access to resource
      if( ! $this->_acl->isAllowed($role, $resource) ) {
        //No access

        //Back up the original request URI
        $session = new Zend_Session_Namespace('ACLSecurity');
        $session->originalRequestUri = $request->getRequestUri();
```

```
        //Overwrite the controller and action that the dispatch will use
        $request->setControllerName('index');
        $request->setActionName('login');
      }
      // else { access is ok, dispatch normally }
    }
  }
}
```

The next step is to integrate the authorization example from the previous chapter. To do this, add a role column to the database users table and set the value for your role column to 'member'. Then locate this line in your loginAction in your IndexController.php file (Listing 16-10):

```
$this->getHelper('redirector')->goto('index','index');
```

and change it to this:

```
//Try to forward the user back where they were trying to get to
$session = new Zend_Session_Namespace('ACLSecurity');
if(isset($session->originalRequestUri)) {
  $this->getHelper('redirector')
       ->gotoUrl($session->originalRequestUri);
} else {
  $this->getHelper('redirector')->goto('index','index');
}
```

This will make it so that when redirected users successfully log in, they will be taken to the original URL they were trying to access.

Finally, register the plug-in with the front controller:

```
$front->registerPlugin(new YourPrefix_Controller_Plugin_Security($acl));
```

Now try to visit your /articles controller. You should be forwarded to /index/login. Once successfully logged in, you will be sent back to /articles. You now have a basic ACL and authentication integrated plug-in solution.

Using a Two-Step View

Zend_Layout serves to fulfill the common requirement of creating sites where each page has a similar look and feel, often known as a site-wide template, two-step view, or a layout.

The concept of a layout is to avoid having to use prepended and postpended templates. Instead, you use Zend_View_Helper_Placeholder to specify where content created by the controller-action dispatch should be placed in the final output. This allows you to use a layout file that represents the structure of the final page, including both <html> and </html> in the same file.

Creating a Master Layout

In order to use the Zend_Layout component, you need to add the code shown in Listing 17-11 to your bootstrap file.

Listing 17-11. *Bootstrapping Zend_Layout (in index.php)*

```
Zend_Layout::startMvc(
            array(
              'layoutPath' => APP_PATH . '/application/layouts/',
              'layout'     => 'index'
            )
          );
```

This bootstrap process defines a location for the layout script files, as well as the name of the default layout. In this case, to demonstrate the option, you've overridden the default name, layout, with index.

Next, create the layout file, index.phtml, as shown in Listing 17-12.

Listing 17-12. *Master Layout (./application/layouts/index.phtml)*

```
<html>
  <body>
    <?php echo $this->layout()->content; ?>
  </body>
</html>
```

When Zend_Layout is active, all of the output from your actions will be placed into the Zend_Layout->content placeholder. This placeholder can be accessed via the layout helper ($this->layout()), as shown in Listing 17-12.

At the controller and action levels, you can choose alternative layouts by calling setLayout() either from init() or within an action:

```
$this->_helper->layout()->setLayout('alternative');
```

To disable layouts for an action, call disableLayout():

```
$this->_helper->layout()->disableLayout();
```

Using Placeholders

In addition to storing the output of actions, placeholders can be used to place content in predefined locations within the layout. A common use is to place an item in a menu, but to configure it from within a view script.

To create a layout that has a menu system, you would define a placeholder under the Zend_Layout name using a custom key 'menu'. Listing 17-13 demonstrates how to create this as a basic layout template.

Listing 17-13. *A Layout Script with an Included Conditional Placeholder*

```
<html>
  <body>
    <?php
      //Check if a menu placeholder exists
      if($this->placeholder('Zend_Layout')->offsetExists('menu')) {
        //Output the placeholders menu key content
        echo $this->placeholder('Zend_Layout')->menu;
      }
    ?>
    <?php echo $this->placeholder('Zend_Layout')->content; ?>
  </body>
</html>
```

Note In Listing 17-12, you used $this->layout()->content instead of $this->placeholder ('Zend_Layout')->content to access the layout content placeholder. The former form is simply a convenience method for the latter form.

When you want to place a menu item into this placeholder, from the context of a view script, you can simply capture some content, as shown in Listing 17-14.

Listing 17-14. *Capturing Output to a Placeholder (View Context)*

```
<?php
  $this->placeholder('Zend_Layout')
      ->captureStart('APPEND', 'menu');
?>
<li><a href="...">New Menu Item</a></li>
<?php $this->placeholder('Zend_Layout')->captureEnd(); ?>
```

This content will then be placed in the proper location in the document when the layout is rendered. This will allow you to create some advanced view effects that inject code into different sections of the document.

Tip The Zend Framework developers currently have plans for other helpers that build on the placeholder concept. These helpers will be called headScript, headTitle, headLink, and so on, and will be specialized for a specific common addition. As always, for the latest information, check out the Zend Framework manual.

Just the Facts

In this chapter, you learned about the Zend Framework's internal operation, and how to create modules, model libraries, plug-ins, helpers, and layouts.

A Conventional Modular Directory Structure allows you to use modules. You can also create a custom component library and add this library to your bootstrap so the framework can automatically load your classes.

The framework request cycle consists of various routing and dispatching events. You can create custom controller plug-ins, action helpers, and view helpers.

The Zend_Layout component allows you to create a site with a common look and feel.

This completes the Zend Framework part of this book. To continue learning about the Zend Framework, read the framework reference documentation and the mailing list archives. If you are interested in developing with the Zend Framework, you can get assistance at #zftalk on irc.freenode.net or from the official mailing lists at http://framework.zend.com.

PART 5

###

Web 2.0

CHAPTER 18

■■■

Ajax and JSON

Ajax, short for Asynchronous JavaScript and XML, is a combination of technologies, typically JavaScript and XML. It is used to create "rich applications" that can retrieve and submit data through their interface without reloading the web page.

The Ajax term is somewhat controversial. The concept of Ajax has been around for a very long time, but the term is a recent invention and scorned by some JavaScript developers. They continue to call Ajax XHR, short for `XmlHttpRequest`, which is the name of the core JavaScript object that makes Ajax applications run.

In addition to the XHR object, Ajax applications will also typically use the browser Document Object Model (DOM) to access HTML and update the content on the page. It is this binding between the DOM and HTML that makes the Ajax technique so powerful. This technique can be used to create partially updating web sites that are more responsive than a complete page reload.

The XHR component is a way to send data. Usually, this data is encoded in XML; however, there is no hard requirement that XML be used to encode data for transport. Because of this flexibility and the relative weight of processing XML, most applications would benefit from a simpler data format, and thus JSON was packaged.

JSON, short for JavaScript Object Notation, is a data-encoding format that is based on JavaScript itself. In fact, JSON datagrams can be evaluated as if they were code using the `eval()` function, and as such, require almost no processing on the client side to decode. This means that on the client side, you do not need to engage in parsing XML documents, and this may save you significant programming time and some CPU cycles on the client machine.

In this chapter, you will learn about Ajax, JSON, and the PHP JSON extension. You will also learn how to interact with JSON from the Zend Framework classes. Finally, you will create a couple of sample projects that demonstrate `GET` and `POST` processing using these techniques.

JSON and PHP

The detail of the JSON encoding is not particularly important to PHP developers, as most of your interaction with JSON will be calling functions to encode and decode data in JSON format. PHP's responsibility in the Ajax/JSON relationship is to understand JSON datagrams posted to it and return JSON-encoded data back to the browser. What is important to know is that JSON is a replacement for XML in Ajax applications.

> **■Note** If you wish to learn more about the JSON encoding itself, see the excellent online manual at
> `http://www.json.org`.

Unfortunately, one of the biggest issues when working with JSON in PHP is that JavaScript and PHP do not have directly compatible data types. JavaScript contains two collection types: objects that are key/value pair collections and are analogous to an associative array in PHP, and arrays that are strictly lists and are analogous to a numerically indexed array in PHP.

Any JSON implementation must include at least two methods: one to serialize a parameter into a JSON-encoded string, and another to undo this operation and return a JSON string to a variable. You can think of JSON encoding as a type of serialization.

The following sections introduce two alternative ways of using JSON with PHP:

- The JSON PECL extension

- The Zend Framework

Json.org publishes the JSON parser script (`json.js`). You should download this now from `http://www.json.org/json.js`, as most JSON applications require it to operate.

> **■Tip** JavaScript minification can significantly reduce the size of the `json.js` library. See `http://www.json.org`.

The JSON Extension

The JSON PECL extension is enabled by default and ships with PHP 5.2 and later. This extension provides the serialization functions required to convert PHP data types into JSON data:

`string json_encode(mixed $value)`: This method encodes any variable type except a resource and produces a JSON-encoded string representation of the data.

`mixed json_decode(string $json, bool $associative)`: This method decodes a JSON-encoded value into a PHP value. JSON cannot represent an associative array as anything other than an object, and thus the `bool $associative` parameter can be used to cast the object back into an associative array. This function is not an exact reversal of `json_encode` and will decode only an array or object. To decode a simple value, it should first be encoded wrapped in an array. If you try to decode a value that does not contain an array or an object, you will see a return value of null.

> **■Tip** You can convert an already encoded JSON basic data type to an array by padding the string with square brackets: `$var = '['. $var .']'; `.

The usage of these functions is straightforward, as demonstrated in Listing 18-1.

Listing 18-1. *JSON Encoding/Decoding*

```
$original = array('key'=>'value', 'key2'=>'value2');
$json = json_encode($original);
$restored = json_decode($json, true);

print_r($original);
print "\n" . $json ."\n\n";
print_r($restored);
```

```
Array
(
    [key] => value
    [key2] => value2
)

{"key":"value","key2":"value2"}

Array
(
    [key] => value
    [key2] => value2
)
```

JSON in the Zend Framework

The Zend Framework provides a wrapper to the JSON extension, but also contains a fallback for systems that do not have the JSON extension enabled (typically installations older than PHP 5.2).

The functionality for the Zend Framework JSON system is provided through the Zend_Json class and the following methods:

string Zend_Json::encode(mixed $value): This method is an alias of json_encode and provides the same functionality.

mixed Zend_Json::decode(string $json [, int $decodeType = Zend_Json::TYPE_ARRAY]): Unlike the json_decode function, the default mechanism for Zend_Json is to try to turn an object into an associative array. You can pass the constant Zend_Json::TYPE_OBJECT as the $decodeType parameter to override this behavior and return an object instead of an associative array.

See Listing 16-12 in Chapter 16 for an example of using Zend_Json.

JSON and JavaScript

To work with Ajax, JSON, and PHP, you need to know a little about JavaScript. For a moment, let's focus on some useful and required JavaScript libraries and functions.

If you haven't done so already, download http://www.json.org/json.js now. You will need this script to use the examples in this chapter. This script provides the client-side encoding functions and an alternative parser to eval() that will throw exceptions, rather than client JavaScript errors, if it gets bad data. This script provides two key methods that enhance the JavaScript language itself:

string type.toJSONString(): This method applies to most of the built-in JavaScript types. It will return a JSON-encoded string representing the data in the type. Listing 18-2 demonstrates its use.

mixed string.parseJSON(filter): This method restores a JSON-encoded string to a JavaScript structure and will throw an exception if there is a problem decoding the data. Building on Listing 18-2, Listing 18-3 demonstrates how to decode a JSON-encoded value.

Listing 18-2. *JavaScript JSON Encoding*

```
<html>
  <head>
    <script src="json.js" type="text/javascript"></script>
    <script type="text/javascript">
      function showJsonData() {
        original = new Array(0, 1, 2, 3);

        //Encode original in JSON returning a string.
        json = original.toJSONString();

        div = document.getElementById("jsonData");
        div.innerHTML = json;
      }
    </script>
  </head>
  <body>
    <a href="#" onclick="showJsonData()">Show JSON Data</a>
    <div id="jsonData"></div>
  </body>
</html>
```

```
[0,1,2,3]
```

■**Caution** If in the development of your site you have used JavaScript `for..in` loops to analyze the properties of objects, be sure that you've also checked for the proper ownership. All `for..in` loops should contain an `object.hasOwnProperty()` check so that inherited properties are not unexpectedly encountered.

Listing 18-3. *Parsing JSON in JavaScript*

```
<html>
  <head>
    <script src="json.js" type="text/javascript"></script>
    <script type="text/javascript">
      function showJsonData() {
        original = new Array('first', 'second', 'third');
        json = original.toJSONString();
        div = document.getElementById("jsonData");

        //Decode JSON, and set div.innerHTML
        //to the first element in the array
        div.innerHTML = json.parseJSON()[0];
      }
    </script>
  </head>
  <body>
    <a href="#" onclick="showJsonData()">Show JSON Data</a>
    <div id="jsonData"></div>
  </body>
</html>
```

```
first
```

The optional `filter` parameter of `parseJSON()` allows you to create a function that will filter the resulting key/value pairs and apply some sort of translation to the value. Listing 18-4 shows an example of using the optional `filter` parameter to convert the value to a JavaScript date object, where the key is equal to `'date'`.

Listing 18-4. *Using the parseJSON filter Parameter*

```
<html>
  <head>
    <script src="json.js" type="text/javascript"></script>
    <script type="text/javascript">
      function convertDates(key, value) {
```

```
      if(key == "date") {
        return new Date(value);
      } else {
        return value;
      }
    }

  function showJsonData() {
    //Create an object
    original = {'date':'01/01/2007', 'data':'some data'};
    json = original.toJSONString();
    div = document.getElementById("jsonData");
    restored = json.parseJSON(convertDates);
    div.innerHTML = restored['date'].toString();
  }
  </script>
</head>
<body>
  <a href="#" onclick="showJsonData()">Show JSON Data</a>
  <div id="jsonData"></div>
</body>
</html>
```

Mon Jan 1 00:00:00 MST 2007

The XMLHttpRequest Object

The next important part of JavaScript's role in JSON communication is the XMLHttpRequest (XHR) object. This is the object that allows you to communicate JSON data to PHP. The code in Listing 18-5 shows a safe way of getting a cross-browser instance of the XHR object.

Listing 18-5. *Cross-Browser XHR Retrieval*

```
function getXHR() {
  var req;
  if (window.XMLHttpRequest) {
    req = new XMLHttpRequest();
  } else if (window.ActiveXObject) {
    req = new ActiveXObject("Microsoft.XMLHTTP");
  }
  return req;
}
```

The reason for this extra complexity is that older versions of Internet Explorer, while fully supporting XHR, do so through an ActiveX object, rather than with native functionality as occurs in all modern browsers. The script in Listing 18-5 will try the modern route first and will fall back to the ActiveX method if the native XHR object is not available.

Tables 18-1 and 18-2 describe the properties and methods available to the XHR object.

Table 18-1. *XmlHttpRequest Methods*

Method	Description
abort()	Cancels an in-progress request.
getAllResponseHeaders()	Gets all the response headers as a string.
getResponseHeader(name)	Gets a specific header by name.
open(method, url [, async, user, pass])	Creates a new HTTP connection. The method may be any valid request type like GET or POST. The URL should be a fully qualified address. The async method controls whether the send() method will block (wait for data to come back from the server) or return immediately. The user and pass parameters are used if the server resource requires HTTP authentication.
send(content)	Invokes the request to the server. It uses the settings provided to open() and will either return immediately or wait for content to be received from the server based on the open() method's async parameter. The content parameter is used with certain types of requests, like POST to send data to the server.
setRequestHeader(name, value)	Sets a request header by name and value.

Table 18-2. *XmlHttpRequest Properties*

Property	Description
readyState	Indicates the current state of the XHR object. It returns a numeric representation of the state, where 0 = uninitialized, 1 = open, 2 = sent, 3 = receiving, 4 = loaded. This property is most commonly used when working asynchronously. In this case, you should check that readyState equals 4 when the onreadystatechange event fires. The onreadystatechange event is fired whenever there is a change to the readystate property of the object. Most commonly, this is used to discover when the response from the server is complete. Check the readyState property when the onreadystatechange event fires to determine the new state.
responseText	The response from the server as a string.
responseXML	The response from the server represented as a DOM XML object.
status	The HTTP status code of the response (200, 404, and so on).
statusText	A string representation of the status code ('OK', 'NOT FOUND', and so on).

Some Ajax Projects

To get the most from the previous theory, you'll want to create a couple of simple applications. The following two examples demonstrate common GET and POST requests.

GET Requests

When dealing with client/server communications, an effective way to test your data transport and the interaction of all the components is to create a really simple time-fetch application. This application will send out a request whenever a link is clicked, and the XHR object will get a response from the server indicating the current server time.

This example has two key components: a client-side JavaScript script and a server-side PHP script. The client-side XHR object is restricted to operating within a single domain. This means an XHR request may contact only the exact same domain as the HTML file that included the script, so creating an HTML file on your desktop that points to your PHP-enabled web server simply won't work. Both the open() URL and the client HTML file must be served from the *exact* same domain.

Start by creating a PHP script on your server, as shown in Listing 18-6.

Listing 18-6. *A PHP Time Ping-Pong (time.php)*

```php
<?php
echo json_encode(microtime(true));
```

Next, create a client-side script, following Listing 18-7 as a guide.

Listing 18-7. *Client-Side Ajax (ajax.htm)*

```html
<html>
  <head>
    <script src="json.js" type="text/javascript"></script>
    <script type="text/javascript">

      function getXHR() {
        var req;
        if (window.XMLHttpRequest) {
          req = new XMLHttpRequest();
        } else if (window.ActiveXObject) {
          req = new ActiveXObject("Microsoft.XMLHTTP");
        }
        return req;
      }

      function getServerTime() {
        xhr = getXHR();
        rand = Math.random(1);
```

```
        //CHANGE THIS LINE - DOMAINS MUST MATCH!
        url = "http://example.com/time.php?id="+ rand;

        xhr.open("GET", url, false);
        xhr.send();
        json = xhr.responseText;
        time = json.parseJSON();
        div = document.getElementById("jsonData");
        div.innerHTML = time;
      }
    </script>
  </head>
  <body>
    <a href="#" onclick="getServerTime()">Get Server Time</a>
    <div id="jsonData"></div>
  </body>
<html>
```

■**Note** In the client-side script in Listing 18-7, you will see that there is an added `id=` `get` parameter set to a randomized number. This is to avoid HTTP caching of the Ajax URL. You could also achieve the same result by sending the correct cache headers with the response to prevent caching of the open URL.

In this script, you get a reference to the XHR object; set the `open()` parameters `'GET'`, `url`, and synchronous (blocking) mode; and then call `send()` to get the data. When the `send()` call returns, the `responseText` property will be ready. The JSON-encoded data can be retrieved from this property, decoded, and turned back into a real value. Once the real value is obtained, it is written to the screen.

Click the hyperlink a few times. You should get a different time (in microseconds) returned with each click.

■**Caution** If you received an access denied client-side error, the most likely reason is that the domain used to load the `ajax.htm` script is not the exact same as is set in the `open()` URL parameter. Even the difference between `http://www.example.com` and `http://example.com` will result in an access denied error, so take care to make sure they both match exactly.

POST Requests

POST requests in Ajax are somewhat more complicated that GET requests, as they require you to set the proper form HTTP header. To demonstrate their use, you will create a search box that will list suggestions from an array of server-side data. The recipe for this application is to use

JavaScript to *listen* on an input box for a keyup event to be fired. When the event is fired, the JavaScript communicates the data currently in the search box to the PHP script on the server.

You will use asynchronous mode and the XmlHttpRequest.onreadystatechange event to wait for the server's response. If another key is typed while a request is pending, XmlHttpRequest.abort() will be called and a new request created.

Listings 18-8 and 18-9 show how to create this POST-based Ajax application, which consists of the suggest.htm and suggest.php files.

Listing 18-8. *The POST Client Side (suggest.htm)*

```
<html>
  <head>
    <script src="json.js" type="text/javascript"></script>
    <script type="text/javascript">

      //Create a global variable for the XHR object
      var xhr;

      function getXHR() {
        var req;
        if (window.XMLHttpRequest) {
          req = new XMLHttpRequest();
        } else if (window.ActiveXObject) {
          req = new ActiveXObject("Microsoft.XMLHTTP");
        }
        return req;
      }

      function suggest() {

        //If there already is an outstanding
        //XHR request going on, abort it.
        if(xhr && xhr.readyState != 0) {
          xhr.abort();
        }

        xhr = getXHR();

        //Set up an asynchronous POST (CHANGE ME)
        xhr.open("POST","http://example.com/suggest.php",true);

        //Read the search value
        searchValue = document.getElementById("search").value;

        //URL encode the data
        data = "search="+encodeURIComponent(searchValue);
```

```
      //Define the function that will receive
      //notifications about state changes.
      xhr.onreadystatechange = readyStateChange;

      //Set the request header so that PHP
      //knows that this is a form submission
      xhr.setRequestHeader
        ("Content-type", "application/x-www-form-urlencoded");

      //Post the data to the server
      xhr.send(data);
    }

  function readyStateChange() {
    //State 4 means the data is ready
    if(xhr.readyState == 4) {

      //Check if the server sent any data and the request was 200 ok
      if(xhr.responseText && xhr.status == 200) {

        json = xhr.responseText;

        //Parse the server response, creating a JS array.
        try {
          suggestionArr = json.parseJSON();
        } catch (e) {
          //Problem with/parsing JSON data.
        }

        //Create some HTML
        tmpHtml="";
        for(i=0, len = suggestionArr.length; i < len; i++) {
          tmpHtml += suggestionArr[i] + "<br />";
        }

        div = document.getElementById("suggestions");
        div.innerHTML = tmpHtml;
      } //else blank response, 404 request etc.
    }
  }

    </script>
  </head>
  <body>
    <input id="search" type="text" onkeyup="suggest()" />
    <div id="suggestions"></div>
  </body>
</html>
```

Listing 18-9. *The Server-Side Code (suggest.php)*

```php
<?php
$arr = array(
        'Alpha','Bravo','Charlie','Delta','Echo',
        'Foxtrot','Golf','Hotel','India','Juliett',
        'Kilo','Lima','Mike','November','Oscar',
        'Papa','Quebec','Romeo','Sierra','Tango',
        'Uniform','Victor','Whiskey','X-ray','Yankee',
        'Zulu'
    );
$search = strtolower($_POST['search']);

$hits = array();

if(!empty($search)) {
  foreach($arr as $name) {
    if(strpos(strtolower($name), $search) === 0) {
      $hits[] = $name;
    }
  }
}

echo json_encode($hits);
```

If you type a character into the resulting input box, you should see that any matching entry will be shown. Using the same technique, you could show the results of an SQL query, such as a username search or an account number lookup.

Just the Facts

In this chapter, you learned about Ajax and JSON. JSON interaction with PHP can be problematic because JavaScript and PHP do not share identical data types, and what is called an associative array in PHP is actually an object in JavaScript.

The examples in this chapter demonstrated how to use the JSON implementation from Json.org (json.js). In the GET application, you used synchronous communications and received the current server time through an Ajax request in response to clicking a hyperlink. In the POST application, you used asynchronous communications and created an input box that gives suggestions from a list of server-side data as you type.

CHAPTER 19

■■■

Introduction to Web Services with SOAP

Web services allow you to share data between server-to-server systems. They represent automated, machine-readable interactions between machines and typically operate using HTTP.

The Web Services Description Language (WSDL) describes the abilities of the web service. The SOAP protocol encodes and encapsulates the data you wish to share. The purpose of SOAP is to exchange packets of data, which are called *envelopes*, using a common format that is universally understood. This universal understanding is critical to web services, as they may be programmed in vastly different programming languages that have very different expectations and methodologies.

In this chapter, you will learn the basics of WSDL and SOAP, as well as how to create a web service using the PHP SOAP extension. At the end of the chapter, you will connect to Amazon.com and find out some information about this book using the Amazon Web Services API.

Introduction to the PHP Web Services Architecture

The PHP web services architecture has a few key components. First, in PHP, SOAP functionality is provided by an extension. If you already have this extension, you'll find soap listed in your phpinfo() results. If the SOAP extension is not listed, you will need to compile it in, using the -enable-soap configuration argument when building PHP.

The SOAP extension provides two key classes, SoapClient and SoapServer, which form the basis of the web services programming interface for PHP. You'll be introduced to their syntax later in this chapter.

SOAP clients and servers both need to know which methods a web service will expose. To describe these methods, you use a description language called WSDL. This is an XML-based markup language, which you will place in a service WSDL file. Then you will provide this file to both your SOAP server and clients. The purpose of the WSDL file is to provide some basic information about the calling context of your methods, such as the location, method name, parameters, and return value.

SOAP is used to send data between the client and server. Unlike with WSDL, you are not responsible for writing SOAP markup yourself, as it will be generated and interpreted for you by the SOAP extension. However, it is important to be able to understand SOAP, because any problem in the automatic encoding of the SOAP data can result in frustrating and time-consuming errors. In developing any reasonably complex web service, you are likely to experience a problem at least once, so you will want to know how your data should look in encoded form.

Introduction to WSDL

WSDL, an XML format, has its own set of elements and attributes. The WSDL file for your PHP applications will provide information about the service, including the URL of your service, the XML namespace, which methods and parameters are exposed, and the return values you expect to receive.

WSDL Terminology

WSDL documents are no more difficult to write than HTML documents; they just follow a different syntax that tends to be a little less concise. WSDL is designed to be really extensible, so a lot of the concepts will seem to overlap, but each does actually have a slightly different purpose. The following are some WSDL terms that you can expect to encounter when you're working with web services. Just as you know what divs and spans are, you'll want to recognize these WSDL equivalents of common tags.

Types: These represent a format of data, like a string or an integer, or even an object with properties. There are built-in types for most things like integers and strings, and these are inherited from the XML Schema Definition (XSD) language. In the next chapter, you will learn how to create complex types that represent custom objects. In this chapter, we'll stick with the standard, simple data types.

Messages: These provide a definition, or collection, of data that will be transferred. Think of a message as a representation of a parameter list and a description of the return values for a function. There are generally two messages for every method: a request and response message. The request message will define the parameters for the method, and the response message will define what data is returned. Due to the behavior of some SOAP implementations, the name attribute for messages should always end in Request or Response. The names of the parameters and return values in a message are called *parts*.

Operations: These are a way of describing methods. Each operation will define an input message for its parameters list and an output message for its return values. The key information provided by an operation element is a name and what input and output messages are associated with the method. In WSDL jargon, a method is called an *operation* and is sometimes referred to as an *action*.

Port types: These are a way of grouping a set of operations. This step allows you to define one WSDL file that might have operations implemented on multiple servers. A port-type collection is the list of operations that will be implemented on one endpoint URL.

Bindings: These define how the port type will communicate data—in your case, using the SOAP-encoding method and using Remote Procedure Call (RPC) as the style of messaging. Other types of encodings and styles are available, but we won't cover them here.

Port: This combines a binding with an endpoint and provides the URL where the service can be located. The port is the actual fully qualified URL to the PHP script that will host your SOAP server.

Service: This defines a collection of ports that make up your web service.

A WSDL File

Ignoring any purpose, which will come later, let's look at a WSDL file created for a method called demo that takes exactly one string parameter and returns exactly one string value, running on http://localhost/service.php. Listing 19-1 shows this WSDL file.

■**Note** URIs in WSDL files are case-sensitive. http://localhost/demo is not the same as http://localhost/Demo.

Listing 19-1. *A Sample WDSL File (demo.wsdl)*

```
<?xml version ="1.0" encoding ="UTF-8" ?>
<definitions name="demo"
  targetNamespace="http://localhost/demo"
  xmlns:tns="http://localhost/demo"
  xmlns:soap="http://schemas.xmlsoap.org/wsdl/soap/"
  xmlns:soapenc="http://schemas.xmlsoap.org/soap/encoding/"
  xmlns:wsdl="http://schemas.xmlsoap.org/wsdl/"
  xmlns:xsd="http://www.w3.org/2001/XMLSchema"
  xmlns="http://schemas.xmlsoap.org/wsdl/">

  <message name="DemoRequest">
    <part name="param1" type="xsd:string" />
  </message>

  <message name="DemoResponse">
    <part name="Result" type="xsd:string" />
  </message>

  <portType name="DemoPortType">
    <operation name="Demo">
      <input message="tns:DemoRequest" />
      <output message="tns:DemoResponse" />
    </operation>
  </portType>

  <binding name="DemoBinding" type="tns:DemoPortType">
    <soap:binding style="rpc" transport="http://schemas.xmlsoap.org/soap/http" />
    <operation name="Demo">
```

```
        <soap:operation soapAction="http://localhost/Demo" />
        <input>
          <soap:body use="encoded" namespace="http://localhost/demo"
            encodingStyle="http://schemas.xmlsoap.org/soap/encoding/" />
        </input>
        <output>
        <soap:body use="encoded" namespace="http://localhost/demo"
          encodingStyle="http://schemas.xmlsoap.org/soap/encoding/" />
        </output>
      </operation>
    </binding>

    <service name="DemoService">
      <port name="DemoPort" binding="DemoBinding">
        <soap:address location="http://localhost/service.php" />
      </port>
    </service>
</definitions>
```

The `definitions` tag defines a number of standard namespaces. This is where the SOAP encoding, WSDL definitions, and XSD are referenced. The only two that you need to customize are `targetNamespace` and `xmlns:tns`. The `targetNamespace` attribute means that all the child elements will be prefixed with the provided namespace. The `xmlns:tns` attribute will define a URI for this namespace to the prefix `tns`. The rest of the prefixes are standard and can be reused for each WSDL file, just as you would put a `DOCTYPE` declaration in an HTML document.

Next, the file defines two messages, providing "parts" for each that will represent the input and return parameters. Remember that it is important that message names end in `Request` or `Response`, as some SOAP implementations require this naming convention to operate correctly. The part's entries each require a data type, which can be any valid XSD type. There are literally dozens of XSD types, but for now, it is probably best to stick to the following list: `xsd:int`, `xsd:string`, `xsd:boolean`, `xsd:float`, and `xsd:date`.

Next, the file adds a port type and provides a number of operations to define the methods exposed by the service. The `input` and `output` attributes associate messages with the operation, and provide the parameter and return value lists.

After that, the code creates a binding between SOAP, RPC, and the port. This is largely a technicality, so just follow the format-replacing information where it makes sense. What this step actually does is define that you will be using the RPC style and encoding data using SOAP. The only thing to watch for is the `soapAction` attribute, which needs to be set to a unique URI. Usually, this URI is the value for `xmlns:tns` plus the name of the operation.

Finally, the `service` element puts it all together into a web server location. Unlike the namespace URIs, which are just unique information and not actual web resources, the address here must be the URL to the physical PHP file that will host your `SoapServer`.

■**Note** For detailed information about WSDL, refer to the W3C note at `http://www.w3.org/TR/wsdl`.

Introduction to SOAP

SOAP is used to exchange data between the web service and its clients. It encodes both the data and the request. The easiest way to understand SOAP is by looking at an example of how it is generated.

The WSDL file in Listing 19-1 defines an operation called Demo, which has one input parameter that takes a string. If you were to call that method, the SOAP-formatted request would look like Listing 19-2.

Listing 19-2. *An Encoded SOAP Request*

```
<?xml version="1.0" encoding="UTF-8"?>
<SOAP-ENV:Envelope
  xmlns:SOAP-ENV=http://schemas.xmlsoap.org/soap/envelope/
  xmlns:ns1="http://localhost/demo"
  xmlns:xsd="http://www.w3.org/2001/XMLSchema"
  xmlns:xsi="http://www.w3.org/2001/XMLSchema-instance"
  xmlns:SOAP-ENC="http://schemas.xmlsoap.org/soap/encoding/"
  SOAP-ENV:encodingStyle="http://schemas.xmlsoap.org/soap/encoding/"
>
  <SOAP-ENV:Body>
    <ns1:Demo>
      <param1 xsi:type="xsd:string">abcdefg</param1>
    </ns1:Demo>
  </SOAP-ENV:Body>
</SOAP-ENV:Envelope>
```

This message contains a SOAP envelope, which encapsulates the method call. The Envelope element assigns the ns1 prefix to your targetNamespace in order to give it a distinct namespace. In the body, it will call an operation using this prefix, passing along the param1 parameter defined by the WSDL and with the data provided by the application. The PHP equivalent method call would look like $ns1->Demo('abcdefg').

The service will then respond with a SOAP datagram that looks like Listing 19-3.

Listing 19-3. *A SOAP Response*

```
<?xml version="1.0" encoding="UTF-8"?>
<SOAP-ENV:Envelope
  xmlns:SOAP-ENV="http://schemas.xmlsoap.org/soap/envelope/"
  xmlns:ns1="http://localhost/demo"
  xmlns:xsd="http://www.w3.org/2001/XMLSchema"
  xmlns:xsi="http://www.w3.org/2001/XMLSchema-instance"
  xmlns:SOAP-ENC="http://schemas.xmlsoap.org/soap/encoding/"
  SOAP-ENV:encodingStyle="http://schemas.xmlsoap.org/soap/encoding/"
>
```

```
<SOAP-ENV:Body>
  <ns1:DemoResponse>
    <Result xsi:type="xsd:string">
       Request received with param1 = abcdefg
    </Result>
  </ns1:DemoResponse>
</SOAP-ENV:Body>
</SOAP-ENV:Envelope>
```

The function that generated this response looks like Listing 19-4.

Listing 19-4. *A Demo Function*

```
function Demo($param1) {
  return 'Request received with param1 = '. $param1;
}
```

Using the PHP SOAP Extension

Now that you have some understanding of WSDL and SOAP, it is easy to explain how to use the PHP SOAP extension to create and interact with web services.

The SoapServer class allows you to publish a web service using PHP. Using this class, you add functions that will fulfill the defined operations in your WSDL file. Listing 19-5 shows a sample SOAP server.

Listing 19-5. *A Complete SOAP Server (service.php)*

```
<?php

function Demo($param1) {
        return 'Request received with param1 = '. $param1;
}

$server = new SoapServer('demo.wsdl');
$server->addFunction('Demo');
$server->handle();
```

The SoapClient class allows you to remotely call web services—invoke an operation, pass parameters, and receive a response. This class will handle two key tasks: generating a SOAP envelope and sending it to the remote service that you just created. Listing 19-6 shows a sample SOAP client.

Listing 19-6. *A Sample SOAP Client (client.php)*

```
<?php
$client = new SoapClient('demo.wsdl');
$response = $client->Demo('abcdefg');
echo $response;
```

```
Request received with param1 = abcdefg
```

Place the service.php file at http://localhost/service.php, or adjust the WSDL file to reflect your actual script location. The only place you define the service URL is in the WSDL file.

When you run the client, a SOAP envelope is created and sent (posted) to service.php, which will then compute a response and return another SOAP envelope. To see what information is being sent back and forth, use the trace option, as Listing 19-7 demonstrates.

Listing 19-7. *Tracing SOAP Interaction*

```php
<?php
$client = new SoapClient('demo.wsdl', array('trace'=>true));
$response = $client->Demo('abcdefg');

print($client->__getLastRequest());
print($client->__getLastResponse());

echo $response;
```

```xml
<?xml version="1.0" encoding="UTF-8"?>
<SOAP-ENV:Envelope xmlns:SOAP-ENV="http://schemas.xmlsoap.org/soap/envelope/" ➥
xmlns:ns1="http://localhost/demo" xmlns:xsd="http://www.w3.org/2001/XMLSchema" ➥
xmlns:xsi="http://www.w3.org/2001/XMLSchema-instance" xmlns:SOAP-ENC= "http: ➥
//schemas.xmlsoap.org/soap/encoding/" SOAP-ENV:encodingStyle="http://schemas. ➥
xmlsoap.org/soap/encoding/"><SOAP-ENV:Body><ns1:Demo><param1 xsi:type= ➥
"xsd:string">abcdefg</param1></ns1:Demo></SOAP-ENV:Body></SOAP-ENV:Envelope>
<?xml version="1.0" encoding="UTF-8"?>
<SOAP-ENV:Envelope xmlns:SOAP-ENV="http://schemas.xmlsoap.org/soap/envelope/" ➥
xmlns:ns1="http://localhost/demo" xmlns:xsd="http://www.w3.org/2001/XMLSchema" ➥
xmlns:xsi="http://www.w3.org/2001/XMLSchema-instance" xmlns:SOAP-ENC="http: ➥
//schemas.xmlsoap.org/soap/encoding/" SOAP-ENV:encodingStyle="http://schemas. ➥
xmlsoap.org/soap/encoding/"><SOAP-ENV:Body><ns1:DemoResponse><Result xsi:type= ➥
"xsd:string">Request received with param1 = abcdefg</Result></ns1:DemoResponse> ➥
</SOAP-ENV:Body></SOAP-ENV:Envelope>
Request received with param1 = abcdefg
```

SoapClient Class Methods and Options

The SoapClient's constructor takes two parameters: a WSDL file and a list of options.

```
SoapClient::__construct(mixed $wsdl [, array $options])
```

Table 19-1 shows the SoapClient::__construct() options.

■**Note** If you do not want to work with WSDL files on the client side, you can provide null as a parameter to work in non-WSDL mode. If you do that, you will need to set the location and URI options explicitly.

Table 19-1. *SoapClient::__construct() Options*

Option	Description
uri	The target namespace of the web service (http://localhost/demo).
location	The URL where the service exists (http://localhost/service.php).
style	In non-WSDL mode, can be used to provide the document style.
use	In non-WSDL mode, can be used to define the document use.
soap_version	The SOAP version to use. Use the constant SOAP_1_1 or SOAP_1_2.
login	HTTP authentication login.
password	HTTP authentication password.
proxy_host	The host of a proxy to connect through.
proxy_port	The proxy port.
proxy_login	The proxy login.
proxy_password	The proxy password.
local_cert	Used in SSL authentication (covered in Chapter 21).
passphrase	The password for the SSL key provided by local_cert.
compression	Enables the compression of SOAP requests. There are various constants defining different SOAP compression techniques, including SOAP_COMPRESSION_ACCEPT, SOAP_COMPRESSION_GZIP, and SOAP_COMPRESSION_DEFLATE.
encoding	Defines the internal character encoding. Will convert received strings into the provided encoding.
classmap	Maps WSDL types to PHP classes. The format of this parameter is an associative array with WSDL types as keys and class names as values (covered in Chapter 20).
trace	Enables or disables the tracing of SOAP requests. See Listing 19-7.
exceptions	Enables or disables the throwing of exceptions when a SoapFault condition is met.
connection_timeout	Number of seconds to wait for a connection to the SOAP service.

The soapCall() method calls a SOAP operation. Typically, you will just use the operation name as a method of the SoapClient class, but if you need extra functionality, you may use soapCall() instead.

```
SoapClient::_soapCall(string $operation, array $args
          [, array $options, mixed $input_headers, array &$output_headers])
```

The arguments array may be an associative array of named parameters and values or a numeric array of parameters. The options array allows you to define the soapaction and uri options for when you're working in non-WSDL mode or when you're calling an operation in a namespace other than the default. The input and output headers arrays are useful for passing extra information, such as a session identifier or application authentication information.

■**Caution** If the service you are trying to interact with is a .NET service, it is sometimes necessary to place an extra array level to enclose your arguments. To pass named parameters to a .NET service, the arguments should be wrapped in an array key named parameters, as in array('parameters'=>array('a'=>1, 'b'=>2)).

The SoapClient class has several other useful methods and options that can be used when interacting with remote web services, as listed in Table 19-2.

Table 19-2. *Some Other SoapClient Methods*

Method	Description
SoapClient::_getLastRequest()	Returns the last SOAP envelope that was sent as a request. Requires that you enable the trace option when constructing your SoapClient class.
SoapClient::_getLastResponse()	Returns the last SOAP envelope returned from the web service. Requires the trace option to be enabled.
SoapClient::_getLastRequestHeaders()	Returns the SOAP headers that were sent with the last request. Requires the trace option to be enabled
SoapClient::_getLastResponseHeaders()	Returns the SOAP headers that were received with the last request. Also requires the trace option to be enabled.
SoapClient::_getTypes()	Returns a list of SOAP types defined by the WSDL file.
SoapClient::_getFunctions()	Retrieves a list of functions (operations) that are defined by the WSDL file.
SoapClient::_setCookie(string $name [, string $value])	An alternative to using SOAP headers, cookies can be passed to the underlying HTTP transport. On the server side, this information is readable as a normal $_COOKIE variable.

SoapServer Class Methods and Options

Construction of a SOAP server allows you to define the WSDL the service represents and assign various options for the service.

SoapServer::__construct(mixed $wsdl [, array $options])

If you pass null to the $wsdl parameter, you are then required to set the uri option. Table 19-3 shows the SoapServer::__construct() options.

Table 19-3. *SoapServer::__construct() Options*

Option	Description
uri	The URI of the service in non-WSDL mode
soap_version	One of the SOAP_1_X constants
encoding	The internal character encoding
actor	The actor URI
classmap	Allows you to transparently convert WSDL complex types into PHP classes

The SoapServer class has a number of other methods that allow you to expose your web services with fine-grained control, as listed in Table 19-4.

Table 19-4. *Some Other SoapServer Methods*

Method	Description
SoapServer::addFunction(mixed $functions)	Allows you to expose PHP functions to the web service. The $functions parameter can be the string name of a function or an array of function names. The functions must accept parameters in the order they are declared in the WSDL file. To return multiple parts, simply return an associative array with the key names equal to the part names.
SoapServer::setClass(string $class [, mixed $args, ...])	Exposes an entire class to the web service. Any arguments passed after the class name will be passed to the class's constructor. All methods within the class will be accessible by the web service. The methods in the class should be non-static, as an instance will be created.
SoapServer::handle([string $soap_request])	The main method in a SoapServer instance. When called, it will read either the contents of $HTTP_RAW_POST_DATA or the provided $soap_request variable. It will parse the SOAP envelope, determine and call the methods required, and return a response to the client.
SoapServer::fault(string $code, string $string)	Allows you to throw a SoapFault to indicate a server error to the client.

A Real-World Example

Now that you know the theory of web services, let's look at an example of one of the most successful and widely used web service APIs on the Web, Amazon Web Services. Using this API, you can get a ton of useful information.

For this example, you will try to find a list of books that have *Pro PHP* in the title or that are published by Apress. To start, most web services require some sort of key that controls access and that enforces some basic requirements, such as how many queries you use on a daily basis. There's no cost to get this key, but you will need to sign up for one at http://aws.amazon.com. Once you've signed up, you will receive an e-mail confirming your subscription. At the end of that e-mail will be a link to get your access key, which you should follow; you will need this key shortly.

The URL for the WSDL for the Amazon Web Services API is currently http://webservices.amazon.com/AWSECommerceService/AWSECommerceService.wsdl, and the file is immense. You're going to use only a very small subset of this WSDL, specifically the ItemSearch operation. This method has some nested parameters. First, the Amazon Web Services request requires the parameter AWSAccessKeyId to be passed along with another parameter named Request. Request is an associative array of data and can contain many optional keys, which are well documented on the Amazon Web Services site. For this example, you will search for this book by Title and Publisher, using the SearchIndex 'Books' and asking for a small ResponseGroup back from the server.

So without further introduction, Listing 19-8 demonstrates an Amazon SOAP request.

Listing 19-8. *Finding Book Information Using the Amazon Web Services API*

```php
<?php
$wsdl = "http://webservices.amazon.com/AWSECommerceService/AWSECommerceService ➥
.wsdl";

$client = new SoapClient($wsdl);

$namedParameters = array(
  'AWSAccessKeyId'  => 'YOUR_ACCESS_KEY',
  'Request'         => array(
                        'Title' => 'Pro PHP',
                        'SearchIndex' => 'Books',
                        'ResponseGroup' => 'Small',
                        'Publisher' => 'Apress'
                      )
);

$response = $client->ItemSearch($namedParameters);
var_dump($response);
```

In this example, you set the WSDL file to the WSDL provided by the Amazon Web Services and initialize a SoapClient. You create an array following the parameter format defined by the WSDL and the API documentation, and pass along your access key plus an array of request information. You then call the ItemSearch operation on the service and output the response. If everything is working properly, you will see a response that looks like the following:

```
object(stdClass)#2 (2) {
  ["OperationRequest"]=>
  object(stdClass)#3 (4) {
    ["HTTPHeaders"]=>
    object(stdClass)#4 (1) {
      ["Header"]=>
      object(stdClass)#5 (2) {
        ["Name"]=>
        string(9) "UserAgent"
        ["Value"]=>
        string(8) "PHP-SOAP"
      }
    }
    ["RequestId"]=>
    string(20) "0000000000000000"
    ["Arguments"]=>
    object(stdClass)#6 (1) {
      ["Argument"]=>
      object(stdClass)#7 (2) {
        ["Name"]=>
        string(7) "Service"
        ["Value"]=>
        string(19) "AWSECommerceService"
      }
    }
    ["RequestProcessingTime"]=>
    float(0.0457289218903)
  }
  ["Items"]=>
  object(stdClass)#8 (4) {
    ["Request"]=>
    object(stdClass)#9 (2) {
      ["IsValid"]=>
      string(4) "True"
      ["ItemSearchRequest"]=>
      object(stdClass)#10 (4) {
        ["Publisher"]=>
        string(6) "Apress"
        ["ResponseGroup"]=>
        string(5) "Small"
        ["SearchIndex"]=>
        string(5) "Books"
        ["Title"]=>
        string(7) "Pro PHP"
```

```
          }
        }
        ["TotalResults"]=>
        int(1)
        ["TotalPages"]=>
        int(1)
        ["Item"]=>
        object(stdClass)#11 (3) {
          ["ASIN"]=>
          string(10) "1590598199"
          ["DetailPageURL"]=>
          string(173) "http://www.amazon.com/gp/redirect.html..."
          ["ItemAttributes"]=>
          object(stdClass)#12 (4) {
            ["Author"]=>
            string(14) "Kevin McArthur"
            ["Manufacturer"]=>
            string(6) "Apress"
            ["ProductGroup"]=>
            string(4) "Book"
            ["Title"]=>
            string(53) "Pro PHP: Patterns, Frameworks, Testing and More (Pro)"
          }
        }
      }
    }
}
```

You can then extract this information using standard object notation. For example, to get the book title, use $request->Items->Item->ItemAttributes->Title.

This API offers a lot of power, which is also true of many other APIs from other vendors. For example, ESRI (a geographic information system developer) offers a tremendous amount of commercial information through its ArcWeb SOAP services.

Just the Facts

In this chapter, you were introduced to the basics of WSDL, SOAP messaging, and the PHP SOAP extension.

A WSDL file contains types, messages, operations, port types, bindings, ports, and services.

SOAP messaging takes the form of an RPC request. The SOAP extension generates different request and response envelopes during operation.

The PHP SOAP extension provides the classes SoapClient and SoapServer, which offer many methods and options for controlling the use of web services.

In the next chapter, you will learn about some of the more advanced topics that affect the development of web services, such as persistence, authentication, and complex types.

CHAPTER 20

■■■

Advanced Web Services

In the previous chapter, you created a basic web service and made a call to the Amazon Web Services API, which involved passing simple arrays and values. For real-life applications, however, you may need to send objects between two back-end systems. To do this, you will need to use some of the advanced features of WSDL and the SOAP extension to encode and decode objects properly. In this chapter, you will learn about complex types, which enable this functionality by defining the elements in the object in a universal format.

You are probably familiar with how to track sessions and authenticate users for your web applications. When working with web service clients and servers, the syntax for these tasks can be slightly different and sometimes more complicated. In this chapter, you will learn how to create session-based services and use the SOAP API to track session identifiers between requests. You will also learn about persistent objects, which can maintain a server state during a web services session. Finally, you will discover how to transmit binary data, such as images and video, to your web services. To demonstrate, you will send a photo to a web service by encoding it using base64 encoding.

Complex Types

Complex types are the way objects are represented in WSDL. While you don't declare methods in a complex type, you can declare any number of member variables as being part of the structure. Let's look at an example of using complex types.

A Complex Type Example

Suppose you work for a phone company with a lot of resellers who are responsible for billing their clients directly. You need to provide a way for your resellers to get access to their subscribers' call records, and you need to do it in a universal way because your resellers use different programming languages in their systems. Enter WSDL and complex types.

The data you want to provide is all the calling information for a specific subscriber: start time, duration, caller (the phone number from which the call was placed), and the callee (the dialed number). You could just provide a generic array type as a return value in your WSDL, but then your resellers wouldn't know which key names to expect and would need to do extra iterations to convert the result to an object format. With complex types, you can provide an object-mappable data type, as well as an array of records of that type.

Listing 20-1 demonstrates creating two complex types: CallDetailRecord, to represent one record of your calling information, and CallDetailRecordArray, to represent an array of records. A complex type in WSDL is most closely analogous to a PHP class containing only properties.

Listing 20-1. *Creating Complex Types (PhoneCompany.wsdl)*

```
<?xml version="1.0" encoding="UTF-8" ?>
<definitions
  name="PhoneCompany"
  targetNamespace="http://localhost/PhoneCompany"
  xmlns:tns="http://localhost/PhoneCompany"
  xmlns:soap="http://schemas.xmlsoap.org/wsdl/soap/"
  xmlns:soapenc="http://schemas.xmlsoap.org/soap/encoding/"
  xmlns:wsdl="http://schemas.xmlsoap.org/wsdl/"
  xmlns:xsd="http://www.w3.org/2001/XMLSchema"
  xmlns="http://schemas.xmlsoap.org/wsdl/"
>

  <types>
    <xsd:schema
      targetNamespace="http://localhost/PhoneCompany"
      xmlns:tns="http://localhost/PhoneCompany"
    >

      <xsd:complexType name="CallDetailRecord">
        <xsd:all>
          <xsd:element name="StartTime" type="xsd:dateTime" />
          <xsd:element name="Duration" type="xsd:int" />
          <xsd:element name="Caller" type="xsd:string" />
          <xsd:element name="Callee" type="xsd:string" />
        </xsd:all>
      </xsd:complexType>

      <xsd:complexType name="CallDetailRecordArray">
        <xsd:complexContent>
          <xsd:restriction base="soapenc:Array">
            <xsd:attribute
              ref="soapenc:arrayType"
              wsdl:arrayType="tns:CallDetailRecord[]"
            />
          </xsd:restriction>
        </xsd:complexContent>
      </xsd:complexType>

    </xsd:schema>
  </types>

  <message name="GetCallDetailRecordsRequest">
```

```xml
    <part name="Subscriber" type="xsd:string"/>
  </message>

  <message name="GetCallDetailRecordsResponse">
    <part name="Result" type="tns:CallDetailRecordArray"/>
  </message>

  <portType name="PhoneCompanyPort">
    <operation name="GetCallDetailRecords">
      <input message="tns:GetCallDetailRecordsRequest"/>
      <output message="tns:GetCallDetailRecordsResponse"/>
    </operation>
  </portType>

  <binding name="PhoneCompanyBinding" type="tns:PhoneCompanyPort">
    <soap:binding
      style="rpc"
      transport="http://schemas.xmlsoap.org/soap/http"
    />
    <operation name="GetCallDetailRecords">
      <soap:operation
        soapAction="http://localhost/GetCallDetailRecords"/>
      <input>
        <soap:body
          use="encoded"
          namespace="http://localhost/PhoneCompany"
          encodingStyle="http://schemas.xmlsoap.org/soap/encoding/"
        />
      </input>
      <output>
        <soap:body
          use="encoded"
          namespace="http://localhost/PhoneCompany"
          encodingStyle="http://schemas.xmlsoap.org/soap/encoding/"
        />
      </output>
    </operation>
  </binding>

  <service name="PhoneCompanyService">
    <port
      name="PhoneCompanyPort"
      binding="PhoneCompanyBinding"
    >
      <soap:address location="http://localhost/PhoneCompany.php"/>
    </port>
  </service>
</definitions>
```

The `CallDetailRecord` complex type, consisting of a number of XSD elements, defines the structure of the data format. The `CallDetailRecordArray` complex type is then defined as a SOAP-encoded array, where each entry is of your `CallDetailRecord` type. These types give your API structure.

Creating a service for this WSDL is relatively simple. You need only to create a `CallDetailRecord` class with public properties for each element and to return an array of them when requested. To do this, simply look at what elements the `ComplexType` defines (boldfaced in Listing 20-1). Then, using this information, model a PHP class, as shown in Listing 20-2.

Listing 20-2. *Creating a SOAP Server for the Phone Company Web Service (PhoneCompany.php)*

```php
<?php

class CallDetailRecord {
  public $StartTime, $Duration, $Caller, $Callee;

  public function __construct($startTime, $duration, $caller, $callee) {
    $this->StartTime = $startTime;
    $this->Duration = $duration;
    $this->Caller = $caller;
    $this->Callee = $callee;
  }
}

function GetCallDetailRecords($subscriber) {

  /*
    This data would normally come from a database
    using the data in $subscriber as a predicate
  */
  $records = array();
  $records[] = new CallDetailRecord(
                ' 20070509T21:48:00-07:00',
                '3600',
                '123-123-1234',
                '123-123-1235'
              );
  $records[] = new CallDetailRecord(
                '20070509T22:58:00-07:00',
                '3600',
                '123-123-1234',
                '123-123-1236'
              );

  return $records;
}

$server = new SoapServer('PhoneCompany.wsdl');
```

```
$server->addFunction('GetCallDetailRecords');
$server->handle();
```

Listing 20-3 shows an example of calling the server in Listing 20-2.

Listing 20-3. *Creating a SOAP Client for the Phone Company Web Service (PhoneClient.php)*

```
$client = new SoapClient('PhoneCompany.wsdl', array('trace'=>true));

var_dump($client->__getTypes());

try {
  $response = $client->GetCallDetailRecords('A-121-332');
  var_dump($response);
} catch (SoapFault $sf) {
  var_dump($sf);
  print($client->__getLastRequest());
  print($client->__getLastResponse());
}
```

```
array(2) {
  [0]=>
  string(95) "struct CallDetailRecord {
 dateTime StartTime;
 int Duration;
 string Caller;
 string Callee;
}"
  [1]=>
  string(40) "CallDetailRecord CallDetailRecordArray[]"
}
array(2) {
  [0]=>
  object(stdClass)#2 (4) {
    ["StartTime"]=>
    string(23) "20070510T21:48:00-07:00"
    ["Duration"]=>
    int(3600)
    ["Caller"]=>
    string(12) "123-123-1234"
    ["Callee"]=>
    string(12) "123-123-1235"
  }
  [1]=>
  object(stdClass)#3 (4) {
    ["StartTime"]=>
    string(23) "20070510T22:58:00-07:00"
    ["Duration"]=>
```

```
    int(3600)
    ["Caller"]=>
    string(12) "123-123-1234"
    ["Callee"]=>
    string(12) "123-123-1236"
  }
}
```

Some debugging data is included in Listing 20-3. Notice how getTypes() now gives you a detailed description of the data types that exist in the service.

Class Mapping

One thing you will notice in the result data from Listing 20-3 is that the results, despite being objects in the WSDL, were returned as stdClass objects. To resolve this and return proper instances of the CallDetailRecord class, you must map the class to the type in the SOAP client, as shown in Listing 20-4.

Listing 20-4. *Class Mapping (replaces PhoneClient.php)*

```php
<?php

class CallDetailRecord {
  public $StartTime, $Duration, $Caller, $Callee;

  public function __construct(
          $startTime, $duration, $caller, $callee)
  {
    $this->StartTime = $startTime;
    $this->Duration = $duration;
    $this->Caller = $caller;
    $this->Callee = $callee;
  }
}

$classmap = array('CallDetailRecord'=>'CallDetailRecord');
$client = new SoapClient(
            'PhoneCompany.wsdl',
            array(
              'trace'=>true,
              'classmap'=>$classmap
            )
          );

$response = $client->GetCallDetailRecords('A-121-332');

var_dump($response);
```

```
array(2) {
  [0]=>
  object(CallDetailRecord)#2 (4) {
    ["StartTime"]=>
    string(23) "20070510T21:48:00-07:00"
    ["Duration"]=>
    int(3600)
    ["Caller"]=>
    string(12) "123-123-1234"
    ["Callee"]=>
    string(12) "123-123-1235"
  }
  [1]=>
  object(CallDetailRecord)#3 (4) {
    ["StartTime"]=>
    string(23) "20070510T22:58:00-07:00"
    ["Duration"]=>
    int(3600)
    ["Caller"]=>
    string(12) "123-123-1234"
    ["Callee"]=>
    string(12) "123-123-1236"
  }
}
```

The $classmap variable is a map between keys and values, where the keys are WSDL types and the values are PHP class names. I recommend that you keep the names the same whenever possible, as having multiple names for the same objects can become quite confusing.

Authentication

So now that you have developed a bit of an API, you may be thinking about authentication. Just as when you're developing web applications, you have several options for authenticating users: HTTP authentication, communicated-key authentication, and client-certificate authentication.

HTTP Authentication

The easiest way to authenticate users is to use simple HTTP authentication. You can enable this using an .htaccess file, just as you would for any other resource, except that the client must be modified to provide the access credentials automatically. This syntax is simple and is demonstrated in Listing 20-5.

Listing 20-5. *HTTP Authentication in Web Services*

```
$client = new SoapClient(
          'service.wsdl',
          array(
           'login'=>'username',
           'password'=>'secret'
          )
        );
```

Communicated-Key Authentication

For the communicated-key authentication method, you add a subscriber ID token to every method in your web service. This is the type of authentication used by most web services.

   You saw this type of authentication in the example of using the Amazon Web Services API in the previous chapter. Your AWSAccessKeyId is your subscriber ID token, which is handled just like any other parameter to your web service.

Client-Certificate Authentication

The client-certificate authentication mechanism involves using SSL certificates on both the server and the client. This is the most secure form of web service authentication, but is also very complicated to set up.

   The certificate authentication options you need to know are local_cert and passphrase to provide client certificates encoded as Privacy Enhanced Mail (PEM). If you're not familiar with administering certificates, no worries—I'll cover the topic extensively in the next chapter.

Sessions

Using sessions in your web services is no different from using sessions in a regular web application. The SoapClient class will set and track a cookie, which will maintain the session ID. This automatic handling can be thought of as an until-object-destruction cookie. However, some sessions are long-lived, lasting hours or even days, and you may be expected to use the same session ID with each request. To do this, you will need to retrieve the session ID from the SoapClient and store it somewhere for later use. Using session cookies with SoapClient is demonstrated in Listings 20-6 and 20-7, which shows the client and server, respectively. This example reuses the demo.wsdl file from Listing 19-1 in the previous chapter.

Listing 20-6. *Multiple SOAP Clients, Same Session (client.php)*

```
<?php

//Normal session calls, first call creates session
$client = new SoapClient('demo.wsdl');
echo $client->demo('a'); //1
echo $client->demo('a'); //2
```

```
//Get the session id from the client cookies
$session_id = $client->_cookies['PHPSESSID'][0];

/*
  Sometime later, like in another request,
  you might create a new SoapClient.
*/
$client2 = new SoapClient('demo.wsdl');

/*
  To resume the session, set the session
  id for client2 manually using __setCookie
*/
$client2->__setCookie('PHPSESSID', $session_id);

echo $client2->demo('a'); //3
echo $client2->demo('a'); //4

/*
  A new client without setting the session
  cookie will start a new session
*/
$client3 = new SoapClient('demo.wsdl');
echo $client3->demo('a'); //1
```

12341

Listing 20-7. *A Session-Based SOAP Server (service.php)*

```
<?php

function Demo($param1) {
  session_start();
  if(!array_key_exists('counter', $_SESSION)) {
    $_SESSION['counter'] = 1;
  }
  return $_SESSION['counter']++;
}

$server = new SoapServer('demo.wsdl');
$server->addFunction('Demo');
$server->handle();
```

This ability to get and set the session ID manually is very important. It is most commonly used when you are creating some sort of multipage process, like an order or sign-up procedure. In these cases, you may start a web service session on the first page and call methods in that same session with each additional post from your browser.

Objects and Persistence

Until now, you have been using simple functions to handle the operations in your web service. You can, however, create a class to achieve the same results. Instead of specifically adding functions to the SOAP client, you can use setClass() to register an entire class of methods. Each method will automatically map to the corresponding WSDL operation. This saves you from having to register each method separately and can help you better encapsulate your web services. Listing 20-8 demonstrates using an object to handle SOAP requests.

Listing 20-8. *Using an Object to Handle SOAP Requests*

```php
<?php

class Service {
  function Demo($param1) {
    session_start();
    if(!array_key_exists('counter', $_SESSION)) {
      $_SESSION['counter'] = 1;
    }
    return $_SESSION['counter']++;
  }
}

ini_set('soap.wsdl_cache_enabled', '0');
$server = new SoapServer('demo.wsdl');
$server->setClass("Service");
$server->handle();
```

Under normal operation, *this class will get instantiated and destroyed with each SOAP call.* However, this is not usually desirable, as classes tend to track properties between method calls, and there is not a lot of benefit to creating an object instance with each method call.

Ignoring the performance implication, you could use sessions to track information between calls, but there is a better way. This ability is called *persistence*, and it allows you to initialize a class once and have it automatically serialized between requests to the service.

Replacing only service.php with the code from Listing 20-9, you can use the persistence mode without using session_start() or $_SESSION variables. From a SoapServer perspective, the method that turns on persistence mode is setPersistence() with either the constant SOAP_PERSISTENCE_REQUEST (the default, normal mode) or the constant SOAP_PERSISTENCE_SESSION.

Listing 20-9. *Persistence Mode (service.php)*

```php
class Service {

  private $counter=1;

  function Demo($param1) {
    return $this->counter++;
  }
}
```

```
ini_set('soap.wsdl_cache_enabled', '0');
$server = new SoapServer('demo.wsdl');
$server->setClass("Service");
$server->setPersistence(SOAP_PERSISTENCE_SESSION);
$server->handle();
```

Upon the first request to the service, the SoapServer class creates a session for the SoapClient. It then initializes the class and uses it to complete the requested operation. Then, instead of just discarding the class instance as it normally would, SoapServer stores the class instance in the client's session. When the next request is made, instead of initializing the class again, it uses the instance stored in the user's session.

This approach will improve performance if you have any significant construction code, and it can also eliminate the need to use session variables directly.

Binary Data Transmission

To transmit binary data, like images or video, to your web service, it must first be encoded into a text representation. For this purpose, web services use base64 encoding and the base64binary XML Schema type.

Let's walk through an example that uses an image file. This service provides an AddPhoto operation that will allow you to send an image file from your client to your server. The key elements in this example are the base64binary data type and the base64 encoding of the file contents. Listing 20-10 shows the WSDL file for the example.

Listing 20-10. *A WSDL File for Transmitting Binary Data (photo.wsdl)*

```
<?xml version ='1.0' encoding ='UTF-8' ?>
<definitions name='Photo'
  targetNamespace='http://localhost/Photo'
  xmlns:tns=' http://localhost/Photo'
  xmlns:soap='http://schemas.xmlsoap.org/wsdl/soap/'
  xmlns:soapenc='http://schemas.xmlsoap.org/soap/encoding/'
  xmlns:wsdl='http://schemas.xmlsoap.org/wsdl/'
  xmlns:xsd='http://www.w3.org/2001/XMLSchema'
  xmlns='http://schemas.xmlsoap.org/wsdl/'>

<message name='AddPhotoRequest'>
  <part name='image' type='xsd:base64binary'/>
</message>

<message name='AddPhotoResponse'>
  <part name='Result' type='xsd:string'/>
</message>

<portType name='PhotoPortType'>
  <operation name='AddPhoto'>
    <input message='tns:AddPhotoRequest'/>
```

```
    <output message='tns:AddPhotoResponse'/>
  </operation>
</portType>

<binding name='PhotoBinding' type='tns:PhotoPortType'>
  <soap:binding style='rpc' transport='http://schemas.xmlsoap.org/soap/http'/>
  <operation name='AddPhoto'>
    <soap:operation soapAction='http://localhost/AddPhoto'/>
    <input>
      <soap:body use='encoded' namespace='http://localhost/Photo'
        encodingStyle='http://schemas.xmlsoap.org/soap/encoding/'/>
    </input>
    <output>
      <soap:body use='encoded' namespace='http://localhost/Photo'
        encodingStyle='http://schemas.xmlsoap.org/soap/encoding/'/>
    </output>
  </operation>
</binding>

<service name='PhotoService'>
  <port name='PhotoPort' binding='PhotoBinding'>
    <soap:address location='http://localhost/photoservice.php'/>
  </port>
</service>
</definitions>
```

Listings 20-11 and 20-12 show the SOAP server and client, respectively.

Listing 20-11. *SOAP Server for Transmitting Binary Data (photoservice.php)*

```php
<?php

class Photo {
  function AddPhoto($photo) {
    $fileData = base64_decode($photo);
    return md5($fileData);
  }
}

$server = new SoapServer('photo.wsdl');
$server->setClass("Photo");
$server->handle();
```

Listing 20-12. *SOAP Client for Transmitting Binary Data (photoclient.php)*

```php
<?php

$client = new SoapClient('photo.wsdl', array('trace'=>true));

$fileData = base64_encode(file_get_contents('test.png'));
echo "Input: ";
echo md5_file('test.png');

echo " Output: ";
echo $client->AddPhoto($fileData) ."\n";
```

```
Input: cd5ea9e8a94a571508161cd606a72a4b Output: cd5ea9e8a94a571508161cd606a72a4b
```

You will notice that the input md5_file signature matches the return value from the service. The matching of these two hash codes indicates that the service is working correctly and that the file sent was the file received.

Just the Facts

This chapter covered some advanced web service concepts, including complex types, authentication, sessions, persistence, and binary data transmission.

Complex types are the WSDL equivalent of objects. You can define complex types and use them to encode PHP objects. You can also map PHP objects to the SOAP extension for automatic serialization and deserialization.

Methods for handling authentication in your web services include HTTP, keys, and certificates. In the next chapter, you will learn how to implement client-side certificate authentication and bring your API to the next level of security.

You can use session cookies with web services, just as with regular web applications. To use the same session ID with multiple clients, you can get and set the session ID manually using SoapClient.

Another way to track information between web service calls is through persistence. You can use the SoapServer method setPersistence() to turn on persistence mode.

You can transmit binary data, such as image files, using web services by encoding the files using base64.

CHAPTER 21
■■■

Certificate Authentication

Certificate authentication is one of the most powerful methods for securing your web applications and services. It is also one of the most underutilized authentication mechanisms available to PHP developers, probably because it is significantly more complex to set up and manage than any of the other authentication mechanisms. The APIs can be picky, the certificate-generation process can be complicated, and certificates must be deployed to clients. Yet certificate authentication is definitely worth the effort, as your site security will be markedly improved.

SSL certificates are typically used in a one-way validation mechanism, allowing a client to determine that a server is who it says it is. With certificate authentication, this process is expanded, with the server verifying the client's identity.

In this chapter, you will learn how to set up certificate authentication from start to finish, using your very own certificate authority.

Public Key Infrastructure Security

Certificate authentication is a public key infrastructure (PKI) security mechanism. The basic concepts in PKI security for web applications and services include certificate authorities (CAs), web server certificates, client-side certificates, and the root CA certificate.

Certificate Authority

A CA is an organization that is responsible for issuing and revoking certificates for third parties. It is the responsibility of the CA to verify the identity of certificate users. Thus, it is exclusively the CA that is enabled to communicate this authority to the web servers and clients that operate with your certificates.

Most modern web browsers have a list of trusted CAs that are enabled by default. These are the guys you need to pay money to when you want to set up an SSL-enabled web site for public consumption. When interacting with client-side certificates, however, you are the CA, as it would be foolish to trust a public CA to control access to your web application.

This presents a few challenges:

- You must set up the infrastructure required to be a CA.

- You must configure all your software to use your CA to verify client certificates.

- You must handle issuing the client certificate.

Technically, your CA is just another self-signed certificate, which is not inherently trusted by any browser or client. This means that, unlike a commercial certificate, which is already trusted, you will need to distribute your CA. Fortunately, you can embed your CA certificate within the client certificate itself before it is installed into the web browser.

Web Server Certificate

To set up client authentication, you will first need an SSL-enabled web site. Luckily, you don't need a commercial SSL certificate for this server.

A commercial certificate is not required because, when you send your client a certificate for use in authentication, you also provide it with the public CA certificate that was used to sign your server. By exchanging keys in this way, you and your client can verify that each other's computers are actually talking to each other, and not an intermediary web site or client. This process is called *peer verification*.

■**Caution** Verifying the peer certificate using the shared CA is a critically important step in the trust relationship between client and server. Many tutorials do not explain how to properly enable peer verification. Improper peer verification will greatly reduce your security effectiveness.

Client Certificate

A client certificate consists of three parts: a private key, the client certificate, and the CA's certificate. To be imported into a browser, these three parts are rolled into one .p12 file, which will be password-protected. Files with the .p12 extension are in the PKCS 12 format, which is the Public Key Cryptography Standard 12, Personal Information Exchange Syntax Standard.

You have two main options for creating this archive:

- You can create all three parts yourself and send your client the final file.

- You can have your client generate a certificate-signing request (CSR) file, which you will sign and give back to the client, along with your public CA certificate. The client would then be responsible for building the .p12 file.

The benefit of having the client generate a CSR file is that it will not share its private key with you, and you will not need to transmit an archive containing a private key between the client and server.

The entire security model of SSL depends on the private keys remaining private, and as such, the fewer locations in which a private key exists, the better. Ideally, a private key should exist on only one machine and be known to a single party; however, this may not always be possible.

Root CA Certificate

The pinnacle of the CA is the *root CA certificate*. This certificate is extremely important, and you must be very careful with it.

If your root CA certificate is lost, you will not be able to generate any new certificates without redeploying every existing certificate you have ever deployed with the CA. Worse, if your root

CA private key is compromised, you have the worst possible scenario: your entire application is now insecure, and any user can be impersonated.

■**Caution** If I've not made it crystal clear, do not put your root CA private key on your web server! The only time you need the CA key is when signing a new certificate.

Setting Up Client Certificate Authentication

This chapter's example uses OpenSSL, an open source implementation of SSL (tested on a Debian "etch" Linux release with the default packages). The nature of OpenSSL is that things are usually in the right place, but please take a minute to confirm that your CA.pl and openssl.cnf files are the following locations. Also, check that your version is at least 0.9.8:

```
> locate CA.pl

/usr/lib/ssl/misc/CA.pl

> locate openssl.cnf

/usr/lib/ssl/openssl.cnf

> openssl version

OpenSSL 0.9.8g 19 Oct 2007
```

If these values check out, the next step is to proceed to create the CA.

Creating Your Own Certificate Authority

Create your very own CA by executing the following commands:

```
> cd /usr/lib/ssl/misc
> ./CA.pl -newca
```

```
CA certificate filename (or enter to create)

Making CA certificate ...
Generating a 1024 bit RSA private key
....................................................++++++
..........++++++
writing new private key to './demoCA/private/cakey.pem'
Enter PEM pass phrase: <Enter a _strong_ password>
Verifying - Enter PEM pass phrase: <confirm password>


-----
```

You are about to be asked to enter information that will be incorporated
into your certificate request.

What you are about to enter is what is called a Distinguished Name or a DN.

There are quite a few fields but you can leave some blank
For some fields there will be a default value,
If you enter '.', the field will be left blank.

Country Name (2 letter code): CA
State or Province Name (full name): Alberta
Locality Name (eg, city):
Organization Name (eg, company): Kevin McArthur
Organizational Unit Name (eg, section):
Common Name (eg, YOUR name): Kevin McArthur Root CA
Email Address:

Please enter the following 'extra' attributes
to be sent with your certificate request
A challenge password []:
An optional company name []:
Using configuration from /usr/lib/ssl/openssl.cnf
Enter pass phrase for ./demoCA/private/cakey.pem: <type pass again>

Check that the request matches the signature
Signature ok
Certificate Details:
        Serial Number:
            c8:ff:56:7b:d8:e3:18:64
        Validity
            Not Before: May 13 01:52:18 2007 GMT
            Not After : May 12 01:52:18 2010 GMT
        Subject:
            countryName   = CA
            stateOrProvinceName   = Alberta
            organizationName   = Kevin McArthur
            commonName   = Kevin McArthur Root CA
        X509v3 extensions:
            X509v3 Subject Key Identifier:
                91:FB:90:02:A0:76:3E:21:02:FE:B6:97:4C:3C:99:B5:79:63:90:1D
            X509v3 Authority Key Identifier:
                keyid:91:FB:90:02:A0:76:3E:21:02:FE:B6:97:4C:3C:99:B5:79:63:90:1D
                DirName:/C=CA/ST=Alberta/O=Kevin McArthur/CN=Kevin McArthur Root CA
                serial:C8:FF:56:7B:D8:E3:18:64

```
        X509v3 Basic Constraints:
            CA:TRUE <Confirm this reads TRUE!>

Certificate is to be certified until May 12 01:52:18 2010 GMT (1095 days)

Write out database with 1 new entries
Data Base Updated
```

■**Caution** Make sure X509V3 Basic Constraints: CA:TRUE is set. If it is not, your entire CA will not work as expected for peer verification! Some versions of OpenSSL ship with a CA.sh script that appears to do the same thing as the CA.pl script, but it will *not* set this attribute.

This operation creates a new directory structure demoCA and generates your root CA certificate. This certificate is contained in demoCA/cacert.pem. The private key, which must be protected, is placed in demoCA/private/cakey.pem. The cacert.pem file may be shared, as it contains only public-key information.

Next, you will use this certificate to set up an Apache 2.x web server for SSL operation using a self-signed certificate.

Create a Self-Signed Web Server Certificate

Creating a web server certificate using the CA.pl script and your new CA certificate is trivial. Execute the following command:

```
> ./CA.pl -newreq
```

```
Generating a 1024 bit RSA private key
.................++++++
............++++++
writing new private key to 'newkey.pem'
Enter PEM pass phrase: <password>
Verifying - Enter PEM pass phrase: <password>


-----


You are about to be asked to enter information that will be incorporated into
your certificate request.

What you are about to enter is what is called a Distinguished Name or a DN.

There are quite a few fields but you can leave some blank
For some fields there will be a default value,
If you enter '.', the field will be left blank.


-----
```

```
Country Name (2 letter code): CA
State or Province Name (full name): Alberta
Locality Name (eg, city):
Organization Name (eg, company): Kevin McArthur
Organizational Unit Name (eg, section): Web Server
Common Name (eg, YOUR name): localhost
Email Address []:

Please enter the following 'extra' attributes
to be sent with your certificate request
A challenge password []:
An optional company name []:
Request is in newreq.pem, private key is in newkey.pem
```

Caution The Common Name entry must match your web server domain exactly. I've used localhost, but you should use your domain name if you are setting up SSL for non-localhost operation.

At this point, you have a certificate request and a new private key for the server. You have not yet signed this certificate as being authentic according to your CA. To sign this certificate, execute the following command:

```
> ./CA.pl -sign
```

```
Using configuration from /usr/lib/ssl/openssl.cnf
Enter pass phrase for ./demoCA/private/cakey.pem: <enter the CA pass>
Check that the request matches the signature
Signature ok
Certificate Details:
        Serial Number:
            a7:8f:54:aa:74:66:29:4f
        Validity
            Not Before: May 15 02:45:28 2007 GMT
            Not After : May 14 02:45:28 2008 GMT
        Subject:
            countryName               = CA
            stateOrProvinceName       = Alberta
            organizationName          = Kevin McArthur
            organizationalUnitName    = Web Server
            commonName                = localhost
        X509v3 extensions:
            X509v3 Basic Constraints:
                CA:FALSE
```

```
        Netscape Comment:
            OpenSSL Generated Certificate
        X509v3 Subject Key Identifier:
            46:40:6A:B4:56:B6:73:3A:5B:F8:0F:89:C2:89:AD:3D:07:99:52:2A
        X509v3 Authority Key Identifier:
            keyid:0F:3C:EF:06:9D:10:7B:17:81:A9:E5:74:4F:B4:72:1D:C4:4E:22:E2


Certificate is to be certified until May 14 02:45:28 2008 GMT (365 days)
Sign the certificate? [y/n]:y



1 out of 1 certificate requests certified, commit? [y/n]y
Write out database with 1 new entries
Data Base Updated
Signed certificate is in newcert.pem
```

Now you have several files, including one that contains a signed certificate. Since CA.pl overwrites the files it creates when it is rerun, you need to move these files to files with unique names. Execute the following commands:

```
> mv newcert.pem server.pem
> mv newkey.pem server.key
```

Currently, you have your web server certificate in server.pem and the private key in server.key. The only problem here is that your server.key file is encrypted with a pass phrase, and you will need to enter the password every time the server starts. If you don't want this to happen, you can decrypt the key and write it out without a password, so you do not need to type a password to start Apache. To decrypt the key, execute the following command:

```
> openssl rsa < server.key > serverkey.pem
```

```
Enter pass phrase: <password>
writing RSA key
```

Now you need to set up Apache with your site.

Configuring Apache for SSL

Start your Apache setup by making a new configuration directory for your SSL certificates:

```
> mkdir /etc/apache2/ssl
```

Then move your server certificates in there.

```
> mv server.* /etc/apache2/ssl
```

■**Note** This step assumes a Debian layout. Your server layout may be slightly different.

Later on, your web server will need to know about your CA certificate, so create a symbolic link to that certificate:

```
> ln -s demoCA/cacert.pem /etc/apache2/ssl/cacert.pem
```

To set up Apache for SSL operation, you need to edit the configuration file. On some systems, this is httpd.conf; on others, it has a different name. On Debian systems, you will find the configuration file in /etc/apache2/sites-available/default.

In your Apache configuration file, you need to enable the SSLEngine, set the Cipher Suite, and point Apache to your new certificate files. You'll do this in the main virtual host section, which will probably look like this:

```
<VirtualHost *>
. . .
</VirtualHost>
```

Add the code shown in Listing 21-1 to your VirtualHost section in your Apache configuration file.

Listing 21-1. *SSL Configuration in Apache Configuration File*

```
SSLEngine on
SSLCipherSuite
ALL:!ADH:!EXPORT56:RC4+RSA:+HIGH:+MEDIUM:+LOW:+SSLv2:+EXP:!eNULL

SSLCertificateFile /etc/apache2/ssl/server.pem
SSLCertificateKeyFile /etc/apache2/ssl/serverkey.pem
SSLCACertificateFile /etc/apache2/ssl/cacert.pem
```

After you've saved your modified configuration file, restart Apache and point your web browser at https://localhost (or the site for which you have configured SSL). If everything is working, you should get an SSL warning saying that the certificate is not trusted. Accept the certificate *temporarily;* do not accept it permanently.

This certificate should be untrusted because it is not signed by a CA that your browser recognizes. Usually, you would pay an SSL company like Go Daddy or VeriSign to sign your certificate, but because you are setting up this site for client-side certificates, that step is redundant and unnecessary.

Creating the Client-Side Certificates

Creating the client-side certificates is slightly more complicated because they must be encoded in the PKCS 12 format. It is also trickier because you have a choice to make. You must decide if you will generate your clients' private keys for them, or if you will ask them to create their own private keys and send you only a CSR file.

First, you or your client will need to determine if the openssl.cnf file you located earlier is configured correctly to create a client-side certificate. This requires opening the file, locating a section, and confirming that it looks like Listing 21-2. If it doesn't, you should add the code in Listing 21-2 to the openssl.cnf file.

Listing 21-2. *Client-Side Certificate Creation Configuration (in openssl.cnf)*

```
[ ssl_client ]
basicConstraints        = CA:FALSE
nsCertType              = client
keyUsage                = digitalSignature, keyEncipherment
extendedKeyUsage        = clientAuth
nsComment               = "OpenSSL Certificate for SSL Client"
```

Creating client-side certificates requires working with the raw openssl commands, which CA.pl was previously doing for you. The first step is to create a new CSR and private key for your client. If your client is generating the CSR, it should execute this command and send you the resulting client.pem, while keeping the client.key private.

```
> openssl req -new -sha1 -newkey rsa:1024 -keyout client.key -out client.pem \
> -subj '/O=Kevin McArthur/OU=Kevin McArthur Web Services/CN=Joe Smith'
```

The subj parameters can be slightly confusing. The O parameter stands for Organization, OU is for Organizational Unit, and CN is for Common Name. The O and OU parameters must be the same for every client, and the CN must be distinct. This is because the O and OU fields will be used by Apache, along with the authority given by your CA certificate, to determine who may access a resource. Changing the OU field will allow you to create different "zones" of access.

Once you have the client.pem, either generated by this command or received from your client, you need to sign it with your CA. This signature is what your web server will use to trust that the O and OU fields are actually valid. In this step, you are certifying these values, so be sure that they are correct!

To sign the certificate, execute the following command:

```
> openssl ca -config /usr/lib/ssl/openssl.cnf -policy policy_anything \
> -extensions ssl_client -out client.signed.pem -infiles client.pem
```

```
Using configuration from /usr/lib/ssl/openssl.cnf
Enter pass phrase for ./demoCA/private/cakey.pem: <enter CA password>
Check that the request matches the signature
Signature ok
Certificate Details:
        Serial Number:
            a7:8f:54:aa:74:66:29:50
        Validity
            Not Before: May 15 03:19:04 2007 GMT
            Not After : May 14 03:19:04 2008 GMT
```

```
      Subject:
          organizationName          = Kevin McArthur
          organizationalUnitName    = Kevin McArthur Web Services
          commonName                = Joe Smith
      X509v3 extensions:
          X509v3 Basic Constraints:
              CA:FALSE
          Netscape Cert Type:
              SSL Client
          X509v3 Key Usage:
              Digital Signature, Key Encipherment
          X509v3 Extended Key Usage:
              TLS Web Client Authentication
          Netscape Comment:
              OpenSSL Certificate for SSL Client
Certificate is to be certified until May 14 03:19:04 2008 GMT (365 days)
Sign the certificate? [y/n]:y

1 out of 1 certificate requests certified, commit? [y/n]y
Write out database with 1 new entries
Data Base Updated
```

Caution It is essential in this step to verify the O and OU information. Do not blindly sign the certificate.

You will now have a `client.signed.pem` certificate. Now, if you are doing this for a client, you will need to send this certificate and your `cacert.pem` file back to the client. In any case, these two certificates will be combined with the private key into a PKCS 12 certificate.

To create the PKCS 12 certificate, execute the following command:

```
> openssl pkcs12 -export -clcerts -in client.signed.pem -inkey client.key \
> -out client.p12 -certfile demoCA/cacert.pem -name "Joe Smith"
```

```
Enter pass phrase for client.key: <client's key pass>
Enter Export Password: <a new pass for the p12 archive>
Verifying - Enter Export Password: <confirm>
```

You now have the final `.p12` file. The trick now is exchanging this file. If your client created the `.p12` file, you don't need to exchange it; however, if you created it, a security issue presents itself.

The file contains a private key, which is really important to keep secure. At this point, it is password-protected, and presumably you used a password that is hard to crack, so it would be difficult to use the file if it were intercepted. Still, if intercepted, this archive might be opened by brute force.

My advice is to communicate the file to your client securely, either via an encoded Secure/Multipurpose Internet Mail Extensions (S/MIME) e-mail message, Secure Copy/Secure FTP (SCP/SFTP), or on physical media of some sort. Then, separately, via a different medium, such as a phone call or letter, communicate the password that was used to encrypt the archive. For extra security, consider deploying smart cards or tokens, so that private keys are not left on client machines while not in use.

■**Caution** The absolute worst thing you could do with certificate authentication is to send the .p12 file along with the archive password via standard e-mail. Not only can this defeat the mechanism if the data is intercepted, but it may give you a false sense of security. Under no circumstances should you transfer the file and communicate the password via the same medium.

The .p12 file will work with web browsers and Subversion clients, but it will not work with PHP. To use SSL authentication from a PHP script, such as a web service for opening remote files, you will need to use the PEM-encoded certificates. To get that working, you will need to merge the client private key with the client certificate file. Execute the following commands:

```
> mkdir /var/www/ssl
> mv /usr/lib/ssl/misc/client.* /var/www/ssl/
> cd /var/www/ssl
> cat client.signed.pem > services.pem
> cat client.key >> services.pem
```

You will now have a services.pem with both the signed client certificate and the client's private key in it.

The next step in creating your authentication mechanism is to allow access only to SSL-authenticated clients.

Permitting Only Certificate Authentication

Allowing access only to SSL-authenticated clients requires editing your Apache configuration files again. Place the code shown in Listing 21-3 in your configuration file, adjusting the location tag as necessary, and then reload Apache.

Listing 21-3. *SSL Restrictions*

```
SSLVerifyClient require
SSLVerifyDepth 1

SSLOptions +StrictRequire +StdEnvVars

<Location />
  SSLRequireSSL
  SSLRequire %{SSL_CLIENT_VERIFY} eq "SUCCESS"
  SSLRequire %{SSL_CLIENT_S_DN_O} eq "Kevin McArthur"
  SSLRequire %{SSL_CLIENT_S_DN_OU} eq "Kevin McArthur Web Services"
</Location>
```

This code tells Apache to require the client to present an SSL certificate. It then says it must be verified by an immediate CA certificate. The 1 represents one degree of separation, which means that the certificate must be directly signed by the SSLCACertificateFile that you specified earlier.

Next, the SSLOptions StrictRequire option overrides any of the Apache Satisfy rules, and the StdEnvVars creates some environment variables you will use with SSLRequire.

The SSLRequire statements state that SSL is required, that the client must verify successfully against the CA, and that the O and OU properties must match the provided values. If any of these properties are not satisfied, access will be denied to the location. By varying the values for the O and OU fields in this configuration and in your client certificates, you can create different areas of access.

Reload your web server, and proceed to testing.

Testing the Certificate

Now it's time to test the certificates. Web browsers will require the .p12 certificate.

For Internet Explorer, you will need to execute the .p12 file by double-clicking it and following along with the on-screen instructions, accepting the default options.

In Firefox, you will need to configure the certificate, as follows:

1. Select Edit ➤ Preferences (Linux) or Tools ➤ Options (Windows) from the menu bar.

2. Select the Advanced tab, and then the Encryption subtab. On this tab, click View Certificates.

3. Click Import. Locate your p12 file, and then click Import. You will be prompted for the export password you specified earlier.

4. After the certificate is imported, click the Authorities tab. Find and select your root CA certificate, and then click Edit.

5. Check the box that says "This certificate can identify web sites" and click OK.

You have configured your client to provide the client certification when requested and that your root CA can sign certificates to identify web sites. It is this latter step that makes a commercial CA redundant for SSL sites with client certificates.

Visit https://localhost. You may be prompted for a password for your certificate store if one is set and it is your first login this session. You should not receive any warnings about the site, as you did during your initial visit. Your web server now knows that the client it is talking to has the certificate, and the client knows that the server is who it says it is because its SSL certificate matches the one contained in the .p12 file.

Everything is now very secure, but everything has occurred at the web server-level, and it has verified only the O and OU fields, and not the CN field. Now you probably will want to implement some sort of PHP authentication control that inspects the CN field.

PHP Authentication Control

You will find a complete list of `SSL_CLIENT_*` variables in your `$_SERVER` variable. You can use the information from these variables to identify clients by name, and since you certified the certificate, you can be sure that the user has access to that certificate and does not just know a username and password.

That said, certificate authentication guarantees only that the user has access to the `.p12` file; it does not confirm identity. Therefore, you will want to use multiple authentication controls, such as adding a username and password login, for sensitive operations.

Binding PHP to a Certificate

Once you are communicating with your server via certificate authentication, a script like the one shown in Listing 21-4 can bind PHP to the presented certificate. In this case, you will access the Common Name field from the SSL certificate. This data can be trusted because Apache has already verified the certificate with your CA certificate.

Listing 21-4. *PHP and SSL Interaction*

```php
<?php

//The user's name is stored in the certificate's Common Name field.
echo "Hello, ". $_SERVER['SSL_CLIENT_S_DN_CN'];
```

```
Hello, Joe Smith
```

Setting Up Web Service Authentication

PHP web services authenticate using client certificates by setting transport options with the HTTPS protocol wrapper. This is commonly known as a *stream context*, and allows you to provide advanced options to stream-interacting calls like `fopen` and the `SoapClient` class. Stream contexts have a lot of other options; however, for this purpose, you will need to use only the SSL subset of options.

Continuing from the examples in the previous chapter, you will need to change your `PhoneCompany.wsdl` file to use HTTPS instead of HTTP for `soap:address`, as shown in Listing 21-5. You don't need to change the namespace or any other options.

Listing 21-5. *Switching the WSDL Port to Bind with HTTPS (in PhoneCompany.wsdl)*

```
  </binding>

  <service name="PhoneCompanyService">
    <port
      name="PhoneCompanyPort"
      binding="PhoneCompanyBinding"
```

```
    >
      <soap:address location="https://localhost/PhoneCompany.php"/>
    </port>
  </service>
</definitions>
```

Next, add the code in Listing 21-6 to your PhoneClient.php script, replacing the $client assignment.

Listing 21-6. *Using a SoapClient with an SSL Stream Context (in PhoneClient.php)*

```
$contextDetails = array(
  'ssl'=> array(
    'local_cert'=>'/var/www/ssl/services.pem',
    'cafile'=>'/usr/lib/ssl/misc/demoCA/cacert.pem',
    'verify_peer'=>true,
    'allow_self_signed'=>false,
    'CN_match'=>'localhost',
    'passphrase'=>'password'
  )
);

$streamContext = stream_context_create($contextDetails);

$client = new SoapClient(
                'PhoneCompany.wsdl',
              array(
                'classmap'=>$classmap,
                'stream_context'=>$streamContext,
              )
            );
```

This code tells SoapClient to use the services.pem certificate you created earlier and also enables peer verification. As in the browser, this ensures that the remote server is not being impersonated and that the server is who it says it is. This can prevent many DNS poisoning and man-in-the-middle attacks, so it's very important that you use peer verification in any deployed application.

Without peer verification, the SOAP client would happily talk to any web server that presented any SSL certificate; it would not know, or care, who it is talking to and would proceed to send the SOAP envelopes without any verification. This would make your application's security entirely dependent on DNS and the network infrastructure between your client and server. With peer verification, only the server that has a certificate signed by the CA will be considered acceptable to the SOAP client.

The CN_match field is part of this peer verification, and ensures that the certificate presented by the remote server contains a Common Name (CN) field that matches the value you expect. This value will typically be the same as the web server address.

The passphrase option is the password for the client.key file you created earlier. This is because the services.pem file incorporates the encrypted private key.

With this code in place and the WSDL updated, you should now be able to call the web service through a secure tunnel. The PhoneCompany.php file does not need to be modified, as it performs no additional authentication. If you do want to authenticate the client's SSL parameters, you can use the $_SERVER approach presented in the previous section.

Just the Facts

The techniques presented in this chapter aren't for the faint of heart, but if mastered, they will provide your applications and clients with an added level of security.

The basic concepts in PKI security include CAs, web server certificates, and client-side certificates. Verifying the peer certificate using your shared CA is a critically important step in the trust relationship between client and server. Peer verification is important to preventing DNS poisoning and man-in-the-middle attacks from affecting your web applications.

In setting up an application for client authentication, you create your own CA. You use this CA to generate a self-signed web server certificate, and configure Apache to use this certificate.

You can issue a client certificate, in multiple formats, and deploy these certificates in your web browser and web services clients.

At the administration level, you limit access to Apache locations by inspecting the properties in client-side certificates.

Index

■Symbols

$ symbol, 16

&$matches data, 149

:: (scope resolution operator), 11, 47

_ (underscores), 260

■A

abort( ) method, 279

abstract classes, 3–6

abstract keyword, 10

abstract modifier, 4

AC (action controller), 203

accept( ) method, 148, 157, 158, 169, 170

access control, 265–267

access control list (ACL), 265

action controller (AC), 203

action helpers, 226–227, 263–264

Action suffix, 220

actions, MVC, 203

actor option, 294

addAction( ) method, 228

addCar( ) method, 5

addHelper( ) method, 264

addPath( ) method, 264

AddPhoto operation, 309

admin modules, 259

Ajax (Asynchronous JavaScript and XML), 273–284

  JSON

    JavaScript and, 276–279

    PHP and, 273–275

  overview, 273

  projects, 280–284

    GET requests, 280–281

    POST requests, 281–284

ajax.htm script, 281

ALL_MATCHES option, 149

ALLOW_EMPTY metacommand, 232

allowOverrides directive, 207

AllTests command, 114

Alpha filter, 231

Amazon Web Services, 295–297

Amazon Web Services API, 299

Apache, configuring for SSL, 319–320

append($value) method, 181

AppendIterator, 147–148

application/controllers directory, 220

application/controllers/index.php file, 212

apt command, 63

apt-get install function, 41

areEqual( ) method, 157

areIdentical( ) method, 157

array overloading
    ArrayAccess interface, 130–131
    counting and ArrayAccess, 131
    SPL, 179–188
        ArrayAccess, 179–180
        ArrayObject, 180–182
        building SPL shopping cart, 182–184
        overview, 179
        using objects as keys, 184–187
array type, 299
array xdebug_get_code_coverage( )
    function, 123
ARRAY_AS_PROPS flag, 211
array_merge( ) method, 147
ArrayAccess, 179–180
    counting and, 131
    exceptions, 189–198
        Bad Function and Method Call
            Exceptions, 192
        Domain Exceptions, 192
        Invalid Argument Exceptions, 194
        Length Exceptions, 194–195
        Logic Exceptions, 189–191
        Overflow Exceptions, 195–196
        overview, 189
        Range Exceptions, 193–194
        Runtime Exceptions, 191–192
        Underflow Exceptions, 196–197
ArrayIterator, 144, 146, 161, 187
ArrayObject, 180–182
ArrayObject class, 180, 182, 188, 211
ArrayObject::ARRAY_AS_PROPS
    constant, 181
ArrayObject::STD_PROP_LIST constant, 181
/articles controller, 267
asort( ) method, 181
async method, 279
async parameter, 279
Asynchronous JavaScript and XML. *See* Ajax
attach( ) method, 132
Attribute class, 100
Attribute type, 100
attributes, 58, 99, 102
authentication, 305–306
AuthenticationTest, 112
__autoload( ) function, 137, 138
autoloading SPL, 137–140
AWSAccessKeyId Id parameter, 295
AWSAccessKeyId ID token, 306

■**B**

BadFunctionCallException class, 192, 198
BadMethodCallException class, 192, 198
base class, 3
base64binary XML Schema type, 309
<batchtest> element, 117
binary data transmission, 309–311
Bindings tag, 286
blockquote tag, 70
bookinfo element, 67
bookinfo node, 63
bookinfo tag, 67
bool $associative parameter, 274
bootstrap file, 203
bootstrapping, 207–208, 217–219
BREAK_CHAIN metacommand, 232

<builder> element, 119

build.xml document, 116

build.xml file, 119

built-in, 227–228

built-in action helpers, 226–227

built-in view helpers, 227–228

∎**C**

CA (certificate authority), 313–317

cacert.pem file, 317, 322

CachingIterator, 152

__call( ) functionality, 50

CallDetailRecord class, 304

CallDetailRecord type, 300, 302

CallDetailRecordArray type, 300, 302

__callStatic( ) method, 50, 52

CA.pl file, 315, 317

$cart object, 184

CA.sh script, 317

catch keyword, 32

catch statement, 31

CATCH_GET_CHILDREN class constant, 154

certificate authentication, 313–327

   overview, 313

   PHP authentication control, 325–327

   public key infrastructure (PKI) security, 313–315

      certificate authority (CA), 313–314

      client certificates, 314

      overview, 313

      root CA certificates, 314–315

      web server certificates, 314

   setting up, 315–324

      configuring Apache for SSL, 319–320

      create self-signed web server certificates, 317–319

      creating certificate authority (CA), 315–317

      creating client-side certificates, 320–323

      permitting only certificate authentication, 323–324

      testing certificates, 324

certificate authority (CA), 313–317

certificate-signing request (CSR) file, 314

chapter element, 67–68

chapter1.xml file, 66, 67

chapterinfo tag, 68

checkout, 106

CHILD_FIRST class constant, 154

CHM:default:default option, 62

chunk.xsl stylesheet, 65

Cipher Suite, 320

cittitle tag, 70

class attribute, 70

class mapping, 304–305

class_exists( ) method, 139

classes, static, 12–18

classmap option, 292, 294

$classmap variable, 305

$classnameinvar::somemethod( ) operator, 18

$client assignment, 326

client certificates, 314

client-certificate authentication, 306

  setting up, 315–324

    configuring Apache for SSL, 319–320

    create self-signed web server certificates, 317–319

    creating certificate authority (CA), 315–317

    creating client-side certificates, 320–323

    permitting only certificate authentication, 323–324

    testing certificates, 324

client.key file, 321, 326

client.pem file, 321

client-side certificates, 313, 320–323

client.signed.pem certificate, 322

__clone( ) method, 22

CN (Common Name) field, 326

CN parameter, 321

CN_match field, 326

code directory, 111

coding conventions, 55–56

collations, Unicode, 46–47

CollectionObject class, 185

comma-separated value (CSV) data, 163

_comment member variable, 92

Common Name (CN) field, 326

Common Name entry, 318

communicated-key authentication, 306

compareIterators( ) method, 157

complex types, 299–305

  class mapping, 304–305

  example of, 299–304

compression option, 292

computeMenu( ) function, 78

configure line, 42

config.xml file, 119, 120

connection_timeout option, 292

__construct( ) method, 22, 149

construct( ) method, 231

content parameter, 279

Content-Type header, 226

continuous integration, 105–124

  overview, 105

  Phing for deployment, 115–118

  PHPUnit testing, 110–114

  Subversion (SVN), 105–110

    committing changes and resolving conflicts, 108–109

    enabling access to, 110

    overview, 105

  Xdebug for debugging, 120–124

    checking code coverage, 123

    installing, 120–121

    overview, 120

    profiling, 123

    remote debugging, 124

    tracing, 121–122

Controller class name, 219

Controller layer, 199, 201, 208, 209, 210

/controller/action directory, 203

controllers, MVC, 203–211

conventional modular directory structure, 259–260

count( ) function, 131, 141, 188

Countable interface, 131, 141, 180

counting, ArrayAccess and, 131

CSR (certificate-signing request) file, 314

CSV (comma-separated value) data, 163

CSV operation, 172–176

CSVFileObject object, 173

curly braces, 59

current( ) method, 129, 144, 166

custom exceptions, 35–36

custom file filter iterators, 169–171

creating plug-in directory, 170–171

operating on CVS directory, 171

using reflection with directory
iterators, 171

customers table, 222, 224

customers/add.phtml view, 228

CustomersController.php class, 228

/customers/redirect directory, 227

/customers/show directory, 227

CVS directories, 171

CVSFileObject object, 177

■D

database element, 70

DatabaseException class, 34

DatabaseFactory class, 29

databases

configuring Zend Framework to use,
222–223

portable, 27–29

setting up, 221–222

DBA, accessing flat-file databases with,
159–160

DbaReader, 160

IniGroups, 160

DbaReader, 160, 161

debug_backtrace( ) function, 33, 122

debugclient command-line debugger, 124

debugging. See Xdebug

$decodeType parameter, 275

DEFAULT metacommand, 232

default modules, 259, 260

/default/index/index directory, 260

definitions tag, 288

$demo = new Demo( ) method, 113

Demo class, 111, 114

demo method, 287

Demo operation, 289

demoCA directory, 317

demoCA/cacert.pem directory, 317

demoCA/private/cakey.pem directory, 317

demodb database, 221

DemoTest class, 112

DemoTest.php file, 117

demo.wsdl file, 306

deploy target, 116, 117

description tag, 60

deserialization, 311

Design role, 202

Development role, 202

directory iterators, using reflection with, 171

DirectoryIterator, 166–167, 177

dirname( ) method, 165

disableLayout( ) method, 268

dispatch( ) method, 261

dispatchLoopShutdown request, 262

docblock extension, 82

docblock tokenizer, installing, 81–82

docblock_token_name($token) function, 83

DocBook, 62–71

    elements of, 67–71

        bookinfo element, 67

        chapter element, 67–68

        overview, 67

        para element, 68–71

        section element, 68

    overview, 62

    parsing files, 63–67

    XML files for, 62–63

doccomments

    accessing data, 82–83

    tokenizing data, 83–84

DOCTYPE declaration, 63, 288

DOCTYPE tag, 66

Document Object Model (DOM), 51, 273

Document Type Definition (DTD), 62

documentation, 55–71

    coding conventions and, 55–56

    DocBook, 62–71

        bookinfo element, 67

        chapter element, 67–68

        elements, 67–71

        overview, 62–67

        para element, 68–71

        parsing DocBook files, 63–67

        section element, 68

        XML files for, 62–63

    overview, 55

    PHP comments, 57–59

        doccomments, 57–58

        lexing and, 58

        metadata, 58–59

reflection-based data, 81–86

    accessing doccomment data, 82–83

    docblock tokenizer, 81–82

    overview, 81

    parsing tokens, 84–86

    tokenizing doccoment data, 83–84

DocumentingReflection* class, 96

DocumentingReflectionClass class, 94

DocumentingReflectionMethod class, 88

DocumentingReflectionParameter class, 94

DocumentingReflection.php file, 86, 89, 94

DOM (Document Object Model), 51, 273

Domain Exceptions, 192, 198

DTD (Document Type Definition), 62

DualIterator, 156–157

DualIterator iterator, 158

dynamic static methods, PHP 6, 50

■E

echo calls, 81

EDITOR environment variable, 107

EmptyIterator, 152

encoding option, 292, 294

&entity syntax, 66

ENTITY tag, 66

$entry SPLFileInfo object, 169

Envelope element, 289

envelopes, 285

/etc/apache2/sites-available/default
    directory, 320

/etc/xinc file, 119

eval( ) function, 273, 276

Exception class, 31, 32–34, 127

exceptions, 31–40

  implementing, 31–35

    catch keyword, 32

    Exception base class, 32–34

    extending exceptions, 34–35

    overview, 31

    throw keyword, 32

    try keyword, 31

  logging, 35–37

    custom exceptions, 35–36

    defining uncaught exception handler, 36–37

    overview, 35

  overhead, 37

  overview, 31

  rethrowing, 39

  type hinting, 38–39

exceptions option, 292

exchangeArray($array) method, 181

export( ) method, 74

extending, 86–102

  adding attributes, 99–102

  exceptions, 34–35

  integrating parser with, 86–88

  overview, 86

  reflection classes, 88–96

  updating parser for in-line tags, 96–99

Extensible Stylesheet Language (XSL), 62

■F

factory convention, 24

factory( ) method, 29

factory pattern, 21

factory patterns, 23–29

FastCar class, 4

FC (front controllers), 203, 208–210

FIELDS metacommand, 232

file iteration, 172

fileperms( ) function, 165

files, searching, 176–177

<fileset> element, 117

filter parameter, 277

FilterIterator, 148–149, 156, 161, 169

find command, 216

FindFile, 168–169

findPlugins( ) function, 78

$flags parameter, 154

flags parameter, 168

FlashMessenger helper, 227

flat-file databases, accessing with DBA, 159–160

float xdebug_time_index( ) function, 123

$foo argument, 59

foo value, 137

footnote element, 70

fopen( ) function, 47

foreach loop, 133, 145, 161, 172

foreach statement, 143, 172

for..in loops, 277

formText and formSubmit view helpers, 228

frameworks, MVC

  creating, 207–212

    bootstrapping, 207–208

    controllers, 210–211

    front controllers, 208–210

    overview, 207

    URL parameters, 212

    views, 211–212

selecting, 204–205

architecture, 204

community, 205

documentation, 204

flexibility, 205

support, 205

setting up virtual hosts, 206

front controllers (FC), 203, 208–210

FrontController class, 208

■G

GET requests, 280–281

get target, 116, 117

get variables, 225

get_called_class( ) function, 49, 52

get_class( ) function, 94

get_declared_classes( ) function, 74, 77, 102, 171

GET_MATCH mode, 149

get_object_vars( ) function, 137

getAllResponseHeaders( ) method, 279

getArrayCopy( ) method, 181

getChildren( ) method, 145

getCode( ) method, 33

getData( ) method, 102

getDocComment( ) method, 88

getFile( ) method, 33

getFileInfo( ) method, 166

getFilename( ) method, 169

getHeader( ) method, 225

getHelper( ) method, 227

getInnerIterator( ) method, 145, 158

getInstance( ) method, 22, 23, 29

getIterator( ) method, 144, 161

getLHS( ) method, 157

getLine( ) method, 33

getMaximumSpeed( ) method, 4, 5

getMessage( ) method, 33

getMethod( ) method, 78

getMethods( ) method, 96

getName( )function, 77

getParam( ) method, 225

getParameters( ) function, 93, 96

getPathInfo( ) method, 166

getPathname( ) method, 169

getPrice( ) method, 184

getResponseHeader(name) method, 279

getRHS( ) method, 157

getTrace( ) method, 33

getTraceAsString( ) method, 33

getTypes( ) method, 304

goto( ) method, 226

■H

h option, 62

hard metadata, 75

has function, 76

hasChildren( ) method, 145, 159

hasMethod( ) method, 78, 102

headLink helper, 269

headScript helper, 269

headTitle helper, 269

help option, 42

helper functions, 129–130

HelperBroker: notifyPreDispatch( ) method, 263

helpers, 263–264

hosts file, 206

.htaccess file, 207, 217, 305

HTML:frames:default option, 62

HTML:Smarty:default option, 62

HTTP authentication, 305

httpd.conf file, 43, 320

■I

IController implementing class, 208

id attributes, 65

IDatabaseBindings interface, 29

IDatabaseBindings-compatible object, 29

ifsetor syntax, 50, 52

IImage interface, 26

image factory, 24–29

    overview, 23–24

    portable database, 27–29

Image_* class, 26

ImageFactory class, 26

implements ISpeedInfo interface, 7

implements keyword, 6, 10

implementsInterface( ) method, 77, 102

.inc extension, 138

include file, 218

index controllers, 219–224

index directory, 220

indexAction default action, 220

indexAction method, 220

IndexController.php file, 220, 267

index.html document, 66

index.php file, 114, 217, 222

index.phtml file, 268

InfiniteIterator, 152

.ini file, 159

ini_set( ) method, 36

inifile handler parameter, 160

IniGroups, 160, 161

init( ) method, 261, 268

input and output attributes, 288

installing

    docblock tokenizer, 81–82

    PHP 6, 41–43

    Zend Framework, 215–216

instanceof operator, 8–9, 38, 77

int xdebug_memory_usage( ) function, 123

int xdebug_peak_memory_usage( ) function, 123

Integration role, 202

interfaces, 6–8

    ArrayAccess, 130

    iterators, 128–129, 143–145

        IteratorAggregate, 144–145

        OuterIterator, 145

        RecursiveIterator, 145

        Traversable, 143–144

Invalid Argument Exceptions, 194

InvalidArgumentException exception, 194, 198

Inversion of Control (IoC), 18

invoke( ) method, 79, 102

IoC (Inversion of Control), 18

IPlugin interface, 77

is function, 76, 225

isDot( ) method, 167

isParamTag( ) function, 92

ISpeedInfo interface, 7

isStreetLegal( ) method, 5

isUserDefined( ) method, 76, 102

itemizedlist tag, 70

ItemSearch operation, 295, 296

Iterator class, 173

Iterator interface, 127, 141, 143, 161, 167, 186

iterator_count($iterator) function, 130

iterator_to_array( ) method, 129, 145, 147

IteratorAggregate class, 146

IteratorAggregate interface, 127, 143, 144–145, 161, 186

IteratorIterator, 151–152

iterators, 128–130, 146–158

    AppendIterator, 147–148

    ArrayIterator, 146

    CachingIterator, 152

    custom file filter, 169–171

    DualIterator, 156–157

    EmptyIterator, 152

    FilterIterator, 148–149

    helper functions, 129–130

    InfiniteIterator, 152

■J

JSON (JavaScript Object Notation), 226

    and JavaScript, 276, 278–279

    and PHP, 273, 274–275

JSON parser script, 274

json.js library, 274

■K

key( ) method, 129, 144

KeyFilter iterator, 160

KeyObject class, 185

keys, using objects as, 184–187

keyup event, 282

ksort( ) method, 181

■L

language attribute, 70

late binding, 16, 48–49

lazy loading, 29

LEAVES_ONLY class constant, 154

Length Exceptions, 194–195, 198

lexing, 58

libapache2-svn package, 106

library directory, 260

LIMIT syntax, 152

LimitIterator, 146–147, 161

Line class, 47

link tag, 96

literal tag, 70

local_cert option, 292, 306

localhost operation, 318

location option, 292

<Location> tag, 110, 323

log( ) method, 35

LoggedException class, 36

logging exceptions, 35–37

    custom exceptions, 35–36

    defining uncaught exception handler, 36–37

    overview, 35

Logic Exceptions, 189–191

login option, 292

loginAction parameter, 267

■M

magic_quotes_gpc function, 41

md5_file signature, 311

member variables, 299

members, static, 12–13

$menu array, 79

menuItem class, 78

MESSAGES metacommand, 232

Messages tag, 286

metacommands, 232

metadata, 55, 58–59

methods, static, 16–18

.mine file, 109

mixed docblock_tokenize($comment, $terseMode=false) method, 83

mixed json_decode(string $json, bool $associative) method, 274

mixed string.parseJSON(filter) method, 276

mod_rewrite directive, 207

$mode parameter, 154

Model layer, 201

models, 221–224

    configuring Framework to use databases, 222–223

    creating, 223–224

    MVC, 203

    setting up databases, 221–222

models directories, 260

Model-View-Controller (MVC) architecture, 201–213

    application layout, 203–204

    frameworks

        creating, 207–212

        selecting, 204–205

        setting up virtual hosts, 206

    overview, 201

    reasons to use, 201–203

Model-View-Controller architecture. *See* MVC architecture

<modificationsets> element, 119

/module/controller/action format, 259

modules, 259–261

modules directory, 260

multiline comments, 57

multiple inheritance, 6

MVC (Model-View-Controller) architecture, 201–213

    application layout, 203–204

    frameworks

        creating, 207–212

        selecting, 204–205

        setting up virtual hosts, 206

    overview, 201

    reasons to use, 201–203

mychapter.html file, 66

MyExtendedObject method, 18

myfirstrepo directory, 108

myfirstrepo2 directory, 108

myLoader( ) method, 138

MyObject class, 15

myOtherMethod method, 18

MyOtherObject class, 15

MySQL class, 29

myVariable class, 16

■N

name attribute, 286

name variable, 220

namespace constructs, 47

namespace statement, 52

namespaces, PHP 6, 47–48

natcasesort( ) method, 181

natsort( ) method, 181

new EmptyIterator( ) method, 157

new keyword, 4

new operator, 4, 23

newfile.txt file, 108

newInstance( ) method, 79, 102

next( ) method, 129, 144, 145

NoCvsDirectory filter, 171

nocvsdir.php file, 171

NoRewindIterator, 152

note element, 70

notify( ) method, 132

notifyPostDispatch( ) method, 263

ns1 prefix, 289

■O

o option, 62

O parameter, 321

Object class, 188

object operations, SPL files, 171–177

    CSV operation, 172–176

    file iteration, 172

    searching files, 176–177

object.hasOwnProperty( ) method, 277

object-mappable data type, 299

objects, 184–187, 299, 308–309

observer pattern, 131–135

observers, 132

offsetExists( ) method, 131, 179

offsetGet( ) method, 131, 179

offsetSet( ) method, 131, 179

offsetUnset( ) method, 131, 179

onreadystatechange event, 279

OOP classes, 86

$op_mode parameter, 149

open( ) method, 279, 280

opendir( ) function, 166

openFile( ) method, 166

openssl commands, 321

openssl.cnf files, 315, 321

Operations tag, 286

OU parameter, 321

OuterIterator interface, 145, 161

Overflow Exceptions, 195–196, 198

■P

.p12 file, 314, 322, 324

paamayim nekudotayim, 13–16

para element, 63, 68–71, 91

param1 parameter, 289

parameters, 224

parameters key, 293

parent:: class, 15

parent scope, 14

parent::__construct construction, 89

ParentBase::render( ) method, 49

ParentIterator, 156

parse( ) method, 3

ParseDocComment class, 88

parseJSON( ) method, 277

parsers

    integrating with reflection API, 86–88

    updating for in-line tags, 96–99

parsing

    reflection-based documentation data, 81–86

        accessing doccomment data, 82–83

        installing docblock tokenizer, 81–82

        overview, 81

        parsing tokens, 84–86

        tokenizing doccoment data, 83–84

    XML with SimpleXML, 158–159

pass parameter, 279

passphrase option, 292, 306, 326

password option, 292

pathinfo( ) function, 26, 170

patterns, 21–29

   factory, 23–29

      image factory, 24–27

      overview, 23–24

      portable database, 27–29

   overview, 21

   responsibility, 21–23

   singleton, 21–23

PDF:default:default option, 62

PDO (PHP Data Objects) extension, 151

PDOStatement class, 151

pear.phpunit.de channel, 110

pecl command, 81

pecl extension, 103

peer verification, 314

PEM (Privacy Enhanced Mail), 306

perms mask, 165

persistence, 308–309

persistent objects, 299

pg_last_error( ) method, 34

PGSQL class, 29

Phing, 115–118

phing binary, 116

phing command, 117

PhoneClient.php script, 326

PhoneCompany.php file, 327

PhoneCompany.wsdl file, 325

PHP

   authentication control, 325–327

   comments, 57–59

      doccomments, 57–58

      lexing and, 58

      metadata, 58–59

      overview, 57

      types of, 57

   and JSON, 273–275

   SOAP extension, 290–294

      overview, 290–291

      SoapClient class, 291–293

      SoapServer class, 294

   web services architecture, 285–286

PHP 6, 41–52

   Dynamic Static Methods, 50

   installation, 41–43

   late static binding, 48–49

   namespaces, 47–48

   overview, 41

   ternary assignment shorthand (ifsetor), 50

   Unicode in, 44–47

      collations, 46–47

      semantics, 44–46

   XMLWriter Class, 50–51

PHP Data Objects (PDO) extension, 151

.php extension, 112, 138

php -i command, 44

PHPDoc, 59–62

phpdoc command, 62

phpinfo( ) function, 43, 121, 285

php.ini file, 44, 45, 82, 120, 123

phpunit test runner, 112

PHPUnit testing, 110–114

PHPUnit_Framework_TestCase class, 112

PKI (public key infrastructure) security,
313–315

    certificate authority (CA), 313–314

    client certificates, 314

    overview, 313

    root CA certificates, 314–315

    web server certificates, 314

placeholders, 268–269

plug-in directories, 170–171

PluginBroker class, 262

PluginBroker methods, 262

plug-ins, 262–263

polymorphism, 21

Port tag, 287

portable databases, 27–29

POST requests, 281–284

postDispatch( ) method, 263

postgres user, 221

postgresql daemon, 221

preDispatch( ) method, 263

$preg_flags parameter, 151

preg_match( ) function, 149

PRESENCE metacommand, 232

print_r calls, 81

printsummary attribute, 117

Privacy Enhanced Mail (PEM), 306

private keys, 323

Product class, 182

profiling, with Xdebug, 123

programlisting tag, 70

programming by contract, 9–10

<project> element, 117, 119

properties, 308

$property value, 49

prototype, 3

proxy_host option, 292

proxy_login option, 292

proxy_password option, 292

proxy_port option, 292

public key infrastructure security. *See* PKI
(public key infrastructure) security

■R

r2 file, 109

Range Exceptions, 193–194, 198

readdir( ) function, 166

readyState property, 279

RecursiveArrayIterator, 153

RecursiveCachingIterator, 158

RecursiveDirectoryIterator, 166, 167–168,
169, 176

RecursiveDualIterator, 158

RecursiveFilterIterator, 157

RecursiveIterator, 145, 153–154, 156, 158,
161, 176

RecursiveRegexIterator, 158

RecursiveTreeIterator, 153, 154–155

Redirector helper, 226–227

reflection API, 73–103

    extending, 86–102

        adding attributes, 99–102

        integrating parsers with, 86–88

        overview, 86

        reflection classes, 88–96

        updating parser for in-line tags, 96–99

    overview, 73

parsing reflection-based documentation data, 81–86

  accessing doccomment data, 82–83

  docblock tokenizer, 81–82

  overview, 81

  parsing tokens, 84–86

  tokenizing doccomment data, 83–84

retrieving user-declared classes, 74–76

understanding reflection plug-in architecture, 76–81

Reflection class, 86

reflection classes, 88–96

Reflection extension, 102

reflection plug-in architecture, 76–81

Reflection* class, 96, 99

reflection-based documentation data, parsing, 81–86

  accessing doccomment data, 82–83

  installing docblock tokenizer, 81–82

  overview, 81

ReflectionClass, 76, 78

Reflection::export( ) method, 74

ReflectionExtension interface, 74

ReflectionMethod class, 78, 88

ReflectionParameter class, 88

reflector interface, 74

RegexFindFile, 168, 169

RegexIterator, 149–151, 161

RegexIterator::MATCH mode, 149

register_globals function, 41

registerPlugin( ) method, 263

remote debugging, with Xdebug, 124

Remote Procedure Call (RPC), 286

render( ) method, 49, 220

REPLACE option, 149

repository, 106

request cycle, 261

request object, 225

  response object, 226

  setting up, 215–219

    bootstrapping, 217–219

    creating virtual hosts, 216

    installing, 215–216

  two-step view, 267–269

    master layout, 267–268

    placeholders, 268–269

  validating input, 229–232

    metacommands, 232

    Zend_Filter_Input class, 229–**231**

  views, 220

Request. Request parameter, 295

require_once function, 137, 170, 207

response object, 226

responseText property, 279, 281

responseXML property, 279

responsibility patterns, 21–23

rethrowing exceptions, 39

rewind( ) method, 129, 144

root CA certificates, 313, 314–315

routeShutdown request, 262

RPC (Remote Procedure Call), 286

runtime exceptions, 191–192, 198

RuntimeException class, 189

■ S

safe_mode function, 41

Satisfy rules, 324

scope resolution operator (::), 11, 47

SCP/SFTP (Secure Copy/Secure FTP), 322

SearchIterator, 158, 176

sect5 tags, 63

section element, 68

Secure Copy/Secure FTP (SCP/SFTP), 322

Secure/Multipurpose Internet Mail Extensions (S/MIME) e-mail message, 322

SeekableIterator, 152, 161

self:: class, 13

self keyword, 22

self scope, 13

SELF_FIRST class constant, 154

self-signed web server certificates, 317–319

send( ) method, 279

Serializable class, 135

Serializable interface, 128

serialization, 135–137, 311

serialize( ) method, 135

$_SERVER variable, 325

server.key file, 319

server.pem file, 319

Service tag, 287

service-oriented architecture (SOA), 180

service.php file, 291

services.pem file, 323, 326

$_SESSION array, 184

session identifiers, 299

sessions, 306–307, 308

set_exception_handler( ) function, 36, 40, 190

setClass( ) method, 308

setDefaultAdapter( ) method, 223

setFileClass method, 165

setHttpResponseCode( ) method, 226

setInfoClass method, 165

setLayout( ) method, 268

setPersistence( ) method, 308, 311

setRequestHeader(name, value) method, 279

setting up
    databases, 221–222
    virtual hosts, 206
    Zend Framework, 215–219
        bootstrapping, 217–219
        creating virtual hosts, 216
        installing, 215–216

setUp( ) method, 113

shopping cart, building, 182–184

SimpleXML, 158–159

SimpleXMLIterator, 161

single-line comments, 57

singleton patterns, 21–23

__sleep method, 135

S/MIME (Secure/Multipurpose Internet Mail Extensions) e-mail message, 322

SOA (service-oriented architecture), 180

SOAP, 289–290

SOAP_PERSISTENCE_REQUEST constant, 308

SOAP_PERSISTENCE_SESSION constant, 308

soap_version option, 292, 294

soapaction and uri options, 293

soapAction attribute, 288

soapCall( ) method, 292

SoapClient class, 285, 290, 291–293, 306

SoapClient operation, 295

SoapClient::__construct( ) method, 291

SoapClient::__getFunctions( ) method, 293

SoapClient::__getLastRequest( ) method, 293

SoapClient::__getLastRequestHeaders( )
    method, 293

SoapClient::__getLastResponse( )
    method, 293

SoapClient::__getLastResponseHeaders( )
    method, 293

SoapClient::__getTypes( ) method, 293

SOAP-encoded array, 302

SoapServer class, 285, 290, 294, 309

SoapServer::__construct( ) method, 294

SoapServer::addFunction(mixed $functions)
    method, 294

SoapServer::fault(string $code, string
    $string) method, 294

soft metadata, 75

SPL (Standard PHP Library), 81, 127–161

    accessing flat-file databases with DBA,
        159–160

    array overloading, 130–131, 179–188

    autoloading, 137–140

    files, 163–178

        and directory information, 163–166

        iteration of directories, 166–171

        object operations, 171–177

        overview, 163

spl_autoload( ) function, 138, 141, 261

spl_autoload_call( ) function, 139, 141

spl_autoload_extensions( ) function, 138, 141

spl_autoload_functions( ) function, 139, 141

spl_autoload_register( ) function, 138, 141

$spl_flags parameter, 150

spl_object_hash( ) function, 140, 185

SplFileInfo class, 163, 177

SplFileInfo object, 166, 177

SplFileObject class, 171, 172, 177, 190

SPLIT mode, 149

SplObjectStorage class, 133, 141

SplObserver interface, 132

SplSubject interface, 132

SSL, configuring Apache for, 319–320

SSL_CLIENT_* variables, 325

SSLCACertificateFile file, 324

SSLEngine file, 320

SSLOptions StrictRequire option, 324

SSLRequire statements, 324

Standard PHP Library. *See* SPL; SPL
    (Standard PHP Library)

static debate, 18

static keyword, 18, 49

static members, 11–13

static scope, 13

static:: scope, 16

status property, 279

statusText property, 279

stdClass objects, 304

str_word_count( ) function, 47

stream context, 325

stream-interacting calls, 325

Street class, 5, 10

string json_encode(mixed $value)
    method, 274

string type.toJSONString( ) method, 276

string Zend_Json::encode(mixed $value)
    method, 275

StripTags filter, 231

strlen( ) function, 44, 47

style option, 292

subj parameters, 321

subtitle tag, 67

Subversion. *See* SVN

Subversion checkout, 119

suggest.htm file, 282

suggest.php file, 282

Sum( ) method, 112

sum( ) method, 113

SVN (Subversion), 105–110

    committing changes and resolving conflicts, 108–109

    enabling access to, 110

    overview, 105

svn add command, 107

svn checkout command, 106

svn commit command, 107, 109, 111, 114

.svn directory, 107

svn export command, 107

svn import command, 106

svn revert command, 108

svn rm command, 111

svn status command, 108, 114

svn update command, 107

svnadmin create command, 106

<svnupdate> element, 117

■T

targetNamespace attribute, 288

targets, 116

tearDown( ) method, 113

ternary assignment shorthand (ifsetor), 50

testing certificates, 324

testing( ) function, 12

Test.php file, 117

tests directory, 112

testSum( ) method, 112

test.xml file, 159

throw keyword, 32, 34, 40

throwExceptions( ) method, 219

title tag, 67

tns prefix, 288

tokens, parsing, 84–86

__toString( ) method, 33, 166, 191

trace option, 291, 292

tracing, with Xdebug, 121–122

Traversable interface, 128, 143–144, 151, 161

try keyword, 31, 40

try statement, 31

try target, 116, 117, 119

two-step view, 267–269

    master layout, 267–268

    placeholders, 268–269

type hinting, 38–39

_type member variable, 92

Types tag, 286

■U

uasort($compare) method, 181

uksort($compare) method, 181

ulink elements, 70

uncaught exception handler, defining, 36–37

Underflow Exceptions, 196–197

UnderflowException exception, 197, 198

underscores (_), 260

Unicode, in PHP 6, 44–47

    collations, 46–47

    semantics, 44–46

$unicode string, 45

unicode.runtime_encoding setting, 45

unicode.semantics setting, 44

unicode.semantics statement, 52

unit testing, 110

unserialize( ) function, 136

update( ) method, 132

uri option, 292, 294

URL parameters, 212

use constructs, 47

use option, 292

use statement, 48

USE_KEY class constant, 150

$use_keys parameter, 148

user database table, 27

user parameter, 279

user-declared classes, 74–76

/usr/share/php/ZendFramework/ZendFra
    mework-1.0.3/, 216

■V

valid( ) method, 129, 144

validating input, 229–232

$_values array, 187

var_export( ) function, 191

varchar column, 27

$variable variable, 16

variables, static, 11–12

Vector namespace, 47

VersionControl_SVN package, 115

View class, 211

view helpers, 264

View layer, 199, 201, 211, 212

views, 220

    creating, 223–224

    MVC, 203–212

virtual hosts, 206, 216

void xdebug_stop_code_coverage( )
    function, 123

void xdebug_stop_trace( ) function, 122

■W

__wakeup method, 135, 137

web server certificates, 313, 314, 317–319

web servers, 203

web services, 285–311

    Amazon Web Services, 295–297

    authentication, 305–306

        client-certificate, 306

        communicated-key, 306

        HTTP, 305

        overview, 305

    authentication, setting up, 325–327

    binary data transmission, 309–311

    complex types, 299–305

        class mapping, 304–305

        example of, 299–304

    objects, 308–309

    overview, 285–299

    persistence, 308–309

    PHP SOAP extension, 290–294

        overview, 290–291

        SoapClient class, 291–293

        SoapServer class, 294

    PHP web services architecture, 285–286

    sessions, 306–307

    SOAP, 289–290

    WSDL, 286–288

        file, 287–288

        overview, 286

        terminology, 286–287

Web Services Description Language. *See*
    WSDL

WebServiceMethod attribute, 102

WebServiceMethodAttribute class, 100

wget command, 215

wheel group, 216

while loop, 173

writing deployment script, 116–118

WSDL (Web Services Description Language), 286–288

   file, 287–288

   overview, 286

   terminology, 286–287

WSDL extension, 299

$wsdl parameter, 294

■X

Xdebug, 120–124

   checking code coverage, 123

   installing, 120–121

   overview, 120

   profiling, 123

   remote debugging, 124

   tracing, 121–122

xdebug_break( ) command, 124

xdebug_get_function_stack( ) method, 122

XHR (XMLHttpRequest) object, 278–279

Xinc server, 118–120

   configuration file, 119–120

   installing, 118–119

   overview, 118

   starting, 120

XML files, for DocBook, 62–63

XML, parsing with SimpleXML, 158–159

XMLHttpRequest (XHR) object, 278–279

XmlHttpRequest object, 273

XmlHttpRequest.abort( ) method, 282

XmlHttpRequest.onreadystatechange event, 282

xmlns:tns attribute, 288

XMLWriter class, 41, 50–52

xsd:boolean type, 288

xsd:int type, 288

xsd:string type, 288

xsd:stringtype, 288

XSL (Extensible Stylesheet Language), 62

xsltproc command, 65, 67

xsltproc tool, 64

■Y

yourfile.html file, 64

yourfile.xsl file, 65

YourPrefix class prefix, 264

YourPrefix_Controller_Plugin_Security plug-in, 266

YourPrefix_Controller_Plugin_Statistics class, 262

■Z

Zend Framework, 215–270

   built-in action helpers, 226–227

   built-in view helpers, 227–228

   helpers, 263–264

   implementing access control, 265–267

   index controllers, 219–220

   models, 221–224

      configuring Framework to use databases, 222–223

      creating, 223–224

      setting up databases, 221–222

   module and model setup, 259–261

      conventional modular directory structure, 259–260

      model libraries and Zend_Loader, 260–261

   overview, 215, 259

   plug-ins, 262–263

   request cycle, 261

Zend_Acl class, 265

Zend_Controller_Action class, 219

Zend_Controller_Action_Helper_Abstract
    class, 264

Zend_Controller_Dispatcher_Standard
    class, 261

Zend_Controller_Plugin_Abstract class, 262

Zend_Controller_Plugin_Broker class, 262

Zend_Db infrastructure, 229

Zend_Db_Table instances, 223

Zend_Debug object, 228

Zend_Filter and Zend_Validate class, 229

Zend_Filter_Input class, 229–231

Zend_Json class, 275

Zend_Json::TYPE_OBJECT constant, 275

Zend_Layout class, 259

Zend_Layout component, 267, 270

Zend_Layout->content placeholder, 268

Zend_Loader class, 259, 260–261

Zend_Request class, 228, 261, 262

Zend_Request::getActionName( )
    method, 263

Zend_View_Helper_ class, 264

Zend_View_Helper_Placeholder class, 267

ZFW_VERSION constant, 218

You Need the Companion eBook

Your purchase of this book entitles you to buy the companion PDF-version eBook for only $10. Take the weightless companion with you anywhere.

We believe this Apress title will prove so indispensable that you'll want to carry it with you everywhere, which is why we are offering the companion eBook (in PDF format) for $10 to customers who purchase this book now. Convenient and fully searchable, the PDF version of any content-rich, page-heavy Apress book makes a valuable addition to your programming library. You can easily find and copy code—or perform examples by quickly toggling between instructions and the application. Even simultaneously tackling a donut, diet soda, and complex code becomes simplified with hands-free eBooks!

Once you purchase your book, getting the $10 companion eBook is simple:

1. Visit **www.apress.com/promo/tendollars/**.

2. Complete a basic registration form to receive a randomly generated question about this title.

3. Answer the question correctly in 60 seconds, and you will receive a promotional code to redeem for the $10.00 eBook.

eBookshop

2855 TELEGRAPH AVENUE | SUITE 600 | BERKELEY, CA 94705

Offer valid through 9/08.